A Primer
of Dutch Seventeenth Century
Overseas Trade

Embarkation of Company troops at Amsterdam
Painting by Abraham Storck. Amsterdam Historical Museum.

D. W. DAVIES

A Primer
of Dutch Seventeenth Century
Overseas Trade

MARTINUS NIJHOFF · THE HAGUE · 1961

To Ida and Homer

Preface

This volume is an attempt to give the American reader an idea of the extent of the Dutch network of trade in the seventeenth century. Although some effort is made to sketch out, however briefly, the activities of the Dutch in various regions throughout the century, emphasis has been placed on their first entrance into these areas in that period. In each area the goods which the Netherlanders received have been indicated as well as the products they traded for them.

The arrangement of the chapters calls for an explanation. Students of Dutch history will think of Surat and Persia as a natural unit, and of Malabar and Ceylon, Japan and China, West Africa and Brazil as being other entities which one would naturally discuss together. I have adopted the more obvious national divisions, Persia, India, Japan, Brazil, etc., as being more easily comprehensible for the casual reader. Within the chapters I have then explained the trade connections between West Africa and Brazil, Surat and Persia, and so forth.

The spelling of proper names has offered some problems. English readers sometimes have an aversion to the abbreviation of proper names. Dutchmen, contrarily, might dislike seeing Cornelisz. written as Corneliszoon, but since this book is for Americans primarily, it seemed best to bear the wrath of Dutchmen, as being farther away, and to spell out such names. Aside from this vagary, I have endeavored to spell the names of Frenchmen, Spaniards, Portuguese, and Dutchmen as their compatriots would prefer to see them spelled. In the spelling of place names, the *Times Atlas* has generally been used as a guide, although in some instances it was necessary to depart from the usage in that work.

In preparing this work I have been above all indebted to J. G. Van Dillen,

Preface

Professor Emeritus of Economic History, University of Amsterdam; W. Ph. Coolhaas, Professor of Netherlands and European Overseas Relations, University of Utrecht; and B. H. M. Vlekke, Professor of Contemporary International Politics, University of Leiden. Professor Coolhaas has been especially generous and untiring in his assistance, saving me from many a grievous error. He is the model of the kind and generous scholar. Professor Pieter Geyl has been, as always, most kind and helpful. Frederick Mulhauser, Professor of English, Pomona College, has given valuable advice on English style. Walter B. Smith, Professor of Economic Institutions, Claremont Men's College, has corrected errors in the field of economics. Hubert Herring, Professor Emeritus of Latin American Culture, Claremont Graduate School, has read those chapters which touched upon his field. William L. Schurz, Professor of Latin American History, American Institute for Foreign Trade, has read the chapter on Brazil, and David M. Ellis, Professor of American History, Hamilton College, has read the chapter on New Netherland. A most valuable critic has been my friend H. W. Pittenger, a skilful master of language. Mrs. Umbra James has typed several versions of the book and corrected many lapses. My wife has taken time from her own absorbing activities to read the manuscript and proofs. Lastly, I must acknowledge a very great debt to the trustees of the Ralph B. Lloyd Foundation for their unwavering aid and encouragement.

Whatever merit the volume may have is due to my wife and my friends and colleagues, here and in The Netherlands. I am, of course, solely responsible for all errors and other failings.

D. W. DAVIES

Honnold Library
Claremont, California

Contents

List of Illustrations

at the end

CHAPTER I

The Herring Fishery

We have been so accustomed to think of England, France, or Spain as the great powers in European history that it is sometimes difficult for us to remember that in the seventeenth century Holland was the greatest commercial power in Europe. A simple catalogue of places where Dutchmen were doing business in that period gives a clue to the strength, complexity, and wealth of their commercial structure. They hunted whales off Spitsbergen and traded for furs with the natives on the shores of the White Sea. In Iceland they bought falcons and fish and sold hooks, lines, nets, and cooking utensils, as they did in the Shetlands and the Orkneys. The herring which they caught off the English coast, to the great distress of the rain-sodden natives, they peddled in Catholic France, Spain, and Italy, where religion gave an impetus to fish-eating. To get salt for salted herring, they voyaged to the Canary Islands and the coast of Venezuela. Once established in this latter region where the slave trade was already prospering, they did a fairly brisk business in African slaves.

The Baltic area to the east of the Dutch was the great granary of Europe, and to the south of them was the great grain market. They poured into Italy the grain they bought in Baltic ports and loaded the empty grain ships in the Italian ports with marble. The visitor to Livorno will see the centuries-old graves of Dutch merchants and will see in Amsterdam, that city surrounded by peat, sand, and water, canals lined with stately houses with marble stairs, marble floors and wainscot, all a by-product of the grain trade. When Louis XIV built Versailles, he procured the marble from Holland, a country which had none.

But the Dutch moved ever farther afield: they bought furs along the Hudson River and established a settlement there which continues to be a place of some

importance. They established themselves in the East Indies and secured eventually a monopoly of the trade in cloves, mace, nutmeg, and pepper from those islands, trading for these spices the cotton cloth which they bought at their own factories in India. They had Company branches in Malaya and Formosa, where they bought silk and porcelain from Chinese merchants, which they traded at their posts in Japan for copper, lacquer work, and silver. They flooded Asia and Europe with literally millions of pieces of Chinese porcelain, and the flotsam and jetsam from that inundation may still be found in many museums.

From their establishments in India they chased the Portuguese from the ports of Ceylon and cornered the trade in cinnamon, elephants, rubies, and garnets. The merchants of Bengal had done a lively business in cotton cloth, elephant tusks, rice, and other goods with various ports in Burma; this trade too the Dutch gathered in, as they did the Indian-Siamese trade. Along the western coast of India trade between northwest India and Persia had flourished, but the Dutch established themselves in both places and took over the business in silk, cotton, and indigo.

There was scarcely a region where they did not trade: they were firmly entrenched in the Turkish domains; they traded with the Barbary pirates, with their arch enemies the Spanish, and with the English; they cut sugar cane in the West Indies and ebony in Mauritius; they freighted goods out of Moscow, and built warehouses in Brazil. Their vast commercial network is surely one of the wonders of commercial history.

Although this complex of trade was formed comparatively rapidly, the means to construct and maintain it had accumulated over centuries. Actually the Dutch, like other great sea traders, the Venetians, for example, had begun by going fishing. Although they did not neglect the profits in cod, ling, and whales, the great sea industry was the herring fishery, and it is of great importance to the present day. Some three billions of the fishes are presently caught every year, and eaten with relish by English, Dutch, Germans, Scandinavians, Russians and many other peoples. These three billions are an inconsiderable fraction of those in the sea. Herring are adaptable and ubiquitous. They spawn in fresh water as well as salt; they spawn in the Firth of Forth in winter, on the coast of Norway or elsewhere in the spring, on the northeast English coast in summer, or in the North Sea in autumn; they breed in a few feet of water or a few hundred. They feed on plankton, on other fish, or even on their own offspring, and consist of a number of races, each

2

with a local habitation and a name. There are Norwegian, Baltic, Icelandic, and various other varieties, and they are caught by Icelanders, Norwegians, Dutch, English, and the Baltic peoples, as they have been caught and eaten by them for centuries.

Great impetus was given to the fishery by the religious injunction to abstain from meat on Fridays. Certainly by 1400, the pious people of the Rhineland, Netherlands, England, France, Spain, Prussia, Livonia, Poland, and Russia were dutifully and industriously consuming herring according to the precepts of their Holy Church. Where there have been so many consumers, there have been likewise industrious suppliers. Before the ninth century, French and Spanish herring traders were buying fishes from the people on the west coast of Scotland. In the twelfth and thirteenth centuries the Germans of Rügen plied a profitable trade in herring, as did the Swedes of Marstrand. In the fourteenth century, the men of the French channel ports, Dieppe, Calais, and Fécamp, were doing a thriving business in the article and shipping the fish all over northern France. In the latter part of the fifteenth and early part of the sixteenth centuries, the Danes at Falsterbo and Skanör entered the business on a large scale, catching their herring in the Sound; and naturally the keen traders from Bremen, Hamburg, Lübeck, and the Wendish cities, finding this profitable business on their doorstep, were trading in herring. But the fishing by all others wilted before the competition of the Dutch, between whom and the herring there was a natural affinity. 'God has made of Holland and the herring business an example of his blessing for all the world,' observed Meinert A. Semeyns, a seventeenth century herring historian, who doubtless felt that he was merely stating an obvious fact. By the time Semeyns wrote, Netherlandish preoccupation with the fishes was already centuries old. In 1177, for example, Margaret of Elzas, Countess of Flanders, issued regulations for the salting of herring, and before the end of the twelfth century, fishermen from the Dutch towns of Kampen and Harderwijk were fishing in the neighborhood of the Schoonen peninsula. At the end of the following century (in 1295) the fact was brought to the notice of King Edward I of England that Hollanders, Zeelanders, and Frisians, in a word, Dutchmen, were fishing off Yarmouth, and thus began what was later considered the reprehensible Dutch habit of taking fishes out of English seas. In increasing numbers throughout the fourteenth century, Netherlanders, the distinction between Dutchmen and Belgians not yet having been invented, took to their boats and fished off the English coast. Despite these early efforts, it was really in the fifteenth century that

destiny and the herring began to conspire in favor of the Netherlanders. In the city of Hoorn in 1416, it was discovered how to make bigger, better, and stronger herring nets; and, to make full use of this improved equipment, the small boats called *flabberts* were abandoned, and much larger boats called *buizen* (or, in English, busses) were brought into use. Of all Dutch fishing towns, Brielle on the island of Voorne at the mouth of the Rhine gradually became pre-eminent. Between the years 1436 and 1470, it was said that the docks of Brielle were so crowded with fishing busses that ships coming to the port had to anchor off shore, and merchants from Mechelen, Antwerp, 's Hertogen-bosch, Dordrecht, Cologne, Frankfurt am Main, Magdeburg, Stendal, Riga, and Revel crowded into the town to buy herring. The pre-eminence of Brielle was of short duration. Soon Rotterdam, Schiedam, and Vlaardingen had respectable fishing fleets; and in the great age of the fishery, in the sixteenth century, the chief herring cities were Enkhuizen, Delft, Rotterdam, and Schiedam. During the first part of the sixteenth century, as has been indicated, the Dutch fishery enjoyed prosperity, but in the latter part of the century the Netherlanders revolted against Spain and there began the long Eighty Years War which resulted in the independence of the United Provinces. The attention of the Netherlanders, consequently, was to some extent diverted from the herring. As a result, for a number of years there was a rival fishery off the Norwegian coast, chiefly exploited by the Germans from the Baltic cities. Fortunately for the Dutch, these fisheries were controlled by the Danes, whose regulations were so oppressive that they actually made the fishery unprofitable and brought about its decline. Thus, by the end of the century when the Dutch were free to give their full attention to it, the whole herring market was again theirs.

In the years of the late sixteenth and early seventeenth centuries, weeks before the fishing season opened, the Dutch fishermen swarmed to the Shetland Islands to await the opening of the season on the English coast. Their activities have been recorded by a number of Englishmen of whom the saltiest, probably, was Tobias Gentleman. This author wrote of the Dutch fishermen in the Shetlands that 'they frolic it on land, until that they have sucked out all the marrow of the malt and good Scotch ale, which is the best liquor that the island doth afford.' It was complained that the Dutchmen rode the horses, milked the cows, teased the girls, fought the young men, and plagued the population in a variety of other ways until it was time for them to sail slowly southward following the shoals of herring. Gentleman lamented that while

4

the Hollanders were scooping up nets full of herring, the English had no fish, and the Lowlanders would only sell them 'the roope-sick herring that will not serve to make barrelled herrings [and which] by their own law, they must not bring home into Holland; wherefore they do sell them for ready money or gold unto the Yarmouth men....'

This writer, and many another contemporary, could see the wealth and power the fishery was bringing to the Netherlands. While the busses were hauling in herring, ships were busily fetching salt to Dutch ports from southern France, Spain, and South America to salt the herring. Still other boats were employed carrying salt and empty casks to the fishing fleet. A great number of vessels carried the packed herring to Bordeaux, La Rochelle, Nantes, Saint Malo, Caen, Rouen, Paris, Amiens, Calais, and the ports of Spain and Portugal. Other ships headed for the Mediterranean, carrying fish for the good Catholics of Italy. Large herring cargoes were shipped to the Baltic. Barges took the same cargoes up the Rhine, and quantities of fish were shipped to Greece, Alexandria, Venice, and even to Brazil. From all these places the freighters returned with cargoes.

Maintaining and maintained by this vast agglomeration of Dutchmen on deep and shallow waters, there was on land an army of boat builders, provisioners, ship chandlers, hemp winders, rope makers, sail makers, packers, coopers, lightermen, warehousemen, brokers, speculators, wholesale and retail merchants. Tobias Gentleman called upon his countrymen to note that because of herring, the Dutch had not only made the King of Spain weary of wars 'and brought him to good terms and reasonable Composition,' but in spite of the huge charges of the long war with Spain, the Dutch had emerged from it rich and strong, and trading and trafficking with all other nations. The Dutch had, observed the Englishman, 'so increased and multiplied their shipping and mariners, that all other nations and countries in the world do admire them.'

The Netherlanders were, and had been for centuries, fully conscious of the fishery's importance. Their rulers watched over it with paternal care. As early as the Burgundian period of Dutch history, laws forbade salting herring in casks before a certain date each year, and described the kinds of salt to be used. In 1519, in the time of Charles V, there were laws to ensure sound herring casks, it being decreed that each barrel was to bear a stamp indicating its soundness, and if the fish packed were caught early in the season, there was to be another stamp indicating the fact. Later, in 1580, another law observed

that there had grown up a reprehensible practice among certain selfish entrepreneurs of fishing for herring before the legal date, and of packing and selling these bad and unseasonable herring, whereby the merchants made huge profits, but developed in the peoples of foreign countries a loathing for herring to the great prejudice, injury, and ruin of the whole trade. Consequently this early fishing was strictly forbidden.

In the years 1580–1621 at least twenty-two laws were proclaimed to regulate the fishery. The date to commence fishing was fixed anew; the men were forbidden to interfere with each other's nets; the manner of placing the herring in the casks was prescribed; the amount of salt to be used and how it was to be used were laid down; the working conditions of sailors were regulated. Skippers were prohibited in certain circumstances from selling herring at sea, nor were they to place herring caught by foreigners in casks marked with the Dutch brand. Salt, fishing tackle, and nets were not to be sold to foreigners, and no herring buss might put to sea which did not have on board a full set of forty nets in good condition, and a sufficient supply of casks. Herring were required to be sold in Dutch markets and if the fish were repacked on land, it was to be done in proper buildings where the doors were left open, or on high streets, or on the docks. When a buss returned from a fishing voyage, both skipper and crew were required to appear before a magistrate and swear that all the laws and regulations had been observed. Thus all fishermen were made to remain honest fishermen, both by the laws of the land and by the regulations of the College of the Great Fishery at Delft, a representative body composed of men from the fishing ports.

Inevitably the folkways and language of Dutchmen were permeated with herring. Where a dullard in our own New England might be called a pumpkin head, or in the South might be thought to resemble a jackass, in Holland it would be said that he hadn't the brains of a pickled herring. He might be also so unfortunate as to sing like a pickled herring, or so undependable that one could not trust him with five cents' worth of herring. There was plenty of proof, naturally, that one of the most healthful foods in the world was herring. Just as it was discovered in Scotland that whisky had great therapeutic value, and found by the California grape growers that raisins put iron in one's blood, wonderful properties were discovered in herring. An Amsterdam burgomaster averred that sickness vanished before herring as mist before the sun. An Amsterdam physician, Nicolaas Tulp, declared that a good herring benefited the digestion, increased the appetite, loosened the phlegm, and made

the body limber. An ulcer of the stomach could be cured simply by eating a herring heart each morning for a month. The gall of a herring mixed with honey prevented dysentery, and the liver mixed with honey would cure a toothache. Herring gills burned to powder would infallibly cure epilepsy, and herring bladders dissolved in hot spring water were good for a stoppage of the urine. Herring scales and wild plums ground up together and drunk in red wine were good for the stone. The roe placed in linen was good for hemorrhoids, and crushed roe was a valuable cosmetic. If one suffered from deafness, it was only necessary to mix eel gall and oil from herring roe and drop the concoction into the ear in order to hear again. The eminent seventeenth century lawyer of Enkhuizen, Meinert A. Semeyns, historian of the herring who has already been quoted, pointed out that God had in the herring fishery given the Dutch such a head start that no nation had ever been able to lead them, and as a result Holland would doubtless go on 'increasing in honor, prosperity, and trade.' He called attention to the fact that The Great Mighty States of Holland had called the herring fishery the Great Fishery, the source of prosperity and the mine of the land, thereby recognizing that the whole of the shipping trade depended upon it and without it would vanish. Semeyns asked soberly 'if we might not declare truthfully if it be not the principal commerce of the world, since world trade without Holland and Holland without herring would be negligible,' or to put it differently, 'Herring makes Holland, and Holland makes world trade.' Tobias Gentleman marveled that even the Dutch fishwives had 'their aprons full of nothing but English Jacobuses, to make all their payments....' Herring, then, bred seamen, provided the basic skills and equipment, and brought the wealth to make the Netherlanders a maritime power. It was said previously that the Dutch began their climb to wealth, like the Venetians, by going fishing. Those first Venetians, settled on the islets and in the swamps of the Adriatic, accumulated surplus fishes and then traded them on the mainland for grain. The Netherlanders too began to trade for grain and this took them eastward to the Baltic ports, behind which lay the rolling plains which were the great granary of Europe.

CHAPTER II

Sweden, Russia, and the Baltic Ports

Dutch ships, as has been indicated, obtained important cargoes of wheat and rye in Baltic ports. This trade, together with the trade to Sweden and Russia, constituted what the Dutch called the trade to the eastward. Of the three branches of commerce the most important was the Baltic grain trade. Although only grain has so far been mentioned, actually four commodities were involved in the development of the Dutch grain trade, and the interplay of these four articles had a history of hundreds of years. The four all-important articles were grain, salt, herring, and cloth.

The medieval demand for fish inspired by the Church and the longing of mankind for fresh meat in an era of scarcity acted like adrenalin on the cod and herring fisheries. In the thirteenth and fourteenth centuries the Norwegian fishing population grew so rapidly as a result of the demand for fish that it could no longer produce enough grain for its needs. The Hanseatic cities, more specifically the cities on the Baltic, found a golden opportunity in the need of the fishermen. They transported great quantities of wheat and rye to the northern fisheries, trading the grain for cod and herring. The Hansa merchants also supplied grain to the herring fishers in the Sound. The relation of the first two of the four factors, fish and grain, was thus established, but obviously if herring are to be preserved salt is needed. The Hansa merchants, having the necessary shipping and commercial relations with the fishing fleets, were so obliging as to bring to them salt from southern France.

Fortunately for the Netherlanders the commerce was not to be a simple fish-grain-salt exchange, for the Baltic peoples also wanted cloth, and the great center of the medieval cloth industry was in Flanders. To supply the Baltic demand, the Hansa merchants bought Flemish textiles, and they developed the trade to the point of their undoing. Before 1300 they had been

content to buy cloths of great price in limited quantities, but after that year they exchanged this luxury trade for a large volume lower quality trade. The effective demand for cloth among the Russians and other Baltic peoples grew enormously. In the single year 1368, the Easterlings bought 20,000 pieces of cloth in south Netherlands, most of it originating in Poperinghe, which they sold later in Sweden, Russia, and the Baltic ports. The industrial cities of the south Netherlands grew with explosive violence. By 1450 the Lowlands textile towns had outrun the supply of grain from adjacent areas, and wheat began to be imported from the Baltic. Similarly these expanding populations consumed enormous quantities of fish. Netherlanders dwelling on the coast, stimulated by the demand of their fellow countrymen in the cloth trades in the interior, went fishing in increasing numbers. Actually they were in a far better strategic position than were the Hansa merchants. The cloth industry was at their back door, the fishery was immediately off shore, and they were closer to the salt supply. As early as 1400, instead of waiting for the Germans to deliver grain the Dutch were going to fetch it, and Dutch rivalry in the trade was sufficiently important to cause a war with the Wendish seafaring cities (1435–1441). A century later a large number of the ships passing through the Sound were Dutch, bound for the Baltic to load grain, and the importance of the trade had greatly increased. Theodorus Velius, councilman and city physician of Hoorn, wrote a chronicle of his native city and noted that up to about 1522 the Easterlings had brought their goods to the Netherlands. He said that up until that time the Dutch could not compare with the Easterlings in the number of their ships, but shortly thereafter the Dutch went to fetch their own goods from the Baltic, and in a very short time, the shipping was largely in Dutch hands. There are a number of indications of how swiftly the eastern trade grew. In 1580, 54% of the ships passing through the Sound were Dutch. In the year 1601, said Emanuel Van Meteren, a famous contemporary Dutch historian, in the space of three days there sailed out of Holland to the eastward between eight and nine hundred ships. By 1615, of the ships passing through the Sound, 67% were Dutch. At the midpoint in the seventeenth century (from 19 June to 16 November 1650) of 1,035 ships passing into the Baltic from the North Sea, no less than 986 were from Netherlands ports. By that time, Dutchmen were beginning to forget the miracle of the herring fishery in contemplation of the even greater miracle of Baltic trade. An anonymous Dutchman, in 1646, referred to it as 'the soul of all trade,' and as that 'on which all other trades and routes depended.' A keen foreign observer, Bishop

9

Huet of Avranche, observed that the Baltic trade was the most important and necessary trade of the Republic. The merchants of Amsterdam were especially deep in this traffic, the wheat and rye trade of that city being greater than that of all other Dutch cities combined. Johan De Witt, Holland's great statesman of the middle years of the century, estimated that if no grain were imported into Amsterdam for seven years, there would be enough in the city to feed the population for that period. De Witt called it 'the mother trade' because all other trade depended on it. It was said that more than half of the warehouses of the town were used for wheat storage. In thinking of the Dutch commerce of those days, we are apt to think automatically about the products of the Orient, or the Netherlanders on the Hudson rather than of grain. In the pages that follow, Dutch activities in those distant regions will be described, but when other commodities and trades are discussed it will be well to keep in mind the fact that more capital on the Amsterdam bourse was employed in grain than in any other commodity. Next to grain, the fishery (herring, whaling, and sealing) was the most popular investment; and the capital employed in the West and East Indies trades was considerably less than that employed in grain and fish.

Thus far only wheat and rye have been mentioned, but other valued products were also obtained from the Baltic. Naval stores such as hemp, tar, pitch, and timber were available as was finished lumber (wainscots and clapboards). Wood ashes, needed in the preparation of potash, were brought home to Holland as was bar-iron, and osmund, a bloom or grade of iron. There were also miscellaneous items to be freighted such as wax and tallow.

The great majority of the commodities which have been mentioned are bulky and heavy. It will be easily apparent that it would be difficult to find cargoes to carry to the Baltic which would be equal in bulk to the grain, timber, and other goods being shipped from there. As a matter of fact, as G. W. Kernkamp has shown, down to 1622 the majority of the ships going into the Baltic were in ballast. After that date the rapidly developing network of trade began to make itself felt; the Lowlanders had a greater variety of goods to offer their Baltic customers. From 1622 to 1650 the greater number of ships had cargoes, and from the latter date until 1657 laden vessels and those in ballast going to the Baltic were about equal in number. In bulk, salt was by far the most important commodity carried to the Baltic, and in many years constituted 40% to 70% of all freight transported on the eastward voyages. French wines, herring, raisins, spices, lead, and of course cloth,

found a ready market. In previous centuries the last-named commodity had been in great demand, but in the first years of the seventeenth century and until 1620, herring and wine were the most popular cargoes, although cloth continued to be shipped in large quantities. After 1620 the effects of the growing East India trade began to be apparent. For example, the value of spices exported to the Baltic in 1635 surpassed the value of herring. The Baltic cities concerned in the trade were chiefly Danzig, Königsberg, and Riga, in that order. About 1600 these three cities enjoyed approximately 80% of the trade, but the Dutch also traded in Revel, Libau, Pernau, and other towns.

The second branch of the trade eastward was the commerce with Russia, the vast land lying at the back door of the Baltic ports, chiefly attractive for the furs to be procured, and the manufactured articles to be sold there. A long tradition of west European-Russian trade existed. The commerce had been carried on by two principal routes, either by sea around the North Cape to the White Sea and the mouth of the Dwina, or overland to Novgorod and Moscow. The Norwegians had used the sea route to the mouth of the Dwina as early as the tenth century and were trading there in the thirteenth and fourteenth centuries. The overland route was utilized by the merchants of the middle ages in the thirteenth to fifteenth centuries, when they did a thriving business through the great city of Novgorod. The Hanseatic League had one of its more important factories in that city.

In the sixteenth and seventeenth centuries, the story of west European-Russian trade is a tale of the rivalry of Dutch and English. At first the English were in the better position by far to control the trade, but the Netherlanders overcame the initial advantages of their competitors and finally surpassed them. The trade of the Dutch is more easily comprehended if a few facts concerning their English rivals in Russia are kept in mind. The English effort began with a group of London merchants who in 1553 got together six thousand pounds for the 'discovery of the northern part of the world.' Of three ships sent out by them under Sir Hugh Willoughby and Richard Chancellor, two met disaster. The third vessel with Chancellor aboard entered the White Sea in the summer of 1553, where the Englishmen wintered. From there, Chancellor, 'a man of great estimation for many good parts of wit,' made his way overland for an audience with the Czar. That monarch promised him that English merchants would be welcomed in Russia. As a result, the English Muscovy Company was chartered in 1555 and given the monopoly of trade with Russia. In the same year the Czar granted the Company liberty

to trade in his dominions. Speedily thereafter a colony of Englishmen was established on Rose Island near Kholmogory. In 1567 the Czar confirmed the monopoly of the English Muscovy Company. 'None beside, out of what kingdom soever it be, England or other,' the privilege read, 'should come in trade of merchandise,' under penalty of forfeiting ships and goods. Russian trade was then, at least nominally, an English preserve. Each year the Muscovy Company sent thirteen or fourteen ships to the mouth of the Dwina, mainly bartering cloth for furs, oil, timber, cordage, and some wheat. The English company grew fat, but also complacent.

The Netherlanders, in point of time at least, were not behind the English in trade with Russia. While the Lowlands were still part of the dominions of Charles V, Netherland traders reached Russia through Narva, a medieval town on the Gulf of Finland, exchanging cloth for talc, furs and hides, and so great was their influence that the port officials of the town came to use Dutch in their correspondence and dealings with any foreigners. Dutch as well as English ships also went around the North Cape to the White Sea. In the early years of the trade, Russian coasters brought furs, stokfish (dried cod), and other trading goods to a number of ports such as Kola and Kegor (near Vardö) where ships from both the North and South Netherlands awaited them. There they traded their cargoes for cloth, beer, and household hardware. What was supposedly an English trading area then was actually infiltrated by the Lowlanders.

Beginning in 1562, Filips Winterkoning, a remarkable merchant of Ooltgensplaat in Zeeland, began trading in the White Sea, and after his death, one of his associates, Cornelis De Meyer of Antwerp, continued his efforts. The latter even set out for Moscow, but got no further than Novgorod, since the English had bribed the governor of Novgorod to allow him to proceed no further. Such was the perfidy of the English even in those days. But the bookkeeper of the Winterkoning-De Meyer firm, Simon Van Salingen, stayed at Novgorod, and beginning with the jewels and pearls he had with him, established himself as a trader. He was able to induce a number of merchants to send their goods to the northern coast where his associates met the Russians and exchanged tin, cloth, and spices for the Russian products. Van Salingen travelled over the lands around the White Sea in reindeer sled and developed Dutch trade there with great rapidity.

Another Netherlander in the Russian trade was Olivier Brunel, a merchant of Brussels or Louvain. Sometime after 1557 on a voyage to the mouth of the

Dwina he was treated discourteously by the English at their factory there. Later the English turned Brunel over to the Russians as a spy. After languishing in a Russian dungeon at Jaroslaw for a few years, Brunel entered the service of the great Russian trading house of the Stroganoffs, and returned a number of times to the Netherlands to purchase goods for his Russian employers. Later, in 1577, with his partner Jan van der Walle, he journeyed overland to Kola to trade on his own account. Following these pioneer efforts, the Dutch traders grew rapidly in numbers, resources, and importance. As early as 1604 there was an English complaint that 'the Hollanders have grown in a short time from two ships to above twenty; this Spring they are gone to Muscovy with near thirty ships, and our men with but seven.' A few years later it was lamented that one of the best trades had been lost, that it formerly employed seventeen ships, but now only two, while the Dutch employed thirty-five and those of much greater burden than the English. From being birds of passage and clandestine traders, the Lowlanders so strengthened their hold on the trade that they were emboldened to remain ashore in Russia. The first Dutch factory or trading post at Archangel was established by Balthasar de Moucheron, one of the Netherlands' most colorful and imaginative entrepreneurs, and by 1600 there were representatives of several Dutch commercial houses there. By 1608, a company to trade in the White Sea had been formed in Holland and by 1619 it was on a firm footing. Archangel rapidly replaced Narva as an outlet for Russian goods and by 1648, says a Dutch historian, although his words are an exaggeration, there were two hundred Dutch factors or commercial agents there. The fur trade was eventually in Dutch hands. An Englishman who had returned from Russia complained in 1667 that, 'the numerous Dutch middlemen swarm here like locusts, and take the bread out of English mouths.'

The last of the three principal areas in the east which attracted Dutchmen was Sweden. There were Netherlanders in that country long before the seventeenth century, but that was the era of great Dutch opportunity. For seventy-five of the hundred and twenty years between 1600 and 1720 the Swedes were at war, and while they were absorbed in this exciting and highly expensive entertainment, there were plenty of Netherlanders who were willing to take over Swedish commerce and to supply the materials of war. Sweden was easily the most important producer of copper and iron, but the leading entrepreneurs in these and other industries were Dutchmen, such as Elias Trip and Louis De Geer. Consequently Amsterdam became Europe's

great copper market. The Dutch entrepreneur par excellence in Sweden was De Geer, an Amsterdamer. He was the leading exporter of Swedish copper, and at times his holdings in the metal were so extensive that he could control the price of copper on the market of his home city. He was not only the manager of Sweden's national armories, but could equip whole armies out of his own stocks of arms and armor. He was the leading smelter of iron. He manufactured brass, steel, tin, wire, paper, and cloth. He was a shipper and ship builder, and neglected no other opportunity to turn an honest dollar. 'While old de Geer,' says B. H. M. Vlekke, 'cast guns and equipped armies and navies, his daughters in Stockholm sold copper kettles, knives, and kitchen utensils over the counter.'

Not only the metal industries but the Swedish carrying trade passed into Dutch hands. We may think of the Swedes as a seafaring people, but in that century the Swedish idea of a fine seaman was a Dutchman. The Swedes averred that a Dutch ship could make three voyages while a Swedish ship made one, and that a Dutch crew of six was equivalent to a Swedish crew of ten. When Swedish laws of the sea were formulated they were on Dutch models. A striking example of the extent to which Dutch influences were felt in Sweden is afforded by the city of Göteborg. When the new city was laid out it was provided with canals and sluices in the Dutch fashion. As the famous Swedish economic historian, Eli F. Heckscher, has pointed out, the first Göteborg city council was composed of five Dutchmen, two Germans, two Scots, and three Swedes. Construction of the port was directed by two Dutchmen who hired Dutch labor. The fishery and fishpacking was in Dutch hands. A Dutchman was head of the first tar company. The fields of the city were accorded to immigrating Dutch peasants. The physicians were usually Dutch, and when the city needed a midwife, it imported a Dutch widow.

It should perhaps be repeated that of the commerce in the three regions discussed, the Baltic ports, Russia, and Sweden, the grain trade from the Baltic was by far the most important. As has been noted, the wheat and rye pouring out of that region filled the warehouses of Amsterdam. Obviously this is only half of the story, since the grain had to be sold somewhere. Actually the complement to the trade to the eastward was the trade to the west, by which the Dutch meant the traffic with France and the Iberian peninsula. It was there they sold their grain, gathered salt, bought wine, and watched for opportunities to develop other enterprises.

CHAPTER III

France

As has been said, the grain purchased in the Baltic was sold in the west. Actually, although the westward trade comprised both the trade to France and to the Iberian peninsula, the grain went principally to the latter place. The commodities which drew Lowland ships to France, as a magnet draws iron filings, were wine and salt. The presence of the Dutch vessels in French ports resulted in the usual exchange of goods, but the role of the Dutch in France was elaborate and more complicated than the transactions of sea trade. The two countries were near neighbours, having relations by land as well as by sea, and neither set of relationships is quite understandable without reference to the other. For the purpose of discussing sea trade, the multifarious commercial contacts between the two peoples may be summarized in a few sentences by saying that the Netherlanders progressed from visiting French ports to taking over the French carrying trade. As the commercial life of France became more familiar to them, the Lowlanders settled in French ports and elsewhere in the country. As Dutchmen established themselves in commerce, there was sometimes a decline in the profits accruing to Frenchmen. As a result, the presence of the foreigners was resented by some. Actually their entrance into the country had been made easy and successful by the benevolent attitude of the French government. The great ministers of the crown in the seventeenth century were under the influence of mercantilist precepts, one of which was that the country's commerce should be increased, even if necessary by the importation of skilled foreigners, and the Dutch certainly possessed commercial skill. The expansion and elaboration of Dutch activity took place throughout three quarters of the seventeenth century, but at the beginning of the era Dutch sea trade was probably most concerned with the simple problem of salt.

This commodity, whose enormous importance is not always realized, is more easily produced in hot countries than in northern Europe. In the middle ages when the demand was moderate, most regions could supply their needs from home sources. At Lüneberg in Germany, for example, there were salt springs, and the spring water was boiled until the salt crystallized out of the solution. In various parts of the British Isles, also, there were extensive salt-boiling centers. In the Netherlands, salt was obtained by burning peat which had become impregnated with salt by being immersed in sea water. After burning the peat, the salter had a mixture of salt and ashes. The mixture being placed in water, the salt went into solution and the ashes settled as a residue. The solution was decanted and the brine was boiled until salt crystals formed.

Such methods, while adequate to supply domestic needs, could not produce the immense quantities needed in the business of catching and salting herring. The demand created by the great catches of the late fifteenth and early sixteenth centuries far outran the salt resources of northern Europe. The northerners then turned to the south where a better method, requiring a hotter and longer season than they experienced, was in vogue. The method is to run sea water into shallow ponds. As the water evaporates and the brine thickens, it is run into yet shallower ponds where the sun has even greater effect, and so by employing shallower and shallower ponds, the brine becomes increasingly thick until the salt crystals form. Not only is a hot sun required, but there must be salt sea marshes which can be dammed to create ponds. Along the French and Spanish shores of the Bay of Biscay, one finds both the hot sun and the necessary low lying land. Here, since the days when France was a Roman province, salt has been made. These salt works, flourishing mightily by the latter half of the sixteenth century, were the principal European sources for salt; and here the Hansa merchants and later the Dutch obtained cargoes. The particular region favoured by both Lowland and Hansa merchants in the fifteenth and sixteenth centuries was the Bay of Bourgneuf near the mouth of the Loire. The Lowland ships brought herring to French ports and loaded cargoes of salt with which to pack yet more casks of herring. Soon they were bringing to the ports of their southern neighbor all of the products which they had gathered in their trade with the Baltic, Russia, and Sweden. They transported and sold there the goods they had gotten in the two Indies, in Japan, the Near East, and even to a limited extent in Iceland. Having profitably delivered such cargoes, the Hollanders loaded their ships, not only with salt, but with wines, fine cloth, linen, haberdashery, iron ware, paper, glass,

sewing thread, lozenges, pastels, saffron, preserved fruit, honey, and French tapestries; and sold the articles profitably elsewhere. There were eventually so many Dutch ships frequenting French ports, Saint Malo, Dieppe and Nantes, that French vessels began to be superfluous. At mid-century, in 1645, the merchants of Nantes complained that in the important harbours of France one found only Dutch bottoms. In their home port not many years before, they averred, their fellow citizens owned a hundred and fifty ships, whereas now they had not more than ten or twelve. The native sailors, these Nantois said, had forgotten the sea routes, and one saw in Nantes only the ships and faces of foreigners, Dutch, English, Scots, Irish, and Portuguese. The year following, in 1646, Jean Eon, a worldly and eloquent monk, declared that France had only six hundred ships while the Dutch had ten thousand. The learned cleric was probably exaggerating for emphasis, but others have said that about this time the French Atlantic ports were bare of French shipping. Twenty years later the situation, at Nantes at least, was hardly better. A document of 1664 states that there were only forty-nine two-decked ships with Nantes as their home port, and of these forty-five were only cod fishing boats. By the time Colbert took control of shipping, even the French coasting trade was in Dutch hands. French ships had disappeared from the Baltic, and even in the Mediterranean most of the shipping was Dutch. The depressed state of French shipping during most of the century reacted unfavourably on ship building. The industry passed out of French hands and even out of France. From the time of Henry IV to the regime of Colbert as the French formed one grandiose maritime trading company after another, they were driven to have the necessary ships built in Holland. Richelieu sought to revive French ship building and even imported Dutch workmen to aid the revival. It was estimated at that time that ships could be built in Holland for three quarters of what they would cost in France, and Richelieu ended by buying a number of ships in the Netherlands. Fouquet, also, in the fifties had ships built there. In 1660, when the French endeavoured to open direct trade with China, the first ship designated for the enterprise was built and equipped in Holland; and, incidentally, the shipmaster and almost all the principal officers were Dutch. Six years later Colbert commissioned the building of two ships in Amsterdam and two in Zaandam. Shortly after 1680, a French envoy arrived in Holland with an order to purchase flutes, the typical Dutch cargo vessels, which were to be loaded in Holland with war materiel needed for the French arsenals. It might be noted incidentally that the French by mid-century had become enormously

dependent on Holland for war materiel. In 1672 when Louis declared war on the United Netherlands with the intention of destroying the little republic, it was found that a good part of the war supplies would have to be purchased in the enemy country. One of Louis XIV's purchasing agents declared that during the war Dutch merchants provided the French armies with the greater part of their powder, match, and lead. Amsterdam bankers financed these French purchases.

In increasing numbers through the first three quarters of the century, Netherlanders settled in France. As has been said previously, they were encouraged to do so by the French monarchs and their ministers. At the very beginning of the century, Henry IV encouraged Netherlanders to enter France and gave them the right to manufacture linen there, a valuable privilege because of the great quantities of the fabric bought by Spain both for sailcloth and for trade in the New World. In Cardinal Richelieu's scheme of things also, the Dutch were favoured since Richelieu saw in them one means of promoting the wealth of the nation. The first great trading company formed by the Cardinal was the *Compagnie du Morbihan*. The king ceded to the company in perpetuity the bay and islands of Morbihan with the right to construct a free port there, and the monopoly of trade in the East and West Indies, and in northern Europe. He also gave the shareholders the right to develop fisheries and mines, to treat with the kings and princes of newly discovered lands, and to do a variety of other things. One of the principal men behind these impressive schemes of the great minister was Nicolaas Witte, a Hollander. The imagination of the Cardinal being now stimulated, the following year he projected the *Compagnie de la nacelle de Saint Pierre fleurdelisée*. This grander company among other things was to deal in all manner of merchandise, develop fisheries, build ships, exploit farm lands, refine, forge and work gold, silver, and iron, and finance voyages. It was formed at Nantes and its principal shareholders were to be Hollanders, and Brabanters, as well as Frenchmen. Any Flemish, Dutch, or other foreigners brought into France by the Company were to be treated as natives, and indeed might be legally Frenchmen simply by swearing allegiance to the King. In 1635, because Richelieu wished it, the Council of State confirmed the right of Dutch merchants to be treated as Frenchmen, and anyone interfering with their activities was liable to a fine of ten thousand *livres*. In Mazarin's time also the Dutch were encouraged to settle in France and to set up manufactures. The later great minister, Colbert, feared the economic power of the United Provinces but was absolutely

benevolent to individual Dutchmen. He persuaded one, Josse Van Robais, a Zeelander, to set up looms at Abbéville; and in the same year, 1665, learning that two Dutch clothmakers had established themselves at Caen, he ordered that they be given all the privileges of citizens and encouraged in other ways. At various times Dutchmen bought and operated paper mills, and also set up looms in various parts of the country. Dutch sugar refineries operated at Marseille, Bordeaux, La Rochelle, Angers, Saumur, Orleans, and Nantes. Dutchmen bought into glass factories. They dyed cloth, distilled brandy, made pottery, and were the moving spirits in the companies which drained and reclaimed land.

The Netherlands immigrants to France naturally were to be found in the largest numbers in the port cities their ships frequented, such as Nantes and Bordeaux. As the Dutch became successful and powerful, resentment on the part of the French citizens increased. Indeed, one of the chief sources of information about Dutchmen in France and about Dutch business methods, an envenomed and prejudiced source to be sure, is the complaints of the Nantois about the Netherlanders in their midst. The citizens of the French port felt that the Dutch succeeded chiefly because of their excellent organization. The Netherlands shippers were all members of a maritime society which manipulated and engrossed the carrying trade. The Dutch merchants in the city met twice a week to exchange information on the market, to decide what should be imported, what was to be the share of each in the importations, and the price at which the goods were to be sold to the French. They also decided what prices were to be offered for French products. Other Frenchmen believed that the kind of cooperation among the Dutch noted by the Nantois was also carried out on a nationwide scale. If there was a dearth of goods in any part of the country, the Dutch established there immediately notified their correspondents of the favourable market. It was explained that Dutch commerce was highly specialized; a merchant dealing in wines and vinegar would not be competing directly with his compatriot in wheat and vegetables. A trader in salt would confine himself to the one commodity as would one in sugar refining. It was thus possible for a number of Dutchmen to aid one another without injuring themselves. There is hardly a shady practice known to business that the French did not lay at the Dutchmen's doors. Of all the foreigners in the marts of commerce, English, Portuguese, Scots, and Irish, they considered the Dutch the most crafty and artful. Dutchmen were said to put sand or starch in the sugar, water in the wine, to adulterate the spices,

and even the drugs. They forged customs marks, put Bordeaux wines in Rhineland casks, and made imitations of French products. They withheld goods from the market until they could demand high prices. Through their shipping association they delayed or accelerated the shipment of cargoes as was most profitable to them. They also combined to offer the French low prices for their goods. As Jacques Savary, a writer on business methods, said, 'They act like upholsterers. If one offers a price for something and it is not accepted on the spot, along comes another to bid, and offers lower than the first.' Their activities in the wine trade particularly drew French ire. They dealt directly with the grape growers, thus driving the French wine merchants out of business, and then treated the growers in a diabolical manner. On first coming to Nantes, according to the Nantois, the Dutch obligingly bought all wines offered them, thereby encouraging the French to turn to the cultivation of grapes. When the great majority of the fields about Nantes were planted to grapes and wine was plentiful, the Dutch cut prices drastically. At the same time the conversion to grapes caused a shortage of grain, and then the Netherlanders shipped in wheat which they sold at exhorbitant prices. The iniquitous foreigners had also been liberal about advancing money on crops, so that eventually they controlled the vintage before the grapes were picked. The Nantois thus attributed to the Dutch a talent for economic planning such as has never been seen even in the welfare state, and a taste for unprincipled intrigue which makes Machiavelli's prince appear a mere dilettante. The exasperating fact was that though Nantes was prosperous there seemed no way for a Frenchman to share in it. Dutch cargoes were brought by Dutch ships, handled by Dutch agents, and sold to Dutch merchants who lived in taverns kept by Dutchmen. These merchants bought wine which was placed in barrels made by Dutch coopers, and transported in Dutch ships to northern Europe where it was sold at huge Dutch profits. When the French complained about these things, the Hollanders pointed out that Frenchmen were perfectly at liberty to trade at Amsterdam or any other Dutch city. This was regarded by the French as merely a bad joke, since the few Nantois who had tried to trade in Amsterdam found themselves in a web of Dutch commission merchants, warehouse owners and wholesalers who skinned them alive and picked the bones. The situation at Nantes, it was said, was aggravated by the fact that a few politically powerful Frenchmen of the city were dealt with generously by the Hollanders whether they were buying or selling, and accordingly those who might have led their fellow citizens in an attack on the foreigners

were, in fact, the Hollanders' best friends. It escaped neither the notice nor the envy of the Nantois that before the middle of the century certain individuals named Bron, Rammelman, Reynier, Velters, Lambert de Grutter, Van Houtte, and Chasteleyn retired to Holland with fortunes of at least a hundred and fifty thousand *livres*.

Actually the French ministers who had so favored the Dutch, and the Frenchmen who had resented them, were in accord in their basic desire. Both wished to see France prosperous. They had merely differed on how prosperity could best be brought about. On the side of government, it might be said that when legislation favoured the native as against the foreign traders, the individual French merchants sometimes defeated the ends of their rulers. At one time the law provided that raw sugar brought from the French West Indies should be refined in France, but at Bordeaux and other French ports, Frenchmen did a vigorous business in selling raw sugar to Dutch shippers who transported it to Holland to be refined at Amsterdam. The great chartered companies were designed to capture trade for France, but when Fouquet organized a whale oil company, instead of catching whales, the company bought whale oil in Amsterdam. When Fouquet was supplanted by Colbert, the latter organized the *Compagnie du Nord* to trade in the Baltic, but these hardy adventurers also bought their Baltic goods in the Amsterdam markets. Without doubt the most effective instruments for recovering French trade for France were Colbert's tariffs. Up until his time customs were still to some extent feudal levies collected at the frontiers of regions or provinces for the benefit of those regions, and to the detriment of foreigners and other Frenchmen alike. Colbert's tariffs of 1664 and 1667 were steps in the direction of national tariffs designed in part to protect Frenchmen and injure Dutchmen, and the latter tariff largely succeeded in this design. Although the Peace of Nijmegen (1678) abolished the measures which had been aimed against the Dutch in the 1667 tariff, there was in the last quarter of the century a gradual hardening of the French heart against foreign merchants, and a growing intolerance of Protestants. Toward the end of the century French-Dutch war marred the traditional French-Dutch friendship of an earlier day. Still, some traffic continued despite war and religion, bringing a livelihood to many Dutchmen and aiding and augmenting the other oversea trades which the Netherlanders developed in the century. Perhaps it should be added that after the War of the Spanish Succession, Dutch-French trade again became very important. The French historian Henri Sée declares that in 1715 the Dutch

maintained their commercial position intact and their superiority and power was such that almost every attempt of the French government and the rulers of Prussia to establish direct commercial relations between the two countries was foiled by the Dutch.

CHAPTER IV

Spain and the Dislocation of the Westward Trade

It is now necessary to go back in time well over a hundred years, and to return also to the beginning of the discussion of the trade with France where it was noted that the quest for salt brought Dutch ships not only to that country, but also to Portugal. By the last half of the sixteenth century, the Hollanders were hauling vast quantities of the precious mineral from the Iberian peninsula. In the less well articulated stages of the trade, ships had cargoes only on the return voyage from Spain; going southward they were in ballast. This was so, for example, in the case of the ship *The Red Lion*. The skipper, Lieven Pieterszoon, agreed with certain merchants to sail to Setúbal in Portugal, and there take on a cargo of salt. He was then to sail to Danzig where he was to deliver it to the representatives of the said merchants, and then within three weeks he was to return to Amsterdam with as much wheat or rye as was delivered to him at Danzig. The sight of empty ships going southward was painful to the Dutch, and they soon discovered ways to fill the cargo holds. Herring cargoes were sold in Baltic ports, and grain loaded for the Spanish or Portuguese cities. In these cities the grain was sold and salt loaded for Dutch ports. The salt was employed to salt down more good red herring, which was again sold in Baltic ports, and so on to the satisfaction of all industrious Dutchmen. Sometimes instead of selling the herring in Danzig, it was sold in Norway, and a cargo of Norwegian timber taken on the southward leg of the three-cornered Baltic-Dutch-Iberian trade. Sometimes timber was loaded in the Baltic rather than grain, and sometimes salt cargoes were taken directly to the Baltic. Grain, timber, herring, and salt formed the solid foundations of the business, but trade in other commodities developed. Cargoes going south from Holland included flax, hemp, wax, cloth, cheese, and hides, in addition to timber. Herring busses or cargo ships selling their cargoes in Norway took on not

only planks, masts, spars, panelling, and clapboards, but also potash, pitch, and hemp. A Dutch ship in Lisbon in 1571 loaded not only salt but fifty thousand oranges and one hundred and sixty-two thousand cork floats for fishnets. Other Dutch ships in that port loaded sugar, spices, and various other articles from the Indies. In Spanish ports Netherlands ships loaded wine, olive oil, fruit, wool, iron and salt. These products of Spain, Portugal, and the Indies had long been familiar in the Netherlands. Spices, for example, were for sale in Dutch markets at least as early as 1508, but the northern entrepôt for far eastern products in the sixteenth century had been the Hapsburg possession of Antwerp. Direct Dutch trade with the Peninsula in the third quarter of the sixteenth century was a new thing. The quantities of spices, pepper, sugar, cloves, figs and other semi-tropical fruits to be found in Amsterdam markets grew larger, and the trade southward became an integral part of the commerce of Holland and Zeeland. Rotterdam, Amsterdam, Enkhuizen, Hoorn, and other ports shared in the trade. In the Iberian peninsula, San Sebastián, Santander, Bilbao, La Coruña, Oporto, Aveiro, Lisbon, Setúbal, Sanlúcar, Sevilla, Santa Maria, and Cadiz were made more prosperous by the presence of Dutch freighters.

The French ambassador to Spain wrote in June 1569 that if the Lowland commerce should cease, nothing would happen in Sevilla, for if the cloth and other merchandise coming from the Netherlands were not sent to the Indies, no gold or silver would be returned, and the merchants in the India trade would be bankrupt. Thus, because Dutchmen plied the European waters, and because Spanish and Portuguese beat across the seas and oceans to the two Indies, Dutchmen, Norwegians, Germans, Spanish colonists, Portuguese, Hindus, Malays, and Persians were bound together in a tolerably comfortable network of trade. A surfeit of useful objects at one end of the earth could be bartered for a plethora of delectable ones at the other, providing a living for many honest merchants situated in between. Unfortunately, before the sixteenth century was over, a whole series and tangle of wars was to make chaos of these commercial connections so industriously built up, and even before the wars were over a whole new pattern of trade was in process of formation. A mere list of the wars gives an impression of the woe into which Europe was plunged.

The revolt of the Netherlands against Spanish rule broke out in 1568, and war between Spain and Holland continued for eighty years, with one brief hiatus, 1609–1621. While the Spanish to the south of them fought with the

revolting Lowlanders to the north of them, the French in between busied themselves with religious wars, which raged intermittently through the last third of the sixteenth century. When, in 1595, it began to appear that both French factions were exhausted, France declared war on Spain. The pugnacious English had been somewhat preoccupied with the equally pugnacious Irish, but in 1585, having their hands free momentarily, an English auxiliary corps under the Duke of Leicester was sent to the assistance of the Dutch, and the English entered vigorously into their role of implacable and bitter foes of Spain. In 1580, Philip II of Spain conquered Portugal, and from that date onward for sixty years, Spain and Portugal had one ruler, though a Portuguese pretender, Don Antonio, until his death in 1594 continued to make efforts to gain the throne.

War might be said to have become the universal pastime in Western Europe, and since, it appeared, grievous injury might be done an enemy by destroying his commerce, such destruction also became a universal pastime. The Netherlands, Spain, England, and France destroyed the sea traffic with almost equal zeal. By cutting off trade, for example, the Dutch sought to deal Spain a mortal blow. Holland and Zeeland in August 1578 forbade trade with Spain, and in 1581, at a time when three hundred ships were ready to depart for Spanish ports, William of Orange again prohibited trade with that country. Two years later it was forbidden by Dutch authorities to send munitions and foodstuffs not only to Spain, but to all places in possession of the enemy, and to all French ports between the Dutch provinces and Dieppe. Methods of fighting the commercial war became more comprehensive as hostilities continued. The year following the last edict mentioned, for example, it was not only forbidden to ship by sea to the enemy in South Netherlands any grain, butter, cheese, or other edibles, or any ammunition or ship fittings, but it also was declared unlawful to send such products into the interior by way of the Maas, Rhine, Leck, or Yssel rivers, or to ship them to France or to England.

In the fourteen years, 1586–1600, the Dutch issued ten laws prohibiting trade with enemy ports. These decrees the Netherlanders knew how to make increasingly severe in language as compensation for a certain laxness in their enforcement. When the Earl of Leicester, commander of the English forces in Holland, became in effect governor of the embattled provinces, he issued an edict which was a model of severity. No one, declared Leicester, whosoever he might be, could forward or transport from the United Provinces or from other lands to the enemy or to any neutral country any grain, butter, cheese,

or other edibles, or any munitions of war, or any ship fittings. The severity of his law, incidentally, was one of the principal reasons why Leicester lost his position in the Netherlands. Other edicts were less sweeping, but more detailed; that of 1591 forbade the export of balls, matches, muskets, bucklers, armour, corselets, lances, spears, halberds, broadswords, sails, cables, anchors, rudders, masts, wheat, rye, barley, oats, buckwheat, or any other grain grown in the United Netherlands.

The Spanish also industriously worked at the task of putting an end to a commerce, without which, averred their great minister, Cardinal Granvelle, the Dutch could not live. The Spanish Commander in the South Netherlands twice issued edicts in 1574 prohibiting commerce with the North Netherlanders. A favourite Spanish device also for discouraging trade was to confiscate the freighters. In order to assemble an armada in 1585, all Holland, Zeeland, German, and English ships in Spanish ports were taken by the Spanish. Somewhat later, although they had been guaranteed free passage to carry grain to famine-ridden Italian cities, twenty-six Dutch ships were confiscated by Spain on the homeward voyage. Four hundred Holland and Zeeland ships in Iberian harbors in 1595 were also taken, and twenty more in Lisbon harbor were lost in the same way the following year. The new young king, Philip III, reflected that the Dutch power to make war on Spain was largely drawn from his own kingdom. He therefore made haste to forbid trade with the Dutch, to confiscate their ships in Spanish harbors, to send the seamen to the galleys, and to imprison Dutch residents in Spain and the Spaniards who had dealings with them. In the year following these actions, in one sweep, all Dutch ships and properties in Spain were seized.

The English also prohibited trade with Spain, but they were more eager to see the edicts against Spanish-Dutch trade enforced than they were to see the enforcement of their own regulations against trade in the Iberian peninsula. Henry IV of France, not to be outdone, prohibited his people to trade with Spain or with the Spanish Netherlands. Also Dutch ships in his harbors were liable to be charged with trading with Spain and confiscated. The situation in France was further complicated at one period by the fact that Dutch merchantmen might also be charged with trading with Henry IV's Catholic enemies, the Leaguers. A Dutch freighter might also be captured by the French Catholic Leaguers, and charged with trading with the adherents of Henry of Navarre. To further muddle the situation, the privateers of Don Antonio, the Portuguese pretender, roamed the seas intent on capturing any ship which might be trading

with the Spanish king, the enemy of Don Antonio. In a word, then, an honest merchant sailing west or south might come to grief at the hands of Spanish, South Netherlandish, French, English, or Portuguese men-of-war, or privateers, and if he had the misfortune to reach his destination, he might lose his ship to Henry of Navarre, to the Leaguers, or to the Spanish crown. The measures to defeat trade which have been mentioned are by no means a complete catalogue for any country, but they are fair samples of such regulations. The laws sometimes affected one area, sometimes another; trade was sometimes permissible upon payment of a fee, sometimes not. Decrees were aimed at a particular commodity, or a group of commodities. They were issued by first one country, and then another, and their enforcement was spasmodic.

The very uncertainty as to what a merchant might expect in the way of regulation was a rather effective deterrent to trade, but in spite of all difficulties, Dutch merchants trafficked with the Iberian peninsula by one means or another, as J. H. Kernkamp in his *Handel op den Vijand* has shown. Certain notaries at Amsterdam were adept at counterfeiting for Dutch skippers the passports issued by the port authorities of Hamburg, Lübeck, and Danzig, and the skippers themselves in Spanish ports were equally adept at passing themselves off as Catholics. Officials of Iberian ports had also their price, and it was usually one which Dutch merchants could afford. If other methods failed, an enterprising skipper intent on getting goods into Spain unloaded them at the French port of Bayonne or at Saint Jean-de-Luz, and arranged with a French confrère to have the goods carried to their destination. The English, like the Dutch, evaded their own prohibitions. Ships bound ostensibly for the Barbary States put in at Iberian enemy harbors, and English goods were shipped on Hanseatic, Holland, or Zeeland vessels. An English merchant in the clutches of the Spanish inquisition in 1593 declared that 'from all parts of the Kingdom of England, and principally from London, Bristol, and Southampton, great quantities of merchandise are sent to Spain, chiefly to Seville. And that in order to insure their safe dispatch they [the merchants] avail themselves of the assistance of various peoples, such as Flemings, Germans, Scotch and Bretons....'

Thus by one means or another commerce was carried on, but because of the wars the network of European trade was a thing of rags and patches. In the zeal to destroy the commerce of others, the simple fact was overlooked that trading is exchanging, and that if one offered nothing, one got nothing. The patriotic virtue of exchanging nothing was rewarded with commercial dis-

aster. Confronted with such an appalling consequence, nations and individual merchants sought a reason, and found it due to the perfidy of their allies or of their countrymen in other branches of trade. It became obvious to the Dutch that their allies, the English, who insisted they not trade with Spain, were anxious to destroy their means of existence, or at best, were oblivious of the fact that by so insisting they were doing so. It was also apparent to the English that the Dutch had no real intention of stopping the commerce. Examining the Dutch decree of 1591 against trade with the Iberian country, the English Privy Council observed that there were 'some wordes of a pretence of a prohibicion... there are wordes of a prohibitinge of rye, wheat, barlie, oates, or other graines growinge in the United Provinces, by which wordes of growinge in those countreyes yt ys apparaunt that nothinge indeed ys to be prohibited, for that at no tyme any quantitie of soch graine hathe ever growen in thos United Provinces sufficient ynoughe to feede half the people there borne.... But yt ys apparently knowne and cannot be denied by any man but that the graine which they of the United Provinces have usually carried or doe at this tyme carrie into Spaine... are the graines which are brought out of other contryes, specially out of Estland....'

About two years before these observations by the Privy Council, the States General had begged the English to remember that the Netherlanders were bearing the brunt of the war, that they had no gold mines in the country to pay for a war, that they had only butter, cheese, and fish which they could and indeed must sell in order to continue the fight. Amsterdam merchants on another occasion reminded their critics that Holland was a warehouse where products brought from one region were briefly stored and sold in another region. If trade to the south were completely stopped, all trade was completely stopped. Before the Spanish war had continued many years the situation had become difficult. Merchants despaired of making a living in the same old way. Theodorus Velius, the contemporary historian of the city of Hoorn, remarks that the capture in Spain of so many Hoorn ships caused his fellow citizens to cast about for other means to employ their vessels, so that various strange voyages were undertaken to the East or West Indies or to Africa. Pieter Christiaanszoon Bor, one of the great historians of the time, also notes that as a result of the vexations in Spain and Portugal, his countrymen began to undertake unusual, far, and strange voyages, and these writers were but two of many who observed and recorded the fact that their countrymen were casting about for profitable means of employing vessels and seamen other than

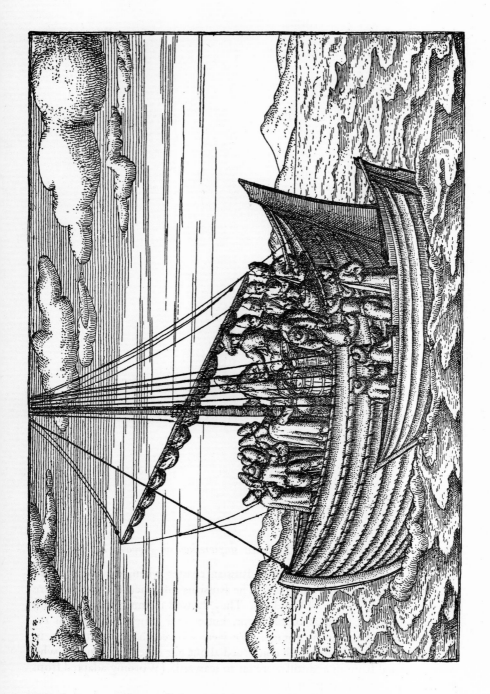

The long voyage home of the Dutchmen shipwrecked on Novaya Zemlya island

The long voyage home of the Dutchmen shipwrecked on Novaya Zemlya island

Picture showing how we came to a Russian coaster when, we thought, we were already across the White Sea. The Russians informed us that we were not yet round the corner of Candinas. They showed us much friendship, and sold us provisions, such as bacon, flour, butter and honey. Being thus re-provisioned gave us much courage. We were showed the right direction in which to sail but we were much concerned about our other companions, who were separated from us and still were far to seaward. (Wording adapted from the original Dutch inscription.)

From Gerrit De Veer's Account of the Three Voyages to the North. Amsterdam, 1598.

in the Iberian trade. The search for new trades and new markets was given impetus by the fact that the Spanish commander in the South Netherlands, the Duke of Parma, by his religious persecutions drove thousands of South Netherlanders to the northern provinces. The number of such refugees has been estimated at 60,000. Among the newcomers to the United Provinces were a great many successful merchants, men with ample capital and far-flung business connections in many parts of the world. The history of Dutch commercial expansion is studded with the names of these refugees from Antwerp, Brussels, Louvain, and other South Netherlands cities. In the effort to develop overseas commerce, ships were sent to find a polar route to the Orient, trade was fostered on the West African coast, opportunities for business in the Mediterranean were exploited, and great enterprises in the East Indies and the New World were carried out. These last two alternatives to the Spanish trade are, of course, the best known, but the others were not insignificant and should be briefly described.

The effort to develop trade with the East by voyaging around the northern shores of Eurasia was led by a remarkable South Netherlandish merchant, Balthasar de Moucheron. One of the most successful of the Antwerp men, he migrated to Middelburg after Antwerp capitulated to the Spanish. From his new home in Middelburg he drove a flourishing trade in wine with the Canary Islands, and before long he was doing considerable business on the West Coast of Africa, and in the West Indies. His ships also fished for cod on the Newfoundland banks. He traded with enemy Spain, and when a grain shortage developed in the countries bordering the Mediterranean, he brought wheat into that region from the Baltic. In 1584, the very year that the Spanish crown prohibited the Netherlanders to trade with Portugal, de Moucheron financed the voyage of Olivier Brunel in search of a north-east passage. The venture was literally wrecked by the shipwreck of Brunel, but it still had important results, for the ships which de Moucheron sent after Brunel discovered a harbor at one of the mouths of the Dwina and through his diligence and talent, the Dutch firmly established themselves at Archangel—so firmly that when the port was burned in the middle of the seventeenth century, the houses were rebuilt in the typical Dutch style. In 1593, de Moucheron again came forward with his plan for reaching the East by sailing to the north, proposing that ships bound for the Orient should pass through the straits of Yugor to the south of Novaya Zemlya. The island of Novaya Zemlya, or Nova Zembla, as it was known to the Dutch, looms large and important in

Arctic voyages, for its vast length (more than six hundred miles) lies athwart the seaway to the East. At its southern end, Novaya Zemlya is separated from the much smaller Vaygach Island by Kara Strait, and the latter island in turn is separated from the Russian mainland by Yugor Strait. In his theory that ships bound for the Orient should pass through Yugor Strait, de Moucheron was opposed by the redoubtable preacher, geographer, cartographer, and theoretical navigator, Petrus Plancius, to give the Latinized form of his Dutch name of Pieter Platvoet, or Anglicized, Peter Flatfoot. It was Flatfoot's contention that if ships passed north of Novaya Zemlya, they would find clear sailing in an open sea. The merchants and officials of the Dutch cities interested in exploring a passage to the north listened to the opposing theories of de Moucheron and of Flatfoot and studied the voyages of the Englishmen, Willoughby, Pet, Jackman, and others. The decision finally reached by them was of a type cherished in academic circles, for it was found that the theories of both Flatfoot and de Moucheron were of such undoubted excellence that an expedition ought to be fitted out to sail both north and south of Novaya Zemlya. In June, 1594, the exploring expedition actually departed from Texel, partly under private and partly under official auspices. Zeeland (Veere) furnished *The Swan*, Enkhuizen the *Mercury*, and Amsterdam *'t Boot*, or simply *The Boat*. The two former vessels were to pass to the south of Novaya Zemlya and the Amsterdamers out of deference to their distinguished fellow citizen, Plancius, were to sail north of the island to the ice-free sea that the clergyman had assured them they would find there. At the end of June, being then far on their voyage to the north, the ships parted company, the Amsterdamers to attempt to sail north around Novaya Zemlya, the other ships to sail through Yugor Strait. With the vessels which were to pass through Yugor Strait was a remarkable man, Jan Huygen van Linschoten, who left an account of the Enkhuizen and Zeeland ships. He described the limitless iceflows and icebergs as large as islands, and noted the prevalence of gams of peaceful whales. He and his comrades saw many Laplanders and Finns, and spoke to Russian traders and hunters who assured them that the neighboring lands teemed with bear, sable, martin, and fox. Ever mindful of the real business of life, Linschoten did not neglect to make a brief market analysis, concluding that one could very easily open up a trade with the Samoyeds but that it could never amount to much, since they were such a poverty-stricken, miserable, misshapen folk.

On the first of August, the ships pushed into the Kara Sea, which was as

The Samoyeds and their King

The Samoyeds and their King

The Samoyeds and their King, showing their situation, clothing and nature, their sledges which travel swiftly, the reindeer who pull them, and how our people have talked amicably with them and parted from them in friendship. (Wording adapted from the Dutch inscription.)

From Gerrit De Veer's Account of the Three Voyages to the North. Amsterdam, 1598.

blue as the Spanish sea, and tasted like pickle salt, sure proof that the Ocean Sea, Japan, and China were not far off, but the season was getting late and reluctantly the ships returned to Holland, arriving at Texel in September. When the word spread that the ships had passed through Yugor Strait into the Ocean Sea, Dutchmen began to calculate the profits of trading to China by the northern route. De Moucheron obtained (for a fee), through the Dutch Consul in England, the historian Emanuel Van Meteren, the opinion of Richard Hakluyt. That English authority assured de Moucheron that China could indeed be reached by Yugor Strait. A second expedition was gotten ready which sailed for the Arctic and China in July 1595. Chief of the super-cargoes was Jan Huygen van Linschoten, and one of his comrades was Jacob van Heemskerck.

Upon going ashore in new countries, Linschoten and his comrades were instructed to explain to kings, governors, or such other persons as they found in authority, that the Dutch trafficked and traded by sea with all the countries of the world in a friendly and upright manner, and that as a matter of fact, the trusty and honest merchants aboard their own ships were ready and willing to begin trading at the very instant. Linschoten and the other supercargoes were then to describe to their prospective customers what commodities and merchandise could be furnished by the Dutch, and to observe and examine the commodities which could be obtained in exchange. But alas, these ships so bravely fitted out, and so well provided with trading goods, found Yugor Strait and the surrounding seas so thick with ice that they could barely get through the Strait to the sea beyond, and so returned to their home ports with no glad tidings, no silks, no spices, only a little rock crystal gathered on Arctic shores. Linschoten for one was undaunted. The adventurers had again, he pointed out, seen from afar the open sea. He urged perseverance, but the only perseverance was shown by the Amsterdamers who sent out two ships on a third expedition, one commanded by Jacob van Heemskerck, the other by Jan Corneliszoon Rijp, with Willem Barents as chief officer or sailing master of the voyage. This expedition, which left the Netherlands in May 1596, is notable for the feats of navigation accomplished, the human fortitude ex-hibited, and the utter lack of any commercial success. As the reader will see by the map, the eastern side of Novaya Zemlya has the appearance of a vast and shallow bay opening on to the Kara Sea. Ice forming off the coast of Western Siberia drifts westward until it is caught by the encircling arms of Novaya Zemlya, and packs against its eastern shore. One of the ships, that

containing Heemskerck and Barents, was caught in this pack ice on the east coast. The hull was crushed and the ship frozen in. The crew spent the winter on the bleak island, and the account of their sojourn has many homely and pathetic touches. With the return of the sun in the spring, the men fitted out two open boats, and pushing off in the icy seas, began an incredible journey toward home, beset by hunger, scurvy, and cold. Barents and a companion died on an iceflow, but the others, after a number of adventures, arrived again in Holland in October 1597. By the time the shipwrecked mariners reached home, the reason for seeking a north-east passage had lost much of its urgency. That same summer Cornelis de Houtman had returned to his native country, the first Dutch merchant to make a voyage to the Indies and return. Further Dutch efforts to find a north-east passage were either by merchants outside the East India Company seeking to break into the India trade, or efforts by the Company itself to ensure its monopoly by charting and utilizing all possible routes.

Though China was not reached, Arctic voyagers gained a knowledge of Spitsbergen, a fact of major importance, for the bays and inlets of that island teemed with whales, polar bear, and walrus. The Northern Company was formed with chambers in several Dutch cities. With minor competition from independent Dutch whalers and with major competition from the English and French, the Company set about exploiting Spitsbergen animal life. Blubber and tusks were taken from the walrus, blubber and pelts from the polar bear, and there was also some trading to be done with the Greenlanders and other Arctic peoples. The principal enterprise was, of course, whaling. At first the Dutch knew little of the business. Harpooners, flensers, even the men who boiled the blubber were Basques, a people who had been whalers for hundreds of years. In season, on the spot most frequented, blossomed the village of Smeerenburg, or Blubbertown, which at its height in the years 1617–1624 counted a thousand inhabitants, bakers, peddlers, and whaling men. When whales became scarce on Spitsbergen, they were sought elsewhere, and in time more whale oil was gotten near the shores of Jan Mayen-eiland than in the bays of Spitsbergen. Occasionally still a ship made an attempt to find a passage to the rich Indies, but usually the skipper was careful to get back in time for the solid profits of the whaling season.

The dislocation of the Iberian trade resulted not only in the killing of whales, but also in a burst of interest in West Africa and the Canary Islands. The Portuguese had exploited these regions since the fifteenth century by granting

Houtman's ships in the harbor of Bantam

Houtman's ships in the harbor of Bantam

How our ships lay before Bantam and fired on the city, how the pinnace then sailed a Javanese junk aground at Pulo Dua and fought against 24 paraos loaded with Javanese, how it beat off the paraos with great losses to the Indians, but without one of us, thank God, having been wounded, how the ships fired upon the city for the second time, causing great fear among the townspeople, and how the ships sailed away from the city turning the junk adrift behind the island of Pulo Lima. (Translation of the original Dutch inscription.)

From the account of the first Dutch voyage to the East Indies. Amsterdam, 1598.

trade concessions for five years on condition that concessioneers explore a hundred miles of West African coastline. At the death of King Affonso V (1481) the exploration had already reached south of the Equator. Along the littoral, Arabs and Berbers bartered with Portuguese, exchanging pepper, gold dust, slaves, salt, and other products for cloth, corn, horses, bowls, pots, combs, looking glasses, and hides. The Portuguese were established at four chief trading centers, and a number of smaller ones. The chief centers were Arguin (Agadir), a small island near Cape Blanco, Santiago, the largest island in the Cape Verde group, São Jorge da Mina, the most important base in Guinea, and the island of São Tomé. The region had long been familiar to Netherlanders, for merchants from Brugge were on the Guinea coast in 1475, and by 1500 Flemings were in the sugar trade in the Canary Islands. Also, before 1540 the *asiento* or contractual arrangement for procuring African slaves for American colonies was in vogue, and the first holders of the *asiento* were Genoese and Flemings. Merchants from Amsterdam, passing by way of Portugal, put in at São Tomé in 1562, and an Enkhuizen ship touched at the Canaries in 1571. These incidents were forerunners of the great Dutch effort to open trade on the coast which came after 1590.

In the fifteen years, 1593–1607, more than two hundred Dutch trading vessels visited the West African coast, and by the end of that period they had broken forever the Portuguese monopoly of trade. Before the end of the century, that indefatigable entrepreneur, Balthasar de Moucheron, attempted to establish a factory on the Gulf of Guinea. In 1611, Fort Nassau was established at Moré and a few years later, in 1617, the Dutch established themselves at Goeree, and at Rufisque. They took Arguin (Agadir) from the Portuguese in 1634, Axim in 1642, São Jorge da Mina and Cabo de Corço in 1637, and São Tomé and São Paulo de Loanda in 1641. Such conquests show that the Portuguese monopoly was destroyed, but they were only the beginning of an exciting game of conquering, losing, and reconquering trading posts which Dutch, Portuguese, English, and French played on this coast for two centuries. Yet throughout the seventeenth century the Dutch drove a profitable trade in the region, and the killings, captures, and robberies which they suffered were not so excessive that they were willing to forego the profits to be made in the region. In their first voyages to the coast, the Dutch were chiefly motivated by the possibility of getting salt without recourse to the dangerous French and Iberian sources. They found that in the Cape Verde or salt islands, cargoes could be scooped up for the labour involved. They were mindful

also that this coast was the great source of slaves, and they exploited the slave trade as far as their own energies and the opposition of their competitors would allow. Also, at the beginning of the seventeenth century, the Portuguese African plantations were the principal source for sugar, and through Dutch efforts, Amsterdam became the chief market for that product. Ivory and gold dust likewise became major concerns of Dutch traders. In the years 1611–1612, one ship returned to the Netherlands with 50,000 pounds of ivory, another with 62,000 pounds, and a third with 96,000 pounds. The same document which reported that two hundred Dutch ships had visited the coast in the period 1593–1607 also recorded the fact that in these years two thousand pounds of fine gold were brought back from Africa each year. Later much more of the metal was gotten from Guinea. This gold was of the greatest importance, for together with the silver streaming in (directly and indirectly) from Spanish America and the gold gotten later from Brazil, it served to make Amsterdam the chief market for precious metals.

The African Negroes welcomed the first Netherlanders with open arms. 'They were wont,' says a contemporary Dutchman, 'to be very simple in their dealings, and trusted the Netherlanders very much, whereat we wondered.' They took the words of Dutch traders for the quality and quantity of the merchandise they purchased, he continues, 'Whereby they were decieved; for, that if they bought ten fathome of linnen, they found but eight....' The Africans learned quickly how to help the Dutch remain honest, and not only remeasured their cloth, but examined carefully the basins and pans which they purchased in enormous quantities. 'We carry them,' said a contemporary, 'great store of Basons, as little Basons, Barbers Basons, Basons to drinke in, Platters of Copper, flat Basons, great broad copper pans, at the least two fathome about, and small Posnets without edges. The small Basons they use to put oil in wherewith they anoint themselves, and the greater of them they set in the graves of the dead & use them to carry divers things in. The Barbers Basons they use to wash themselves.... The great broad Pans, are by them used to kill a Goat or a Hogge in ... and many other such like Basons of Copper, which our ships bring thither in great quantities, and therewith fill the countrie so full... they are sold as good cheape there unto the Negroes as they are bought in Amsterdam....' In addition to basins, milk cans and kettles, the Dutch disposed of large quantities of bar iron from which the Africans made spears, daggers, and cultivators, and sold also tinware, knives, and fishhooks. Such delicacies as oil, lard, sardines, biscuit, wine, brandy, and

good Dutch cheese also went well. There was a lively market for glass, striped glass, crystal and amber beads; copper and tin arm rings; copper leg rings, bells, chains, and knick-knacks of all sorts. Linens and kerseys, and cottons in red, white, yellow, and blue were greatly prized and brought a good return. For such glittering and colorful merchandise, the Dutch got not only slaves, gold, and ivory, but pepper, hides, wax, amber and some dye wood.

The search for alternatives to the Iberian trade resulted, then, in whaling and in the African commerce. It also resulted in ventures into the Mediterranean, and the East and West Indies, as will be explained in the following chapters.

CHAPTER V

The Mediterranean

As the Dutch cast about for ways to employ their ships, and a trade to take the place of the disrupted Spanish commerce, they turned, in addition to the regions that have already been mentioned, to the Mediterranean. There had long been trade between northern Europe and that region which had been carried on via three routes. First, from the eighth to the twelfth centuries, goods from the Levant were carried across the Black Sea up the Dnieper to Kiev and north to Novgorod. The merchants of that city then transported them to Visby on the island of Gotland in the Baltic, and to other Scandinavian and German cities. Second, during the middle ages and into modern times there was a well-worn route for Levantine goods used by the Hansa merchants which ran overland from the Adriatic, via the Alpine passes and the south German cities to the Baltic; and third, there was the route northward by sea around the western edge of Europe. Within the Mediterranean area there might be thought to be three principal trading regions from which goods were drawn. These were the Italian cities, the Levant, and the Barbary states on the North African coast.

Dutchmen casting a speculative eye on the Mediterranean thought naturally of the sea route, and at first only of trade with the Italian cities, for such traffic had a long tradition with the Lowlanders. At the beginning of the fourteenth century and probably earlier, Venetian ships came to Brugge and Antwerp. Long before there was a United Provinces, agents of Antwerp merchants were to be found in the chief Italian cities, and early in the sixteenth century travellers were sometimes astonished to see Mediterranean galleys at the Antwerp docks. Middelburg, the Zeeland city at the mouth of the Scheldt, shared in this commerce as well as Antwerp farther upstream. Apparently, although Italian ships sought these Lowland ports, and Netherlands ships

sailed to Spain and West Africa, the Netherlanders were content not to pass beyond the Straits of Gibraltar until forced to it by the depressed state of their Iberian commerce. Here as in other instances impetus was given to the trade by refugees from the South Netherlands who had business connections in the Mediterranean, and who knew about or had been involved in voyages from Antwerp to Italian ports. When the Dutch did enter the Mediterranean, they began with a few timid and tremulous exploratory voyages. Then, when there was a shortage of grain in Italy, trade developed with a rush. This traffic was badgered and bled by the Spanish until the Dutch defeated their enemy at sea in 1607, and then it expanded extensively during the period of the Dutch–Spanish truce, 1609–1621.

One of the first, though certainly not the first, Dutchmen in the Mediterranean was Steven van der Hagen, who sailed as supercargo on the ship *De Witte Leeuw (The White Lion)* which left the Texel at the end of 1585 bound for Genoa, carrying a cargo of ling for the account of a group of merchants of Hoorn. Part of the cargo was sold at Valencia, and the rest was disposed of at Genoa, where a cargo of treacle, raisins, rice, and almonds was loaded for a return voyage to Valencia. *The White Lion* ran into heavy seas. The barrels of treacle, being improperly stowed, rolled and smashed against each other, and damaged the ship so badly that it was forced to put in at Cadiz. There the hostile Spanish port authorities confiscated the ship, but Van der Hagen was freed and returned overland to Holland. Despite his misfortune, he retained the confidence of his employers, and he was commissioned to outfit an even larger ship for a second voyage. The cargo was again largely fish. After a difficult voyage, the ship reached Alicante, where Van der Hagen sold part of the cargo, and then continued on to Valencia, where he sold the remainder. In the Spanish ports, Van der Hagen witnessed the outfitting of ships for that great armada, which was called Invincible. It occurred to him what with Spain preparing an unprecedented number of warships, and the English holding no mean idea of their maritime prowess, that the narrow seas between the continent and Britain were no place for a peaceful merchantman. Consequently, instead of returning home to Holland from Valencia, he loaded a cargo belonging to Italian merchants and sailed for Genoa out of harm's way. In that port he had the good luck to be hired to proceed to the Balearic Islands and to bring back a cargo of salt from there to Genoa. Thus, in 1588, while Charles Lord Howard and his Dutch allies fought the Armada in the Channel and the English and Spanish were engaged in the exciting business of

killing one another, Van der Hagen passed a pleasant and profitable summer in the Mediterranean. Unfortunately, he did not stay long enough in that region. Returning to Genoa with salt from the Balearics, he there loaded rice, raisins, almonds, anise, and soap for Valencia. In the latter port, he found the Spanish smarting from their defeat at the hands of the English and looking for scapegoats. Through well-wishers, Van der Hagen learned that the port authorities again intended to seize his ship, and when the Spanish arrived, the Dutch crew were elsewhere. Van der Hagen made his way to Genoa and from there overland to Holland.

In the following year, 1589, there was another trading venture into the Mediterranean. The ship, *The Black Horseman*, was financed by North and South Netherlanders and a merchant of Bremen. It was loaded with a heterogeneous cargo of flax, salted salmon, salted eels, sardines, herring, hides, cloths, lance shafts, and pitch, the object being to discover what products sold most easily in Italian ports. If these goods could be disposed of in Livorno or Genoa, then the ship was to proceed to Crete for a cargo of muscatel, a wine more popular then than it is now. Failing to get a cargo of muscatel, the ship's officers were to attempt to buy refined sulphur, alum, rice, or subtropical fruits for the return voyage to Holland. The voyages of *The White Lion* and *The Black Horseman* were only precursors of a tremendous Mediterranean trade. Beginning in 1587, Italy experienced a series of bad harvests, and by 1590 there was a serious famine. The historian Muratori tells us that in that year the poor were reduced to eating grass, and that in the year following, it was even worse. There was weeping and wailing on all sides, he continues, and the Pope, the Dukes of Firenze, Ferrara, Urbino and other princes, and especially the wise republic of Venice, spared no expense to bring grain from the most distant places.

Velius, the chronicler of Hoorn, reported that in 1590 the first ships from his city left with cargoes of grain for Italy, and within the year fifteen or sixteen Dutch ships passed through the Straits of Gibraltar. News of the astounding profits made by these first grain ships spread rapidly, and in the following year two hundred ships made the voyage to Italy. This great and profitable new trade had the usual effect of innovation, that is, it was both pointed to with pride and viewed with alarm. It was attacked by the alarmists, who were circumvented by the prideful pointers, and finally it was accepted as part of the pattern of life.

In spite of continued imports from the Baltic, the new commerce rapidly

depleted the grain reserves in Holland. In 1596 there were numerous complaints that with a grain shortage in Holland itself, the merchants were shipping to Italy every bushel they could lay their hands on, and at a time when the country was at war with Spain and needed all available ships, the owners were recklessly throwing them away in the Mediterranean trade. The States General yielded to this clamor and detained the grain ships bound for Italy. The merchants in the trade pointed out that this action would simply result in neutrals rather than Dutchmen buying the Baltic grain and shipping it to Italy and there were signs that this was actually happening. In the same year also, both Venice and Tuscany placed important grain orders in Holland, and Venice sent a skillful and shrewd nobleman, Francesco Moresini, to the Netherlands to buy wheat. In any event, the prohibition decreed by the States General was not too effective, since the Amsterdam merchants simply sent their ships around Scotland to French ports. There French passports were obtained for Italian ports and the vessels continued on as before. In view of the powerful persuasives to continue the trade, and since it could not be stopped anyhow, the embargo on the trade was conveniently forgotten and the grain ships allowed to sail. In 1597 the number of ships bound for Italy jumped to four hundred and in the same year, voyages direct from the Baltic to the Mediterranean were initiated. In the following year, in one week, six hundred wheat ships arrived in Amsterdam from the east, and in 1601 within three days, between eight hundred and nine hundred grain ships left Dutch ports to load wheat in the Baltic.

The trade persisted and grew despite the many hazards and enemies the ships encountered at sea. The vessels had to run the gauntlet of English, French, and Barbary pirates, and also the risk of being captured by the Spanish enemy. There are records of many grain voyages ending disastrously. The unfortunate experiences of Van der Hagen and the ship, *The White Lion*, have already been mentioned. Although Philip II promised safe passage to ships relieving the Italian famine, he did not apparently think his safe conduct applied to the ships *after* they had relieved the famine. In 1591 a fleet of twenty-six Dutch grain ships on the way home to Holland were taken by the Spanish in the Straits of Gibraltar, and the seamen sent to the galleys. In 1594 a number of grain ships, after surviving a disastrous storm in their home port, were also taken by the Spaniards. The trade labored under the maltreatment of the Spanish as long as the fleets of Spain remained strong and in command of the Straits of Gibraltar. The damage done to the commerce of Holland finally

spurred the States General to send a war fleet to clear the Straits of the enemy. The ships appointed for the task were commanded by that doughty seaman who has already been mentioned in connection with the voyages to the north, Jacob van Heemskerck. The Dutch admiral with twenty-six ships arrived off Gibraltar in 1607. He found the Spanish warships bigger, better armed, and more numerous, but he attacked them without hesitation. Van Heemskerck chose for his own special prey the ship of Juan d'Alvarez d'Avila, the Spanish Admiral , and when he poured a broadside into the Spaniard, the melee became general. There has seldom been as spectacular a sea battle as that which ensued, with both fleets of fighting ships crowded into the narrow Straits of Gibraltar. As De Jonge, Holland's historian of the sea, says, 'the booming cannon, the burning and exploding ships, the shouting of the sailors, the cries of the wounded and dying, the cheers of the victors,' produced a terrifying and awesome scene. The ship of the Spanish admiral drifted helplessly out of control until destroyed by the Spanish themselves. The Spanish vice-admiral's ship burned to the water line, as did two other galleons. A fourth was sunk, and two others blown up. What was left of the Spanish fleet fled to the protection of the shore batteries. Though Van Heemskerck was killed, he had achieved an impressive victory and removed the greatest obstacle to Dutch Mediterranean trade. Two years later when a truce was declared between Spain and the United Netherlands, the last vestiges of Spanish interference with the trade disappeared, at least for a time.

The Mediterranean commerce, as has been said, was also aided by the fact that a number of South Netherlanders who had fled to the northern provinces had agents in Italy, and also by the fact that Spanish and Portuguese Jews in the United Provinces were in touch with friends and compatriots settled in the Mediterranean area. Since Amsterdam was the grain city, the Italian trade was chiefly an Amsterdam trade. On one occasion in 1592, for example, of twenty-two Dutch ships arriving at Livorno, twenty-one were from Amsterdam. Other Dutch cities, Hoorn, Rotterdam, and Middelburg, had also a share, if a minor one, in the commerce. At first the chief trading ports were Livorno (Leghorn) and Genoa. Later Venice, and then Naples, Messina, and Civitavecchia in the Papal States became ports of call for Dutch ships, but Livorno remained by far the most important port for Netherland merchants. A 'Via degli Scali Olandesi' (street of the Dutch wharves) which still exists is evidence of the city's great popularity with Dutchmen. It was a freeport, neither export nor import taxes being levied, and there was also freedom of

religion. Catholics, Calvinists, Lutherans, Moslems, and Jews thronged its busy streets. The foreign merchants were united in brotherhoods or 'nations,' one of the most important of which was the 'Nazione Olandese-Allemana.' The city became the market place for cotton and later coffee, but almost all articles of Mediterranean commerce could be purchased there. In Genoa, trade was principally in silks, carpets, gold and silver cloth, oil, soap, rice, drugs, and marble. Grain was carried to Naples and Messina, and from Civitavecchia the Dutch procured alum, wine, olives, and semi-tropical fruits. Next to Livorno, and perhaps as important for the Dutch as Genoa, was Venice, their voyages there probably beginning before the end of the sixteenth century. In 1609 the Dutch sent an ambassador to the Venetian republic, Cornelis van der Mijle, Curator of the University of Leyden and son-in-law of Oldenbarnevelt. Later, in 1620, the States sent Francoys van Aerssen, and the Venetians sent (in 1616) Christofforo Suriano to The Hague. Reports of Dutch ships at Venice are fragmentary but give an impression of a noteworthy trade. In February 1616, for example, eighteen Dutch ships lay at anchor at Venice, and two months later ten more arrived from Sicily. In March of the following year, the same number of Netherlands merchantmen were at anchor. Half of these returned home with cargoes and the other half entered the service of Venice as fighting ships. From that time on for many years, Dutch merchantmen were regular visitors at the Adriatic port. The first branch of an Amsterdam commercial house was established in Venice about 1617, and others followed. Dutch ships came laden with such goods from the Baltic as wheat, caviar, masts, hemp, and other marine stores. They also brought their own inevitable herring, spices and dyewoods from the Indies, and madder which might have originated in a number of places. At Venice, the Dutch loaded salt, rice, oil, and semi-tropical fruits. They also bought there the famous Venetian glass and mirrors, and such de luxe fabrics as velvet, lace, raw and worked silk. They took home, in addition, some steel, turpentine, sulphur, and anise, the latter much esteemed as a medicine and as flavoring.

There was not to be had at Venice any valuable bulk commodity to make up a profitable return cargo for the Dutch ships. Indeed the lack of return cargoes was the drawback to the whole Italian trade. The Lowland skippers, in order to show a profit, adopted the expedient of carrying cargoes between Italian ports, and in time the great bulk of the Italian carrying trade was in their hands. When they had to return home, very often they took marble as ballast, and this commodity developed into an important business. Two Am-

sterdam capitalists, Gilles and Willem Sautijn, together with Pieter van der Straten, the consul at Livorno, built up a great trade in the stone. These men acquired the sole right to export certain kinds of marble from the lands of the Republic of Genoa, from the domains of the Duke of Massa, and those of the Grand Duke of Tuscany. Although these men were among the leaders in the trade, marble was imported by numerous Dutch merchants. The stately houses which the burghers of Amsterdam built along the Heerengracht and the Keizersgracht with their marble floors, marble wainscots, and marble stairs, are souvenirs of this Italian trade. A seventeenth century traveller to Amsterdam exclaimed that 'There are such vast magazines [of marble] in Amsterdam that a man would think that there were marble quarries near the city gates,' and Amsterdam long maintained its place as a marble emporium. When the palace of Versailles was built, Louis XIV bought his marble in Amsterdam.

After 1648, when the wars in Germany came to a close and overland trade could be resumed, the Dutch sea trade to Italy diminished somewhat, but throughout the century it retained a respectable degree of vigor. There are statistics available, for example, to show that in 1667 considerable quantities of almonds, lemons, and rice were loaded at Genoa for Dutch ports, and that from elsewhere in Italy oranges, sulphur, raisins, currents, gall nuts, and cotton were exported, or re-exported, to Holland.

Previously it was said that in addition to Italy there was trade with two other Mediterranean areas, the Levant and the Barbary States. Of these, the traffic with the Levant was by far the more important. At the birth of the Dutch republic, the Levantine trade was in the hands of the Italians, French, and English, the Netherlanders receiving Levant merchandise only at second hand; but in 1598, thanks to the good offices of Henry IV of France, the Great Lord of the Porte granted Dutchmen permission to trade under the French flag at Constantinople and at other harbors in his domains. The Turks knew that the Dutch were only masquerading as French, but favored them because they had rebelled against Spain. The Hollanders were aided in developing this trade also by the Spanish Jews settled at Amsterdam who had relations and friends in the Levant. In Turkey, Jews, as well as Greeks and Armenians, acted as dragomen or interpreters, and since Turkish merchants refused to do business with foreigners, the dragomen were immensely influential, being in fact commission merchants who received a percentage on all goods bought and sold. Having obtained a foothold, the Dutch sought to become more firmly established in the Near East by appointing Cornelis Haga as 'orator' or spokesman

at the Porte. The English, French, and Venetians did what they could to hinder Haga, but in spite of their efforts, in 1612 he negotiated a treaty with the Turks. The Hollanders were given the right to trade in all the realms of the Sultan which stretched into eastern Europe, the lands bordering the Sea of Azov, and including the island of Cyprus. Soon there were consuls in Dalmatia, Greece, Turkey, Syria, and Egypt, as well as in those Moslem lands not subject to the Sultan, Algiers, and Tunis.

The trade in the Levant was largely conducted in hard money, and the staples of Dutch trade were largely useless. Moslems felt no compulsion to eat fish on Fridays, grain came to them easily from the Ukraine by the inland seas, and the heavy Lowlands cloths were of limited usefulness in many regions of the east, about as useful as burnouses in Amsterdam. The Levantines had long been accustomed to buy the fine cloths of Languedoc, so that Dutch merchants trading to the Near East usually put in at Marseille to barter their northern cloths for the lighter, finer materials of southern France. They then went on to sell other parts of their cargoes in Italian ports for the piastres, sequins, or preferably, Spanish reals which they needed to buy goods at Constantinople, Aleppo, or Smyrna. Though buying for cash was the general rule in the Levant, Dutchmen did manage to sell or barter there a considerable variety of goods obtained elsewhere. The products most in demand were those from India and the Far East, muslins, painted cloths, porcelain, and tea, which the Dutch could actually bring around the Cape of Good Hope to Holland and back to the Levant cheaper than the Levantine merchants could transport these articles overland. The Netherlanders also sold in the eastern Mediterranean the goods which they had picked up on the Italian and Dalmatian coasts. Their ships also carried Russian products, caviar, furs, and Russian leather; Scandinavian products such as iron, steel, and copper; whale oil from the Arctic; coffee, dyewoods, and cacao from the West Indies; elephant tusks from West Africa; the finer cloths of their own country, Flanders, and Silesia; ironmongery from Germany; and a modicum of herring and dried cod. The articles which the Dutch bought in the Levant were largely carpets, Persian silk, Angora wool, camel's hair, fine leather, coffee, tobacco, pearls, perfume, and opium.

As was usually the case, Dutch trade was well regulated and organized. In 1625, Amsterdam created a College of Directors for the Levant Trade and Navigation in the Mediterranean. Soon there were similar colleges in Leyden, Hoorn, Enkhuizen, Medemblik, and in 1670, a Rotterdam College. These

chambers of commerce inspected goods destined for the southern cities, supervised and paid the consuls in the various ports, paid part of the salary of the orator at the Porte, executed the regulations of the States General, requested convoy vessels of the government when they were necessary, and last, but not least, provided gifts for Turkish officials. The consuls employed by the Directors for the Levant Trade saw to the procurement and sale of cargo, the handling of freight, the settlement of freight bills and of damage claims. Their salaries were paid by a two per cent tax on imports and exports, payable in the home port. The shippers sometimes sought to avoid the tax. To this end they declared their cargoes at half the real value, falsified ships papers, and three hundred years before American ships were registered as Panamanian or Liberian, Dutch skippers were placing their vessels under foreign flags.

In the first years of the Levant trade, Aleppo and its port of Alexandretta were the chief market places for the Dutch in the Near East, and a central point for the commercial traffic of Asia Minor, Arabia, and Persia. Netherlands commerce with Constantinople itself declined after the departure of Haga in 1639, and in the following year, there were only two Dutch business houses in the Turkish capital. Egyptian trade had no great appeal for Lowlanders and Alexandria was not of great importance in the trade. Such Dutch ships as frequented the port were largely vessels which had been commissioned or chartered to carry freight between Egypt and the Italian ports. After the Turko-Persian war of 1617, the chief outlet for Persian goods was Smyrna, and by 1640 that was the favorite Dutch port. A Dutch colony grew up in the city, which was at its height in the period 1688–1723, but which endured until the present century.

The third Mediterranean region which interested the Dutch was the Barbary States. In the seventeenth century this coastal strip was principally known as a pirate's den, and the inhabitants, one might say, were not aware of the mutual advantages aspect of trade. Conditions in Morocco and Algiers were so chaotic that it was very difficult to trade actually on the ground, although there was some legitimate business transacted there. Usually the commerce was conducted at Livorno. When the Jews were expelled from Spain and Portugal, they migrated not only to the Netherlands and the Levant, but also to the Barbary States. As a result, Amsterdam Jews frequently had good connections with friends in this region, and these Amsterdam citizens did a thriving business in selling arms in Barbary and in arming Moroccan and Algerine ships which were usually engaged in piracy. While selling arms and munitions

in Barbary, merchants could procure there slaves and booty captured by the pirates. Actually, Amsterdam Jews settled at Livorno acted as fences for the robbers, and it was usually cheaper to buy slaves and plunder at Livorno than it was to buy them in Barbary. Cloths, dyestuffs, Tripolitan silks, and many other articles in addition to slaves could be got in this way.

Despite a great deal of illegitimate and some legitimate trade, the Barbary States were chiefly notable as an obstacle to commerce. There are various indications of the losses inflicted by the pirates of the ports of Salee, Tunis, and Algiers, some being noted by that philosopher of commerce, Pieter de la Court. 'The Algerines,' says this author, 'in the years 1620 and 1621, within the space of thirteen months took of Holland [i.e., the Province of Holland] ships alone 143 sail.' The Dutch had three possible solutions to the pirate problem. First, they set warships to chastise the wicked men, but found this expensive. Second, they bought off the pirates with bribes, and third, they instituted the convoy system. The States General in 1621 ordered that ships going to the Mediterranean were to be well armed and to sail in convoy, and the ordinance remained in force for the remainder of the seventeenth century. Convoys sailed three or four times a year, and dispersed at Livorno and Zante for the various ports, and reassembled at the same harbors for the voyage home. Regularly there were about two hundred ships in a convoy. The system did not altogether eliminate losses to pirates. In 1662 and 1663, for example, Amsterdam lost twenty-nine ships to the Algerine pirates, but the device did have the effect of cutting the losses.

The Mediterranean trade arose because the Spanish and Portuguese had made it difficult for the Dutch to trade in their ports. The action had simply resulted in the Lowlanders going to the Mediterranean source for many of the goods which they had formerly got in Spain or Portugal. It began as a solution to the complex commercial problem which was posed by war with Spain, but the solution was not unpleasant nor unprofitable and possibly too much has been made here of the dangers and difficulties. The region was certainly attractive and pleasant. The commercial relations of South Netherlanders who had moved to the United Provinces were probably numerous. The development of business after the initial disasters of confiscation by Spain was probably relatively smooth and unhindered.

CHAPTER VI

Indonesia

As in the case of the African, the Arctic, and the Mediterranean trade, a description of Dutch commerce in the Orient must begin with the facts that in the last quarter of the sixteenth century, the Netherlands trade to the Iberian peninsula was considerably disrupted by war. When the Dutch could no longer trade freely with Portugal, they were largely cut off from the products of the mysterious East, since all of the Eastern trade, as far as Europeans were concerned, was in Portuguese hands, and had been for most of the century. Portuguese penetration into the Orient began with Bartholomeu Dias, who rounded the Cape of Good Hope in 1488, and Vasco da Gama, who passed that promontory and reached India about ten years later. In 1510 Affonso de Albuquerque conquered Goa and made it a center for Portuguese trade. Cities of Ceylon were first occupied by the Portuguese in 1517, Malacca was captured in 1511, and in the same year the Portuguese reached the Moluccas. They later established themselves in China at Macao, and before the middle of the sixteenth century were trading in Japan. One of their important trading centers was the islands of the East Indies, which were the chief source for pepper and spices.

Until Dutch ships were left without employment, the Lowlanders were content to let the Portuguese gather the goods of the Indies and transport them to their home ports, while the Dutch ships awaited them there to buy what the Portuguese brought home. This apparent lethargy on the part of the Dutch was not simply ignorance of how to get to the Orient themselves. Charts showing the way there were for sale in Portugal, and some were reprinted and offered for sale in Amsterdam by Cornelis Claesz. Portuguese ships bound for the Orient employed great numbers of foreign sailors, and among them were many Dutchmen. Netherlanders were also employed as clerks, mer-

Plants of the East Indies

Plants of the East Indies

A. The coconut tree which can be found growing very abundantly in all quarters of East India, very much to the convenience of the Indians.
B. The banana or Indian fig tree which contributes most of all to the support of the Indians.
C. Pepper growing around a tall cane, called bamboo in Malayan.
D. Indian saffron in bloom. This plant grows in many places in India. (Wording adapted from the original Dutch inscription.)

From the account of the first Dutch voyage to the East Indies. Amsterdam, 1598.

chants, and in other offices, and some of these men talked and wrote of experiences in the eastern lands.

One of the most enthusiastic Dutchmen was a certain citizen of Enkhuizen named Dirck Gerritszoon Pomp. The family of this man had, about 1550, migrated to Lisbon. Young Dirck had entered the Portuguese service and made a voyage to the Far East. In 1590, forty years after the family had left the town, Dirck returned to Enkhuizen. So fond was he of telling travellers' tales of his experiences in the East that his long suffering neighbors nicknamed him 'Dirck China.' Another Dutchman to go to the Orient in the Portuguese service was the remarkable man who has already been mentioned in connection with the voyages to the Arctic, Jan Huygen van Linschoten. 'My heart,' he wrote in 1584, 'is longing day and night for voyages to far-away lands.' His yearnings were fulfilled, for he travelled widely from the Orient to the Arctic. In 1579 he was sent to Spain to learn the practical business of trading. Four years later he sailed to Goa in the service of a Portuguese archbishop, and spent five years in the Indies. Returning to his native land he published his *Reysgeschrift*, dated 1595, a collection of Portuguese sailing directions, and his *Itinerario* (1596), a description of the peoples and products of India, Ceylon and the lands of the Far East. All of Linschoten's information was not got at first hand. Some of it was related to him by his friend, Dirck Gerritszoon Pomp. In his *Itinerario*, Linschoten attempted to give not only a description of the countries of the East, but more specifically a full account of the products to be obtained in the various regions and kingdoms there. The oriental commodities had quite different values for the seventeenth century than they have for us. One gets an idea of the importance of the Orient for the seventeenth century man by reading Linschoten's catalogue of places and their products. He systematically discusses the islands of the East Indian Archipelago, Timor, the Moluccas, the Banda group, Sumatra, Borneo, and Java. Timor, he notes, was the prime source for sandalwood, although the tree grew on the Coromandel coast and elsewhere in India. The wood was greatly prized in India, China, and throughout the East. It was useful for carving, for incense, and yielded an aromatic oil for preparing perfume. More wondrous was the fact that if it were beaten to a pulp and laid on the stomach with rosewater, it was good for burning fevers, and put into cordials it strengthened the heart.

To the north of Timor lie the Moluccas which, says Linschoten, with some exaggeration, 'have nothing else but Cloves, which are carried from thence, throughout the world.... When the Cloves are greene, they make good

conserves in Sugar and are likewise salted in Vineger & so kept in pots and made into Achar in which manner they are carried into Malacca and India....' Linschoten adds that 'The Indian women use much to chawe Cloves, thereby to have a sweete breath, which the Portingales wives that dwell there, doe now begin to use.' Linschoten continues his catalogue with a description of Amboina and Banda which produced nutmegs and mace. 'The fruite,' he says, explaining how the nutmeg grows, 'is altogether like great round Peaches, the inward part whereof is the Nutmegge.... This fruite or Apples are many times conserved in Sugar being whole, and in that sort caried throughout India, and much esteemed....' Linschoten also explains that the seed, or nutmeg, has a red fibrous seed cover from which mace is prepared. Both nutmeg and mace were powerful medicaments, nutmeg being, in fact, a veritable wonder drug. In addition to other therapeutic values, it sharpened the memory, warmed and strengthened the maw, drove wind out of the body, drove down urine, and stopped diarrhea. Mace was good for a cold, aided digestion, and enabled one to break wind. Of the island of Sumatra, Linschoten reports that it yielded gold, silver, brass, precious stones, medicinal herbs, and other products. Of far more importance was the fact that Sumatra was the great producer of pepper, an article which was the firm foundation of Portuguese trade, as it had been of Venetian commerce. For us pepper is only a condiment. We have forgotten what Linschoten and his contemporaries knew, that mixed with various ingredients, it would improve the eyesight, cure the dropsy, and eliminate pains in the liver. Continuing down the list of islands, the geographer-merchant-adventurer explains that from Soekadana on the west coast of the island of Borneo, one could get diamonds, and from the sultanate of Sambas, also in west Borneo, one could procure both gold and diamonds, while Banjermasin in south Borneo supplied tortoise shell. The great island of Java Linschoten described as a trading center where a large variety of articles brought from various places were for sale. In Java grew a certain tree which grew also in Sumatra and Malaya, and from the bark of this tree was procured a resin called benzoin, one of the costliest drugs in the Orient. Bernard ten Broecke, Linschoten's fellow townsman who interpolated many notes in Linschoten's narrative, assures us that benzoin comforteth the heart and sharpeneth the wit. It was valuable also for perfume and incense.

Linschoten had much to say of India and Ceylon. India, he tells us, is the place to get cardamon, a spice much used to dress meats, and to chew upon, very good against stinking breath and evil humours in the head. The same

Foreign merchants at Bantam

Foreign merchants at Bantam

Foreign merchants at Bantam, showing their usual manner of dressing.
D. A Malayan merchant whose business it is to lend money on plantations or
   on voyages.
E. The Quillin (Klingalese) who also handles such transactions.
F. The wife of a merchant.
The merchants pictured also buy the cargoes of the Chinese merchants and
sell them at retail. (Wording adapted from the original Dutch inscription.)

From the account of the first Dutch voyage to the East Indies. Amsterdam, 1598.

country yielded spikenard, which 'comforteth the mawe.... and consumeth cold humors.' Ginger was found in many places in that domain, good in salads with oil, salt, and vinegar, and also on flesh and fish. There also one found tamerind, necessary for chutney and curries, and good against the plague. Snakeroot was also much traded in, good against poison, colic, worms, and more especially the shakes. Bhang and opium, two narcotics in great demand throughout the East, were prepared in India, as was the dyestuff indigo. This country was also the prime source for many kinds of gems, such as sapphires, topazes, diamonds, and rubies. Turning to Ceylon, our commercial reporter declares that there one found literally whole forests of cinnamon trees, a delicious spice, good for the heart, for catarrh, for dropsy, stopping of the kidney, and strengthening of the liver. From China came musk, rhubarb, and all kinds of lacquer work, such as cabinets, chairs, tables, stools, and beds, as well as numerous pieces of porcelain. As was well known, this country was also the source of China root, a sure cure for the pox, piles, cramps, and palsies. By the trade routes to the interior of Asia and Asia Minor many other products were brought to Chinese markets, such as manna, frankincense and myrrh.

These brief extracts from Linschoten's extensive works give an impression of how the east appeared to a seventeenth century European, a source not only of riches, but what was perhaps more important in that era when life was brutish, painful and short, a source for drugs, which would restore health and well being. What Linschoten wrote probably many others reported by word of mouth, and such interesting oriental goods as they described had been brought to Holland from Portugal. Linschoten also avowed, and again probably many others brought the same information, that the Portuguese empire in the East was decayed, rotten and tottering, a structure which would collapse if given even a moderate blow, or to change the metaphor, it was a plum ripe for the plucking. A number of factors, then, lured the Dutch into sending ships to the Far East. They needed employment for their vessels, their customary source for oriental goods was cut off, and there appeared good prospects that they could intrude into the Portuguese preserves with little danger and good profits.

It was almost inevitable, then, that in 1594, in the wine shop of Martin Spil, in the Warmoesstraat in Amsterdam, nine powerful capitalists of the city held meetings wrapped in mystery. They were in the process of forming a 'Company for Far Places,' and were in actual fact planning a trading voyage to the

Far East. Subsequently they contracted with shipbuilders for the construction of four vessels of the type usually employed in voyages to Brazil and the Mediterranean, and outfitted them with three sets of spare masts, and double sets of anchors and cables. When the vessels were ready, their holds were filled with trading goods, woolen cloth, linens, blankets, mosquito netting, glassware, mirrors, amber, miscellaneous ornaments, ironware, knives, padlocks, steel helmets, and cuirasses. In charge of the commercial affairs for the voyage, the stockholders of the Company for Far Places selected a relative of one of their number, Cornelis de Houtman, an experienced business man, who had spent some time in Portugal where, presumably, he had gained some knowledge of Far Eastern trade. The chief navigator for the voyage was Pieter Dirckszoon Keyser.

The ships sailed with the high hopes of the Company directors and of the crews, but affairs went badly almost from the beginning of the voyage. There were quarrels, lack of discipline, and sickness. When the four ships finally reached Bantam, some fifteen months after leaving Holland, the Dutchmen were received with suspicion by the Portuguese but with kindness by the Javanese, and the hopes of the Netherlanders for a happy and prosperous voyage were revived. Javanese, Chinese, and Indian merchants thronged the ships and bought the Dutch goods, and in the words of one Hollander, 'There was nothing missing and everything was perfect except what was wrong with ourselves.' Unfortunately this happy state was of short duration. Keyser died under mysterious circumstances, and de Houtman proved himself a fool and a bully. There were quarrels with the Malays and with the Portuguese. One ship was abandoned because of lack of sailors to man it, and when the three remaining vessels reached Holland with but eighty-nine men of the 248 who had sailed, they carried cargoes which barely covered expenses.

Though a somewhat sorry affair in itself, de Houtman's voyage made apparent to all that profits were possible on voyages to the Orient, and a number of trading expeditions were projected. The old company that had sent out de Houtman united with a new company, and a second expedition was sent out under command of Admiral Jacob Corneliszoon van Neck, which was highly successful. Van Neck established friendly relations at Bantam and in the Spice Islands and brought back cargoes yielding a profit of four hundred per cent. His success brought multitudes into the field. In the single year of 1598, five expeditions totalling twenty-two ships left Holland for the Far East; and before the formation of the East India Company, in 1602, there were fifteen voyages

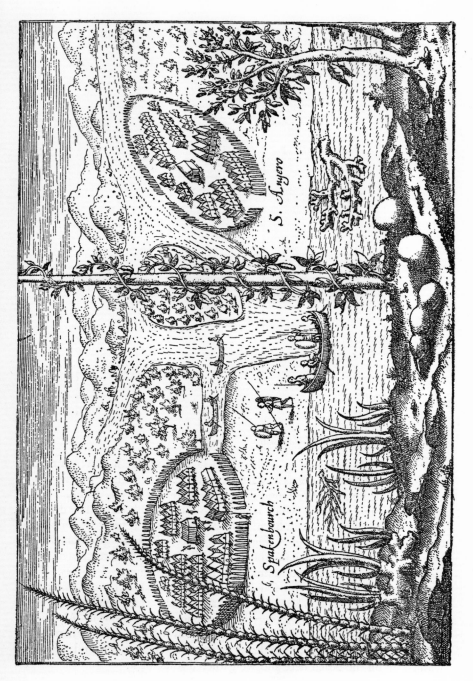

Villages on the Island of Madagascar

Villages on the Island of Madagascar

Two of the villages fenced in with palisades. Each village has two entrances. In each case, one entrance is towards the water. The village on the left is named Spakenbourch. We found their King there and he was drunk. He had us drink of their beverage which is made from rice and honey. The drinking cup was made from an oxen's horn. We made our best profit in Spakenbourch bartering glass beads for great quantities of rice, chickens, goats and fruits. We also traded in a similar fashion in the village of S. Angero shown in the picture. The villages are populous, each having two hundred houses. Their houses are built on poles. We found here also an inn where the sailors went to drink. We show here also how the sugar cane grows, which could be harvested here in great abundance by those who know how to go about it. Also beans grow here very different from ours and that is why we show them here. Ginger also grows here as we have pictured it. Coral, red and white, is washed up on the beach here and we gathered some of it.

From the account of the first Dutch voyage to the East Indies. Amsterdam, 1598.

The Bazaar or Great Market at Bantam

A. Where they sell Melons, Cucumbers and Coconuts
B. Where they sell Sugar and Honey in pots
C. The Bean market
D. The Bamboo or Cane market
E. Where they sell the krisses, sabers, spears, and daggers
F. Where the men sell linen
G. Where the women sell linen.
H. Stalls where they sell all kinds of spices, dry goods, and all kinds of seeds
I. The stalls where the Bengalese and the Gujerats sell many kinds of ironwork and cutlery
K. The stalls of the Chinese
L. The meat stalls
M. The Fish-market
N. The fruit market
O. The green or vegetable market
P. The Pepper market
Q. The Onion and Leek market
R. The Rice market
S. Place where the merchants and adventurers walk
T. The Jewellers' stalls
V. Strange little ships with all kinds of edible wares
X. The chicken market

From the account of the first Dutch voyage to the East Indies, Amsterdam, 1598.

The Bazaar or Great Market at Bantam

to the Orient. Some of these were profitable, others were dismal failures. The average profits could not have been great, but average profits made scant impression when individual voyages yielded fortunes. The natives in the main liked Dutch goods, and even, at first, Dutch prices. The shrewd Dutch set about exploiting the Orient systematically, and one of their first steps was to eliminate competition among themselves. The various groups engaged in the trade were merged in the Vereenigde Oost Indische Compagnie, or the United East India Company, a joint stock company in which all might take part. The controlling body was a board of seventeen directors drawn from a number of Dutch cities, and this body over the years became known simply as 'The Seventeen.' Portuguese ships and traders were literally overwhelmed by the Dutchmen. As B. H. M. Vlekke points out, within three years after the return of de Houtman, Dutch ships had appeared off the west coast of Sumatra, and near Atjeh at the western tip. They had visited Java and the Moluccas, were seen off the northeast coast of Borneo, and off Manila. They explored the coasts of Siam and Indo-China and attempted to establish trade relations with Canton. They were in Japan in 1600, trading in Ceylon in 1602, and explored the coast of Australia in 1605.

The chief base for Dutch activity in the Orient was first the city of Bantam on the island of Java, and later Batavia on the same island, a city erected on the site of the native town of Jacatra. From Batavia, the governors of the company exercised control over the vast sprawling network of trading stations and factories stretching from Arabia to Japan. From their first entrance into the Orient, the Dutch were firmly and frankly bent on establishing a monopoly of trade. This objective involved first, the elimination of other European nations from the East India-European commerce; and second, the procurement of a large share of the traffic between oriental countries heretofore in the hands of native merchants. The elimination of other European nations from the European-East India trade meant primarily the elimination of the Portuguese and the English. As Linschoten noted, the Portuguese had lost their old vigor, which made their commercial defeat easier. In addition, the cruelty of individual Portuguese to the native races had earned dislike for the nation throughout the Orient. The Dutch were also better sea fighters, and armed clashes between the two powers almost always resulted in Dutch victories. The speed with which the Lowlanders spread throughout the East is an index of the speed with which the Portuguese were vanquished. The English constituted a different problem. Like the Dutch, they wished to fall heir to Portuguese

commerce, but they simply had not the shipping or financial resources to compete with the Hollanders. The true state of affairs was revealed by Edmund Scott, an English trader at Bantam who wrote in February 1604 that 'blowe which way the winde would, they [the Dutch] had shipping to come thither, eyther from the East or from the West; insomuch that one woulde have thought they want to carry away the pepper growing on the trees....' He observed sadly that 'pepper now is scarce in Bantam, by reason the Hollanders have men in every place that yields pepper; so that the shipping of these partes [i.e., the native shipping] which was wont to bring it to Bantam, now doe not come.' Slowly but surely the English as a commercial power were squeezed out of the East Indies, and were not an important factor there after the time of the redoubtable Jan Pieterszoon Coen, who was governor from 1618 to 1623, and again from 1627 until 1629. For a short period, 1619–1623, the governing bodies of the English and Dutch East India Companies in Europe agreed to cooperate, but Coen considered this arrangement a mistake in judgment on the part of his employers. In the final analysis, he was the only man who could make the arrangement effective. He observed on one occasion that 'Were the English masters here, we would soon find ourselves out of India,' and he had various devices for circumventing his English collaborators. His most effective method was to make his trading projects so large that the much poorer English Company could not afford to participate. The farcical arrangement between the two companies was ended in 1623. In that year, after a trial, the Dutch tortured and executed eight Englishmen. This was the so-called massacre of Amboina. Shortly before this time, Coen also attacked the English fleet and captured seven ships. The Dutch became preëminent in the Indies, and the English talked for at least two centuries of the perfidy of the Dutch and their cruelty at Amboina. The Britons were bitter about being vanquished. 'Your men have robbed my people of their possessions,' King James complained to the Dutch ambassadors in London; 'you have made war on them, you have killed and tortured several of them. You never considered the benefits you have received from the Crown of England who made and maintained you as an independent nation. You have a man in the Indies [i.e., Coen] who deserves to be hanged. Your people present your Prince of Orange as a great King in the Indies while they picture me as a small ruler and the Prince's vassal. You are masters of the sea wide and large and can do what you want.'

Having largely disposed of both the Portuguese and English in the East

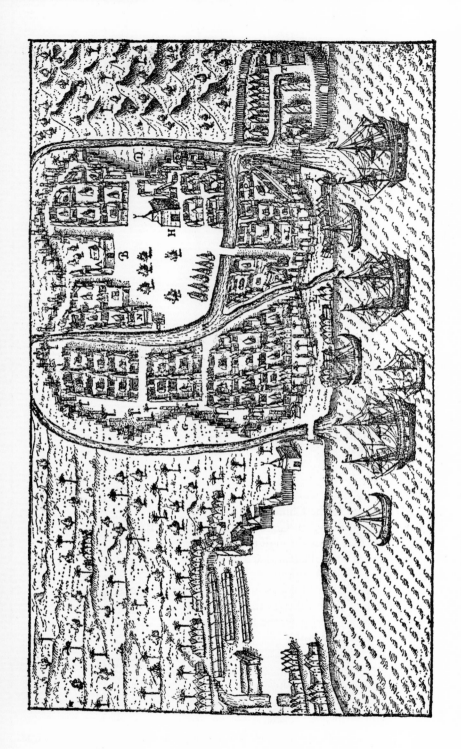

Plan of the City of Bantam

Plan of the City of Bantam

A. The home of the King
B. The forecourt
C. The land gate
D. The mountain gate
E. The water gate
F. The Boom
G. The Tower
H. The Mosque
I. The dwellings of the Chinese
L. The Home of Panyeran Gouban, the Captain of Bantam
M. The River that flows through the City
N. The home of the Sabandar, harbour-master
O. The Home of the Admiral
P. The Home of Satie Moluc or merchant of the Moluccas
Q. The Home of the brother of the Governor
R. The Home of Chenopate, the King's General
S. The Home of Panjansiba
T. The Chinese Market
V. The Home of Andemoin
X. Our lodgings or warehouse
IJ. The houses of the Gujerats and Bengalese
Z. The Munition-depot

From the account of the first Dutch voyage to the East Indies. Amsterdam, 1598.

Indies, the Dutch had solved their major problems as far as Europeans were concerned. The French and Danes were never an important factor in the seventeenth century East Indian trade, and the Spanish from the Philippines were gradually pushed out of the archipelago. A special but minor problem was the flotsam and jetsam of races which had drifted to Amboina—independent Dutch traders, Norwegians, Germans, Scotch, English, French, Portuguese and Flemings. By 1617 such people had begun to buy Chinese junks and to do a little independent trading, but they were not a serious threat to the Company's Orient-Europe trade.

The second objective, as has been said, was the elimination as far as possible of the native shippers, Chinese, Indian, Japanese, and Malay from the trade between the Eastern countries. The Dutch perceived that the banishing of Orientals from ocean trade would, in fact, have two happy results. Not only would it make their monopoly of spices and other desirable items more secure, but it would also place the profitable trade between the eastern countries in their hands. This commerce was a far larger prize even than the European-Oriental traffic, and one which was to prove the mainstay of the Company. The eastern world was crisscrossed with arteries of trade. Over the caravan routes through Tartary and Turkestan were carried silk from China, manna from Usbeq, and many homely necessities for the peoples along the way. The ships from Malabar appeared in Sumatra and Java, bringing cotton and silks for sarongs. Chinese junks brought rice to the Spice Islands and returned laden with condiments. Other sailing craft in Indian ports took on cargoes transhipped from China, Japan, and Malaya which were subsequently unloaded in Persia. Japanese junks plied quietly and profitably between their home ports, Malaya, and the Philippines. That same redoubtable, shrewd, ruthless governor, Coen, who was hard on the English, saw that this commerce must be in Dutch hands. 'Just as,' he explained, 'the teeming populations of the East surpass in number the populations of Europe, so likewise does the trade of the East surpass the commerce of Europe.' In a word then, Coen and his Company aimed not merely at supplanting the Portuguese in trade, but at supplanting everyone else; but for the moment only the effect of this grandiose program in the East Indies need be noted.

The East Indies stretch for a distance of three thousand miles from east to west and for thirteen hundred miles from north to south. The actual land mass of the 3,000 islands is equal to 735,000 square miles, much bigger than Alaska, and twice as big as Texas. It was virtually impossible to eliminate na-

tive trade completely from so vast an area, and as a matter of fact, the small Chinese traders who did business between the smaller islands were actually helpful to the Dutch in their efforts to gather in the products of the islands. The Dutch could only hope to eliminate trading where it occurred on a considerable scale. The Company directors in the Netherlands were insistent on the elimination of competition in the Spice Islands at least. When the first Company governor-general was appointed, his instructions were that 'as far as possible he should see to it that the trade of Amboina, Banda, and the Moluccas should remain firmly in the hands of the Company, so that no nation in the world should have a share in it but ourselves....' It being impossible to police systematically the vast extent of the islands in order to eliminate competition, the Company adopted the policy of stationing ships or men only at strategic points. Thus, the island of Solor was considered such a strategic point, since it lay athwart the trade route to the Island of Timor which was the great source for sandalwood. Governor Coen pointed out that Dutch vessels based on Solor could apprehend any strange ships bound for Timor, and bring them into Solor, where their cargoes could either be purchased or confiscated as prizes. He pointed out also that Solor could serve as a trading center where clothing, cooking utensils, porcelain, and small luxuries could be sold to the thousands of natives on Timor, Solor, and the surrounding islands. Similarly, Adriaen Blocq Martenszoon, at one time governor of Amboina, advised that each year a sloop or a frigate ought to be stationed off Amboina from March to May to intercept the junks which came there to trade. It would be the task of the ship's officers to take the junks as prizes, or buy up their rice cargoes. Little or no official compunction was felt about depriving the native traders of the means of livelihood, since, as one Dutchman put it, these people were 'enemies of Christendom, enemies of the true God, and thus our natural enemies.' Still, difficulties arose as a result of the Dutch attempt to engross trade. First, certain populations which had lived by trading endured very great hardships when deprived of it; second, certain island groups which depended on Javanese and Chinese traders for part at least of their food supply, suffered hunger and famine as a result of the Dutch policy; and third, the Company did not really possess the shipping or the commodities to take the place of the independent traders, with the result that prices were high and goods scarce throughout the islands. Adriaen van de Velde, Commandant on Solor, observed to Governor Both: '....that during the Portuguese regime the island of Solor was an opulent and rich place because the people enjoyed

Inhabitants of the Island of Banda

Inhabitants of the Island of Banda

A. The little Turk from whom we bought many goods, and who showed us much friendship.
B. A nobleman walking in the street with a slave behind him. They fit out the slaves elegantly in their own manner in order to make a brave show.
C. A woman of Banda as she appears when walking in the street. Usually a female slave walks behind her carrying a hat for her mistress to wear when she removes the mantle from her head.
(Wording adapted from the Dutch inscription.)

From the Journal of the Voyage of Jacob C. Van Neck. Amsterdam, 1601.

the right to engage in the Timor trade,' but that since the coming of the Dutch, that happy state was greatly changed. If the Dutch engrossed all of the trade, he observed, 'the result could not be other than that wherever the Dutch conquered, the natives must decline and perish.' Cornelis Dedel, Councilor of the Indies, wrote in May 1617 that 'They [the natives] could buy everything they needed from the Javanese and others at lower prices and get a better choice of varieties and sizes.' Herman van Speult, Lieutenant Governor of Amboina, thought that (July 1618) 'In prohibiting foreigners to trade in Loehoe, Kambelo (on the island of Ceram) or Hitoe (the northern peninsula of Amboina) we have neither right or reason on our side.'

Sometimes the natives attempted to regain their economic balance by charging the Dutch a higher price for their spices than that agreed upon. This happened in the Ceram Islands when the inhabitants asked a higher rate for their cloves than the contract called for. They were promptly called 'greedy, false Moors' by the Company officials, and a fleet was sent to punish them. A greedy, false Moor, as one Dutch historian explains, was any native who tried to get a hundred reals for his cloves, when the Company was paying sixty.

Looming large as part of the difficulty in creating a monopoly was the stubborn fact that pepper and spices were simply so plentiful in the East Indies that if they were allowed to grow freely and be marketed freely, the profits would be too insignificant to interest the Dutch East India Company. The problem of too plentiful a supply of pepper was described by the surgeon Christopher Frick, who was in the Indies in 1681–1686. 'Now tho' pepper is as plenty in India as stones in the streets,' says Frick, 'and only serves for the ballast very often, and to pack up other goods tite; and altho' sometimes several whole shiploads of it be thrown into the sea, and many hundred thousand poundweight of it burnt, yet dares no man in the service of the Company take one single corn of it... and the same rule is observed in respect to other spices.' What was true of pepper, as Frick says, was true also of cloves and nutmegs. The governor of the Moluccas in the period 1622–1627 was Jacques LeFebure, who was instructed by the Governor General on behalf of the Directors of the Company to begin the destruction of the clove trees, but to do it in such a way as not to arouse the suspicions of either the English or the natives. 'For we find,' explained the Directors, 'that yearly there are certainly produced twice as many cloves as are consumed in the whole world.' In 1625 Herman van Speult, Governor of Amboina, sent an expedition to Ceram. Overcoming what little native opposition there was, the Dutch began the

destruction of the clove trees. At a conservative estimate they probably destroyed 65,000 clove trees on this single expedition. By 1656, says the historian of the Indies, E. S. De Klerck, an important goal was reached, for by that year clove culture was restricted to Amboina and the Uliasser Islands, and was allowed nowhere else. The Moluccas, says De Klerck, were transformed into a wilderness and lost their former prosperity. He might have added in fairness that prosperity in the Moluccas never had been great and what there was of it had largely been confined to the courts of princes. Still, the elimination of these islands from the clove trade was not accomplished without difficulty. The story of the kingdom of Goa, or Makassar, illustrates the difficult task confronting the Dutch when they set about limiting clove production and native trade. Makassar, or Goa, was one of the most important regions in the islands, since it produced abundance of rice, which was traded in the Moluccas for cloves. It was also the center for the free traders in cloves, English, Indian, Portuguese, and Chinese. The prince of this kingdom was so ill-advised as to protest to the Dutch against their policy of destroying clove trees. He declared that the Company should not imagine that God had reserved the islands so far removed from their own country for their sole benefit. Makassar was already a thorn in the side of the Company and one may be sure that such utterances on the part of the prince did not ameliorate the situation. The Company sent two notable expeditions against the Makassars, the first in 1660 and the second in 1667. The latter expedition went first to Buton, an island southeast of Celebes, which the Dutch cleared of Makassars. About 5,500 were taken to a neighboring island where they starved to death. Other Makassars were killed or made slaves. The prince was finally brought to terms. His people were forbidden to trade to the Moluccas, and he delivered to the Dutch a huge war indemnity and one thousand slaves.

What happened in the case of cloves also happened to nutmegs. The story of nutmegs is to a considerable extent the story of the Banda Islands. The Bandanese had contracted to sell all their nutmegs to the Dutch, who had advanced payments on the crops, but it is doubtful if the Bandanese had any real comprehension of the transaction, and the Dutch interpreted the agreement to mean that they should have all of the trade of any description carried on in Banda. The Bandanese had long been accustomed to procure the rice which was their principal food by trading with Java, but such trade was, of course, contrary to Company policy. The Company Directors instructed Governor Both, their first governor-general, to stop this traffic in rice. If the Bandanese

The Bandanese playing ball

The Bandanese playing ball

They stand in a circle with one person in the middle and pass the ball to each other. One tosses the ball up and then they throw it at each other. They also kick the ball with their feet, as high as one could throw it. The balls are made of hoops of plaited rattan. If a player misses the ball with his foot, he is much chagrined and the others laugh at him. This game is greatly loved. Some players kick the ball as they jump. Others jump and turn and still kick the ball. (Wording adapted from the original inscription.)

From the Journal of the Voyage of Jacob C. Van Neck. Amsterdam, 1601.

persisted in trading, he was to cut down their sago palms and thus deprive them of their other principal foodstuff. The punitive measures thus begun against the Bandanese under Governor-General Pieter Both were continued under subsequent governors. Laurens Reaal, who was governor in the period 1616–1618, was more than dubious about the Company's action. 'The exclusion of foreign junks,' he wrote in May 1618, 'makes us so odious as is scarcely to be believed, for yearly a hundred junks came to these [i.e. Bandanese] waters. They brought the inhabitants provisions and clothing, and now they go in want, for the Dutch do not bring rice, the clothing is of a kind they cannot use, and the prices of all goods are too high.' When this unduly soft governor, Reaal, was succeeded by the stern man of business, Coen, the latter made short work of the recalcitrant Bandanese. He sent a military expedition to the Banda Islands and proceeded to the massacre of the population. Some natives succeeded in escaping to neighboring islands, but the vast majority were killed or carried off to slavery, and in this way the whole population of Banda, about 15,000 people, was destroyed. The Dutch soldiers were revolted by the task they were called upon to perform. As one Company employee remarked, the tale of the Dutch expedition to Banda would make a book equal to the story of the cruelty of the Spanish to the natives of the West Indies. Certainly such ferocity has seldom been equalled, and has only been surpassed by such spectacles as the Spanish destruction of the Indians on Hispaniola, the destruction of the North American Indians by ourselves, and the destruction of Jews by the Germans. The Bandanese were eventually replaced by Dutchmen who were assigned plots on which they were to grow nutmegs, which were to be sold to the Company at fixed prices. But even after all of these strenuous efforts, the Dutch were having the same problem of too many spices well into the next century. 'In the Spice Islands,' wrote Adam Smith, more than a hundred years after the memorable exploit of the Dutch in the Banda seas, 'the Dutch are said to burn all the spiceries which a fertile season produces beyond which they expect to dispose of in Europe with such a profit as they think sufficient. In the islands where they have no settlements, they give a premium to those who collect the young blossoms and green leaves of the clove and nutmeg trees which naturally grow there, but which this savage policy has now, it is said, almost completely extirpated. Even in the Islands where they have settlements they have very much reduced, it is said, the number of those trees.' It is, of course, possible to be downcast about this aspect of the great Company's activities, but actually a cheerful view

might also be taken, for the Company was doing pioneer work in the techniques of synthetic scarcities, a branch of economics which has become increasingly important.

It is common knowledge that the Dutch in the East Indies gradually brought the native races into subjection and caused the withdrawal of the Europeans, so that until recent years these islands were an important appendage of the Dutch economy. This, their first entrance into the East, was their most successful, and from the beginning Batavia was the capital of the Company's operations in the Orient. To this city were brought the products of China, Japan, India, Ceylon, and Persia before being transshipped to Europe or elsewhere in the East. Each of the regions mentioned was an integral part of the Company's network of trade, and the traffic to and from them will be briefly described.

The Return of Houtman's ships from the In

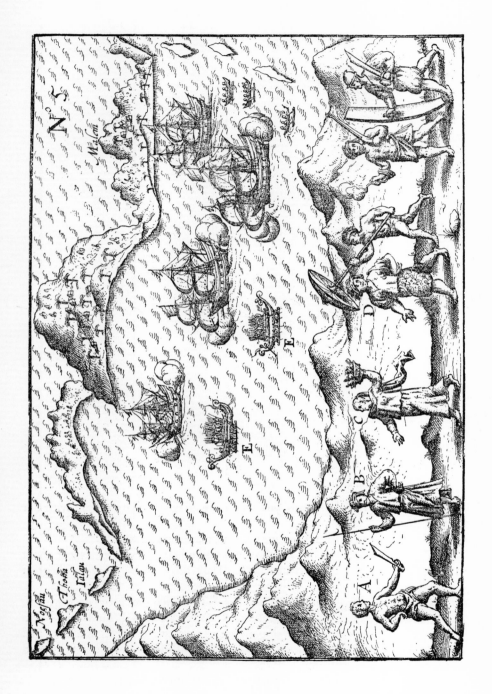

The Island of Amboyna

The Island of Amboyna

Picture of the Island of Amboyna where we arrived 3 March, 1599 with our four ships.

A. Is a simple man of modest means who works in the woods.
B. Is also a commoner but a man of more standing. He carries a spear about one and a half fathoms in length. They throw these spears with great accuracy.
C. A woman going to market to sell her wares which she carries on her hand.
D. The Admiral of the Sea, walking with his servants behind him. This Admiral came aboard our ship asking us what we wanted. We answered that we wanted in all friendship to trade with them, whereupon he said that we were welcome.
(Wording adapted from the original Dutch inscription.)

From the Journal of the Voyage of Jacob C. Van Neck. Amsterdam, 1601.

CHAPTER VII

China and Formosa

Almost as important as spices from the Indies in the plans of the Company were silks, sugar, tea, and porcelains from China. The instructions of the Directors of the Company to their servants in the Indies in 1608 were that special efforts should be made to trade with China in order to obtain increased quantities of silk, since there was a large market for the fabric, and it yielded good profits. Of porcelain, Linschoten says, 'To tell of the porcelains made there [i.e., in China], is not to be believed, and those that are exported yearly to India, Portugal, and Nova Hispania and elsewhere! But the finest are not allowed outside the country on penalty of corporal punishment, but serve solely for the Lords and Governors of the country, and are so exquisite that no crystalline glass is to be compared to them....' The European demand for porcelain in these first years of the seventeenth century increased by leaps and bounds and made the Company all the more anxious for good trade relations with China. Sugar was generally useful, both for Oriental trade and as a cargo for ships bound for Holland. In addition to these commodities, Dutchmen had noted also that the great Chinese trading junks came to the East Indies laden with linen, cotton, gunpowder, sulphur, iron, steel, quicksilver, copper and other metals, as well as meal nuts, chestnuts, dates, biscuits and furniture, and they were anxious to participate in this trade. Of the commodities mentioned silk was the most important.

The Dutch were not the first westerners with a lively interest in China. Indeed, the history of Europeans in China before the seventeenth century is a story stretching over at least five hundred years, and European trade with that country on a considerable scale had begun with the Portuguese. As has been said, the Portuguese navigators spread rapidly throughout the East, and one of them, Rafael Perestrello, reached China in 1516. The following year

Fernando Perez de Andrade arrived with eight ships at St. John's Island seventy-five miles south-east of Macao, and eventually reached Canton, where he received permission to trade. The intrepid Iberian adventurers were soon engaged in commerce as far away as Foochow and Ningpo, but being often unscrupulous and sometimes cruel, they earned the animosity of the Chinese. Eventually they were expelled from the country, but managed to cling to Macao on the tip of a peninsula near Hong Kong. That was their position when the Dutch appeared in the East. The Spanish in the Philippines also enjoyed some Chinese trade even though China lay on the opposite side from the Philippines of the imaginary line by which the Pope had divided the world between Spain and Portugal. Although they dared not intrude on the Portuguese side of the line, the Spanish in the Philippines regularly enticed Chinese trading junks to Manila; and, as a matter of fact, the China-Philippines trade was centuries old. When Magellan reached those islands in 1521, he found the natives of Cebu already familiar with Chinese products, and there was much other evidence of an extensive Chinese trade. Since the Dutch commanded the sea, China-Philippines trade caused the Dutch little uneasiness but they were anxious to oust the Portuguese from the China trade, if possible.

The Netherlanders first appeared off the China coast in 1601 and endeavored to obtain permission to trade at that time, but two facts militated against them. First, the Portuguese at Macao described the Dutch to the Chinese as a very undesirable and barbarous nation; and second, Chinese officials had recently been issued strict orders to prevent such barbarians from penetrating into the kingdom. Consequently, the efforts of the Lowlanders came to nought. Later, in 1603, in an effort to displace the Portuguese, two Dutch ships appeared before Macao, bombarded the town and destroyed a galleon. The Portuguese stoutly resisted, and again the Dutch departed with nothing to show for their efforts. The following year a Dutchman accompanied the Siamese embassy to Pekin to attempt to obtain trading privileges, but met with no success. In the same year a second Dutch fleet set out for Macao under Wybrant Warwijck, but a typhoon forced the ships to put in at the Pescadores. From those islands, Warwijck negotiated with the Chinese authorities of Fukien for permission to trade, but he was told that he must first pay thirty thousand dollars merely for an audience. He remained four and a half months in the Pescadores before he also gave up hope of doing business, and sailed away. The fruitless attempt of Warwijck was succeeded by the bootless attempt of Admiral Cornelis Matelief, who anchored off the island of Lamoa. The Chinese refused

to listen to his proposals to trade unless he first removed himself from Lamoa, but when he sailed from that island to Pehoe in the Pescadores, the Chinese promptly forgot about him. In 1622, another effort was made to get by force what could not be gotten by negotiation. In that year Cornelis Reyerszoon sailed northward from the East Indies with sixteen ships and two thousand troops to capture Macao. He cannonaded the stronghold for five days and debarked his soldiers, but the Portuguese, or more precisely their Christian slaves, resisted so bravely that he was forced to give up the siege. Reyerszoon then established himself at Pehoe. From there he terrorized the Chinese coast, burning villages, capturing junks, and carrying off the people into slavery. The fear inspired by Reyerszoon's raids was heightened by a tradition which persisted among the villages that one day their land would be taken by a people with fair hair. The Chinese whom Reyerszoon captured he transported to Pehoe. There he tied them two and two and set them to carrying earth and stone for the construction of a fortress. When the strongpoint was completed, he shipped fourteen or fifteen hundred of the unfortunates to Batavia. The Dutch somewhat unrealistically endeavored to combine coastal raids and the capture of junks with further negotiations for permission to trade. Needless to say they were unsuccessful. Eventually the Chinese assembled one hundred fifty war junks and four thousand troops off Pehoe, and with these forces in view persuaded Maarten Sonck, Reyerszoon's successor, to remove himself and his countrymen from Pehoe to Formosa. The Dutch dismantled their fortress stone by stone and transported it to the latter island, establishing themselves there in 1624.

This happy isle was happily named, and one of the most fascinating descriptions of it was written by a minister of the Dutch Reformed Church, Georgius Candidius. On the plains on the western side of the island fern trees, camphor trees, palms, and pineapples grew in tropical abundance, while the backbone of the island was a chain of magnificent mountain peaks. Candidius reported that the country was full of deer, wild swine, wild goats, rabbits, woodcocks, partridges, and other kinds of fowl, and averred that although the natives cultivated the soil only to a small extent, it was actually rich and fertile. He found the aborigines to be barbarous, but friendly, faithful, and good natured. They lived in large beautiful houses and were fond of drinking, joviality, and fornication, for, he lamented, 'they are a lewd and licentious people.' In addition to the aborigines, the Dutch found several colonies of Chinese and a considerable number of Japanese. The Chinese had long been

acquainted with the island, for in the first centuries of the Christian era they were a great maritime power, their ships crossing and recrossing the seas about Japan and China. Those Chinese who settled on the island were principally of two groups, the Hakkas, one of the oldest of Chinese racial stocks, a shrewd, industrious, courageous people, and the Fukienese who had migrated from the coastal province on the mainland. The Japanese had come to the island not long before the Dutch and were principally traders, for they also recognized the strategic importance of the island for commerce. Direct traffic between China and Japan was forbidden, and Formosa served as a way station where Japanese and Chinese exchanged goods.

The transported fort which the Dutch established on the south-west coast was first called Fort Orange and then Zeelandia. The first governor was the Maarten Sonck who has already been mentioned, and the second was Pieter Nuyts, who served from 1627 to 1629. The chief commodities dealt in at Zeelandia were those which the Dutch had long wanted to procure from China, namely, sugar, silk, and porcelain, and these goods were procured in two ways. They were either purchased in Formosa from Chinese merchants, or they were bought clandestinely at Amoy on the China coast through the connivance of the Chinese governor-general at Foochow, and of other officials. The latter method was preferred, since even with the necessary bribes, goods could be got cheaper in China than through the merchants on Formosa. As to porcelain, the island became the central distributing point for that article. During the century, the Dutch shipped more than fifteen million pieces to Europe and to the various Oriental countries. Rare and much sought after at first, the world was eventually inundated by Chinese cups and teapots. Although sugar could be obtained from a number of places such as Brazil, the West Indies, Bengal and Java, China sugar was much needed by the Company both for its markets in the Orient and for the sugar refineries in the home country. A great deal was shipped to Northwest India, where it was used in the trade of that region with Persia. As in the case of porcelain, Formosa became the sugar distributing point for the Orient. With regard to silk, the Dutch found that there was a greater market for it in Japan than there was elsewhere. The importance of this market is revealed by the fact that in the year 1627 the value of the silk cargoes shipped from Formosa to Batavia and Holland was in round figures 560,000 guilders, while the value of the silk sent from Formosa to Japan was 620,000 guilders. The quantities of merchandise for sale in China were enormous. Governor Nuyts declared in 1629 that the

volume of trade in Formosa was limited only by the amount of capital at the disposal of the Dutch factors there. He asserted that the whole capital of the East India Company would not be sufficient to purchase one-sixth of the goods available in China. Not only, he said, was there no difficulty in fulfilling the agreement to deliver three-quarters of a million guilders' worth of Chinese goods annually, but he could easily deliver twice the amount.

The Netherlanders did not have this rich field of the Chinese trade for their private preserve. Portuguese, Spanish and Japanese were busily exploiting it also to the best of their abilities. Until they were expelled from Japan in 1638, the mainstay of the Portuguese merchants at Macao was the Chinese-Japanese trade, and their ships passed and repassed Formosa on their way to Japan. The Chinese-Japanese trade was also of course the chief business of the Japanese merchants themselves, and unlike the Portuguese the Japanese were actually established on Formosa. As a matter of fact, the scale of operations of the Japanese traders was so much greater than that of the Dutch that they could easily buy up everything the Chinese had to offer, leaving nothing for their European rivals. This difficult problem the Netherlanders solved by placing a ten per cent tax on all goods traded, the tax being sufficient to make it unprofitable for the Japanese to continue longer in business. The impost was so resented by the Japanese that they sometimes refused to pay it, whereupon the Dutch confiscated their goods. On one occasion the Japanese sought to circumvent the Dutch by having Formosa become a province of their home-land. To this end they transported sixteen native Formosans to the Japanese court. It was arranged that the Formosans would offer their island home to the Emperor, but the Company also sent representatives to Japan armed with a large sum of money and by a series of judicious bribes distributed among the Emperor's entourage, the Netherlanders arranged that the Emperor would refuse the island. There then ensued between the Company and the Japanese a series of moves and counter-moves, provocations and reprisals. Through all of the squabbles the Japanese held the trump card, since the Dutch needed their trade, while there was nothing the Japanese procured from the Hollanders that they could not as easily get from others.

On Formosa, Governor Nuyts wreaked his displeasure with the Japanese traders by ransacking several junks and detaining the crews. In retaliation and desperation, when a number of junks were ready to sail for home, the Japanese crews seized Nuyts. They demanded of him that their ships be allowed to depart in peace, and that reparations be made for the maltreatment they had

suffered in the past. Nuyts' compatriots, knowing full well that they could crush the handful of Japanese who detained Nuyts, were all for doing so and getting back their governor dead or alive. The governor, exhibiting an almost frantic preference for the latter state, was apprehensive that his compatriots might attack the Japanese. He agreed that the latter might depart in peace, that large quantities of silk should be given them as reparations, and that hostages should be exchanged with them, one of the Dutch hostages to be his own son. On being set free, Nuyts seized the cargoes of two richly laden junks which put in at Formosa, and in retaliation the Japanese authorities promptly placed an embargo on the Dutch vessels then at Hirado. The Netherlanders, fearful that their carefully nurtured Japanese trade was in danger, recalled Nuyts to Batavia and imprisoned him. They then turned him over to the Japanese as the cause and author of all the misfortunes which had occurred. Also, and laudably, they sent along to the shogun a plea for clemency on his behalf. The Japanese later released Nuyts and he returned to Batavia. Those who followed him as governor were more circumspect in their conduct, but the Japanese themselves solved the vexed problem on Formosa in 1636 by prohibiting their nationals, with certain almost negligible exceptions, to trade abroad.

The Lowlanders, as has been said, had as competitors in the China trade, not only the Portuguese and the Japanese, but also the Spanish. Formosa lay across the sea route from China to Manila, and Governor Nuyts pointed out that the Dutch strategic position permitted them to cut off the China-Philippine trade whenever they pleased. This fact was also obvious to the Spanish, and they resolved to establish themselves on Formosa also, in order to checkmate the Dutch. Accordingly, Don Fernando de Silva, Governor of Manila, prepared an expedition for the island which, sailing from the Philippines in February 1626, debarked troops at Keelung at the northern end of Formosa several months later. The Spanish called the port Santissima Trinidad, and constructed a fort there which they christened San Salvador. Almost as soon as the Spanish landed, the Dominican fathers accompanying the expedition began the study of the Formosan tongue. The priests were able to reassure the natives who had fled on the approach of the invaders, to coax them back to their former homes and to instruct them in the Holy Catholic faith. Three years later, in 1629, the Spanish built a second fort at nearby Tamsuy, which they called San Domingo. The establishment of the second fort alarmed Governor Nuyts, and he urged that an expedition be sent to destroy the Spa-

nish fortresses. He pointed out that while the Dutch were originally in a position to cut off Spanish shipping, the Spanish were now in a position to cut off Dutch shipping. The Governor also explained that the Spanish, like the Japanese, possessed far more capital than the Dutch. If they were allowed to operate at all, they could quickly engross all of the Formosan trade. Finally he prophesied that the Spanish could and would gain the confidence of the natives and Chinese settlers, and then might incite them to revolt. The cost of providing armed forces to guard against this danger could consume the profits of the Formosan station. Nuyts urged the attack on the Spanish settlements in 1629, but at Company headquarters in Batavia hasty action was eschewed. Mature consideration was the order of the day. Consequently, it was not until 1641 that the Netherlanders' expedition was sent against the fortress of San Domingo at Tamsuy. The weak Spanish garrison fought bravely and the Dutch were repulsed. It was now the turn of the Spanish on Formosa to be alarmed and they pleaded with the Governor at Manila for reinforcements. But a calm and deliberate atmosphere also prevailed at Spanish headquarters. In fact, to digress a little, such tranquility might be called the headquarters, or far-from-wars'-alarms, atmosphere. The authorities at Manila finally yielded to the pleadings of their compatriots on Formosa to the extent of sending them a contingent of eight soldiers as reinforcements. Meanwhile the Dutch were rallying for a second assault, and with commendable alacrity launched it eighteen months later. The Spanish again fought with valor, but despite this and the reinforcements, they were overcome and their establishments with much booty fell into the hands of the Netherlanders.

The energetic efforts of the Dominicans to bring the inhabitants to the Holy Catholic faith by instructing them in their native tongue were probably responsible for a counter effort by the Dutch on behalf of the Dutch Reformed Church. Usually the Company was somewhat casual about religious matters. When, for example, a Dutch clergyman in Batavia complained to the governor that he tolerated heathen idols, the governor replied that 'the laws of the ancient Jewish republics do not apply in the territories of the Company.' Contrarily, Dutch protestantism was pressed on the Formosans with great vigor, even though it proved to be a difficult task.

The Formosans, the Reverend Candidius said, were lewd, adulterous, and bibulous. They proved to be also changeable and wayward. Upon one occasion, for example, several native families who had signified that they wished to live with the Christian community, later moved away from it. It

was only by using force and by placing their leaders in chains that they could be brought back to the Christian settlement. Even more discouraging was the fact that although the natives learned fluently and readily whatever was taught them, it was discovered after a number of years that the vast majority had absolutely no understanding or interest in what they had learned, and apparently had made the effort to learn Christian doctrine only to be agreeable. The Dutch appointed lay teachers who were to inculcate Christianity by teaching in the native tongue. Unfortunately, the persons often assigned to the task were common soldiers, and usually they either died or their terms of service expired before they acquired the necessary linguistic skill. It was lamentable also that although teaching the Christian way of life, these men themselves drifted into the Formosan way of life, and were guilty of drunkenness, fornication and adultery. Even ordained ministers were also attracted to the Formosan way, it being noted on one occasion that two young clergymen had become so addicted to drink as to become useless. By 1658, Dutch authorities on the island had become so exasperated by the religious insincerity of the natives that they decreed that idolatry should be punished by 'public whipping and banishment from this place.'

Meanwhile, the chief concern of the Company on Formosa, namely trade, went steadily forward. In addition to the main items of commerce, silk, porcelain, and sugar, the Dutch utilized a great variety of articles in their trade with Japan. The Netherlanders gathered yearly on Formosa itself seventy to eighty thousand deer skins, some dried fish, and some sugar for shipment to Japan. They imported from Europe for the same trade such familiar commodities as oak planks, whale oil, hemp, and resin. The Japanese also wanted the woolen cloths of England and the Lowlands, as well as the satins, damasks, velvets, taffetas and linens originating elsewhere. From the Company's other oriental stations the Formosan factors requisitioned sappan wood, sandalwood, cambodian nuts, pepper, cloves, and rattan. On at least one occasion also rhinoceros horns and buffalo horns were shipped to Japan. In 1628, Governor Nuyts made the curious request that he be shipped among other items three hundred Japanese dresses, an equal number of pairs of socks and pairs of shoes, and two cravats.

While the Formosan Dutch bought and sold goods, requisitioned supplies, dispatched ships, and punished recalcitrant natives, a series of events were transpiring on the mainland of China which would eventually deprive them of their island trading station. For some two hundred and fifty years China

had been ruled by the Ming emperors. The early representatives of the dynasty had been enterprising, vigorous, and progressive, but over the decades, the government had become corrupt and the emperors weak. By the beginning of the seventeenth century the vassal states on the periphery of the empire had ceased to heed Chinese authority. There were also internal revolts; and, most catastrophic of all, the Manchu Tartar tribes on the border of the empire had united, and were making terrific inroads into the country. The only leader who had any success at all in combating the Tartar enemy was a rich and powerful merchant, pirate, and war lord, usually known as Koxinga. In his battle against the invaders, Koxinga was indomitable. He maintained his fleet and paid his army by foreign commerce, and his trading junks plied to the Philippines, to Cochin China, and to the East Indian Archipelago. From 1648, Koxinga made continuous war on the Tartars and reached the height of his power in 1658, but in that very year he overreached himself. Gathering together an estimated three thousand junks and a considerable army, he sought to capture Nanking, but the expedition was an utter failure, and the greater part of his forces was destroyed. Koxinga was eventually compelled to do what he had long contemplated doing, namely, to invade Formosa. The Dutch had considerable opportunity to prepare themselves for the invasion. In 1646, a Chinese junk arriving at Nagasaki brought the news to the Dutch stationed there that the Chinese, defeated by the Tartars, were turning their eyes toward Formosa. Nearly six years later a Jesuit arriving at Batavia declared that there were rumors current in China that since Koxinga had been forced off the mainland and had taken to the sea, he had set his sights on getting the island. In 1655, the Dutch heard that Koxinga had prepared a great number of storming ladders which, it was suspected, he intended to use against the Fortress Zeelandia on Formosa. Five years later it was noted by the Netherlanders that the Chinese on the island were getting their goods out of the country, and it was suspected that they intended to follow their goods. Influential Chinese also reported that Koxinga intended to land 25,000 troops. A little later the Dutch intercepted letters from Chinese on the mainland advising their relatives on Formosa to flee, with or without their worldly goods. In 1661, the Lowlanders in Siam advised their colleagues on Formosa that Koxinga, in danger of losing his base at Amoy, was gathering his junks for the assault on their island. It was now fifteen years since the Dutch were first warned that this might happen, but they were surprised and aghast one morning to see Koxinga's junks threading their way through the tortuous

channel of Taiwan as if it were their home port, for this super bandit excelled in espionage and fifth column activities. Koxinga landed 25,000 troops and ample artillery, as previously advertised, and after some preliminary skirmishing and parleying settled down to besiege the Fortress Zeelandia.

In the meantime, in far off Batavia, various complaints having been received about the then governor of Formosa, Frederik Coyet, the Company had resolved upon his removal. The successor whom they appointed was one Herman Klenck. Two months after Koxinga opened the siege of Zeelandia, Klenck, filled doubtless with happy thoughts of governing a prosperous station on a happy isle, arrived one morning off Taiwan. The thunder of broadsides from the Chinese junks rolled across the water and the Dutch batteries belched fire and lead in return. With commendable prudence, Klenck sent his commission as governor, together with the Company's letter expressing their disapproval of Coyet, ashore by messenger. Coyet and his council thereupon invited Klenck to come ashore and take charge. Klenck demurred. Coyet pointed out that his successor could not govern the island from a ship. Upon the mention of ships, Klenck was reminded that his ships' stores, more particularly his rice and drinking water, might be running low. He weighed anchor and departed for Japan to replenish them, and never returned.

Back in Batavia news arrived soon after Klenck's departure of Koxinga's invasion of Formosa. Ten ships and seven hundred soldiers were hastily gotten together for the relief of the island, but then the question arose as to who should command the expedition. It became evident that although all of the members of the governor's council and all important officials were ready to endure any danger or hardship for the welfare of the Company, all were prevented from taking charge of the expedition because of pressing duties in Batavia. Finally, after many inducements were offered and generous promises made, the Advocate and Councilor of Justice of Castle Batavia, Jacob Cau, was induced to accept the post. This gentleman, though learned in the law, had limited military experience. In fact, as he himself declared, his sword had only previously been used to pry between the cobble stones in the streets, or to run through the windows of people's houses while he was a student at the University of Leyden. Springing into the breach, as it were, Cau took charge and the expedition sailed away for Formosa, arriving there soon after Herman Klenck had departed. Cau immediately formulated a plan to attack Koxinga by land and sea, but failed to debark his troops. At about this time, the Dutch

received a message from Koxinga's Tartar enemies on the mainland. The Tartars offered troops for the attack on Koxinga if in return the Dutch would furnish two ships to help wipe out the vestiges of Koxinga's power on the China coast. The Formosan Dutch were cheered, and Cau went ashore to reconnoitre, filled with an enthusiasm which was somewhat dampened by a closer view of Koxinga's army. Cau was so impressed by Koxinga's strength that he proposed to Coyet and his council that he return to Batavia for reinforcements. The council pointed out to Cau that as a matter of fact Batavia had sent him and his troops as reinforcements. Cau then suggested that he take his fleet to the assistance of the Tartars on the China coast. It was brought to his attention that he had ten ships and the Tartars had only asked for two. General Cau stood firm in his resolution, and departed with his fleet, but not for the China coast. He anchored in the Pescadores, where he seemed disposed to stay indefinitely until his officers insisted that he up anchor and make sail. He finally sailed, but for Siam rather than China. The Dutch inhabitants of a Siamese port were delighted one day to see his fleet sail in bedecked with flags and firing salutes, as was the custom after great victories, although they were somewhat puzzled later to know where the victory had occurred.

Back on Formosa, Coyet and his compatriots felt themselves forsaken, and at last they were forced to surrender to Koxinga. They abandoned their stores and sailed for Batavia, where, incidentally, the stern spirits in charge accused Coyet and his council of negligence and cowardice, and rigorously punished a number of them, including Coyet. Thus was lost a most valuable station for the Chinese and Japanese trade, but fortunately there were other ways to acquire Chinese goods, and other channels for traffic with Japan. Indeed, the fall of Formosa merely resulted in renewed efforts to get in touch with China directly. Throughout the remainder of the century there was a whole series of Dutch embassies to the court of the Tartar emperors, and Chinese junks plied busily between the mainland and the East Indies, bringing to Batavia the tea which the Company much desired. Other means of securing the products of Japan and China will be noted in the following chapter.

CHAPTER VIII

Japan and the Malay Peninsula

It was said in the previous chapter that there was an avenue for the purchase of Chinese goods and for Japanese trade other than by way of Formosa. That trade route began at the port and state of Patani, on the east coast of the Malay Peninsula, below the Gulf of Siam. The Portuguese had traded there since 1517, and by 1601, even before the formation of the East India Company, Dutch traders were established there. Patani was known as 'the door to China and Japan,' and Chinese silk and porcelains were dealt in extensively. The port attracted shipping not only because of the cargoes available, but also because provisions for the crews were to be had there in abundance. Johann Albrecht Mandelslo, a famous German traveller, says that the inhabitants 'had every moneth several Fruits, and Hens that lay twice a day, by reason whereof the Country abounds in all sorts of provisions for the belly as Rice, Bif, Goat, Geese, Ducks, Hens, Capons, Peacocks, Deer, Hares, Cunnies, Fowl and Venison, and especially in Fruits, whereof they have a hundred several sorts.' It was from Patani that the first Lowlanders penetrated into Siam, and it was by way of this port also that the first Dutch ships sailed for Japan. That the Netherlanders should reach the Flowery Kingdom by this route was not accidental. Japanese junks had visited Patani at least as early as 1592, and in 1599 a Patani junk visited Japan. This maritime commerce continued into the seventeenth century, and the rulers of Patani and Japan exchanged letters, which were carried by the trading junks. Hirado, in Japan, and Patani have been called sister ports because of the brisk trade carried on between them. Trade with several places in Indo-China and Malaya was also established by the Netherlanders from the base at Patani, and so in describing both the Japanese and the peninsular trades, this port or principality is the point of beginning. With regard to Japan, one of the first, if not the first, Dutchman to visit Japan

was that Dirck Gerritszoon Pomp, alias Dirck China, who was so filled with the impulse to describe the wonders of the Orient as to cause his neighbors to flee from him in terror. Dirck made two voyages to Japan, the second in 1584, and the first a few years previously. Much of what Dirck Gerritszoon knew of that land Linschoten set down in his *Itinerario*. Pomp also furnished information on Japan to L. J. Waghenaer for a volume which became widely known—the *Treasure of Voyages (Thresoor der Zeevaert)* which appeared in 1592. The first Dutch ship to reach Japan was *De Liefde (Love* or *Charity)*, of which Jacob Quackernaeck was skipper, Melchior van Santvoort, supercargo, and William Adams, an Englishman well known to students of Japanese history, was pilot major.

After a difficult voyage around the Horn, *De Liefde* reached Japan in April 1600, and the Dutch seafarers were hospitably received. Subsequently, in making a coastal voyage, their ship was wrecked, but both crew and cargo were saved. The Netherlanders journeyed to Tokyo, where they were presented to the Shogun, who gave them a great sum of gold and permission to trade, or to practice trades in Japan. The only incident which spoiled an otherwise profitable and happy visitation was that the Shogun also forbade the Dutchmen to leave the country.

Because of the traffic between Patani and Japan, the twenty-four survivors of *De Liefde* soon learned that their countrymen had established a factory at the former place. Largely through the influence of Adams, who had gained considerable prestige among the Japanese, van Santvoort and Quackernaeck were given a junk and permission to sail to Patani. More important, they carried with them an invitation to the Dutch to trade with Japan. The Netherlanders arrived at the Malayan port in December 1605. The wheels of the Company were set in motion with the usual alacrity, and by July 1609, barely three and a half years later, two Company ships, the *Griffin* and the *Red Lion with Arrows* dropped anchor in Hirado (or Firando) harbor, prepared to take advantage of the invitation to open trade. Company officers aboard the ships journeyed to the court of the Shogun at Tokyo and that august official entrusted to them a letter of greeting addressed to Maurits 'King of Holland' which gave the Netherlanders access to all his lands and islands, and granted them permission to trade and to build houses. Accordingly, a Company branch was established at Hirado, with one Jacques Specx, an excellent administrator, in charge and five survivors of *De Liefde* for his staff. The new factory was stocked with Chinese silk and pepper, which, though desirable merchandise,

did not constitute a sufficiently varied stock to compete successfully with the Portuguese. The energetic Specx sent two of his assistants in a junk to Siam urging that linen, glassware, iron, lead, flints, leather, carpets, and above all, more Chinese silks be shipped to him. His superiors in Batavia, acting with energy, dispatched a cargo to him by the yacht *De Brak (The Beagle)*, which arrived in Japan in 1611. So began a trade which, as has been said in the previous chapter, was of great importance to the Company, and the Netherlanders remained in Japan continuously from this time until 1860.

The principal exports from Japan were gold, silver, and copper. Down to 1668, when its export was prohibited, the Japanese silver pouring into the Company's coffers was of prime importance. The Chinese silk was principally paid for in Japanese silver. Also silver from the same source was used to buy Chinese gold which was much needed in the Company posts in India, both at Surat and on the Coromandel coast. Incidentally, the Chinese obtained gold from the Spanish in Manila who bought Chinese products with gold transported from Mexico, which illustrates the point made earlier that the seventeenth century commercial world was a rather small one. Returning to the narrow path from which this narrative has strayed, in the early 1670's, owing to gold discoveries in Japan, the Company was able to export far larger quantities of gold than they had before obtained. The Lowlanders were thus able to console themselves for the loss of the silver trade which, as has been said, was cut off in 1668. As to copper, other countries in Europe and the Orient, of course, produced the metal, but no other country had such vast quantities available for export. This commodity was especially desirable for trading in the oriental area, but a certain amount of Japanese copper was also exported to Europe from time to time. Of all the articles imported to Japan, easily the most desirable was Chinese silk. Other imports and exports will be mentioned later.

When the Netherlanders first entered the Japanese trade, they encountered the usual rivals, the Portuguese, the Japanese themselves, the Chinese, and, until they abandoned their factory in 1623, the English. The Portuguese had begun trading in Japan in the 1540's and, as has been said, conducted a good trade between that country and their settlement at Macao. Their eventual elimination from this commerce came about suddenly as a result, on the one hand, of their zeal for Christianizing, and on the other hand, of a growing antagonism to Christianity on the part of Japanese officials, which was itself a reaction to the Christian zeal of Portuguese and Spanish. The Portuguese

began proselytizing almost as soon as they arrived in Japan. Francis Xavier landed in that country only seven years after the Portuguese became established there, and he was not the first priest to spread the true faith. At the outset Catholic missionaries encountered no opposition in Japan, because as Oda Nobunaga, who in some measure had unified the country in 1573, remarked, the establishment of one more sect in a land where there were already more than thirty was a matter of no consequence. As the Japanese were converted by the thousands, the missionaries became more and more arrogant in their attitude towards other religions, and increasingly uncompromising in the demands which they made for their own. Japanese authorities grew suspicious of Christianity and Nobunaga's successor to power instituted an investigation of the Jesuits. He asked them to give reasons for: 1) their desire to spread Christianity in Japan; 2) their destruction of shrines and temples; 3) their habit of eating cows rather than using them as work animals; 4) their propensity to persecute Buddhist priests; and, 5) their buying and selling Japanese as slaves. Anti-Christian feeling in Japan increased to such an extent that in 1587 the propagation of Christianity was prohibited. This decree was followed by others ordering the expulsion of the Christian clergy. In the years 1614 to 1635, 280,000 Japanese Christians were punished for their faith. The climax to anti-Christian feeling was the Shimabara revolt of 1637–38. Some historians believe that the revolt began simply as a rebellion of a group of farmers, rather than as a rebellion of Christians, but regardless of its origins, it ended as a battle between Christians and the troops of the anti-Christian authorities. Eventually, 37,000 of the Christian rebels were exterminated. The Venetians had a slogan, 'We are Venetians first, then Christians.' Worthy successors in the great Venetian tradition, the Netherlanders played a modest part in the extermination of their fellow Christians. The chief Dutch merchant at Hirado, Nicolaes Coeckebacker, contributed five cannon, six casks of powder, and one ship to the anti-Christian forces. In fifteen days, the Company ship threw 426 shot into the stronghold of the Christian rebels. The effort was of great service to the anti-Christians since it drove the Christians underground and destroyed their freedom of movement. From the standpoint of Dutch trade, the revolt was not at all a bad thing. As a result of the uprising, all subjects of the Spanish crown, as well as the Portuguese, were forbidden to set foot on Japanese soil, and the Dutch, because of their military assistance, were looked upon with favor.

The second competitor of the Dutch, the Japanese trader, was eliminated

officially by government decree about the same time that the Portuguese lost their right to trade. In the first years of the seventeenth century, the Japanese had been formidable competitors. In those years Japanese were found throughout the Orient. They were traders in the Malay Peninsula, mercenaries in the employ of the Dutch East India Company, and employed in various capacities by the Spanish in the Philippines and also in Mexico. Their ships roamed the Eastern seas, and they were in a fair way to be a respectable commercial power when their activities suddenly stopped. The same dislike of Christianity which had so fortuitously eliminated the Portuguese as competitors also played a part in the Japanese withdrawal from trade. Appalled by the influence of the new religion, and fearful of it as an instrument of Western penetration, in 1633 all Japanese ships were forbidden to make overseas voyages except the so-called nine 'red seal ships' which sailed by special permission of the Shogun. Two years later, in 1635, Japanese were forbidden to go overseas and all Japanese at that time in foreign lands were ordered to return immediately. Those abroad who did not comply with the edict were forbidden to return later on pain of death. The reason given for this ruling was that the Japanese overseas had been so long under the influence of the Pope and the Catholic fathers that they were as ignorant as the priests themselves. The year following the restrictive measure, all seagoing Japanese craft were ordered destroyed. In this anti-Christian, xenophobic atmosphere, the Dutch did not go unscathed. By a decree of 1635, the Portuguese had been confined to a man-made island in the harbor of Nagasaki called Deshima. When the Portuguese were expelled from the country, the Dutch were ordered to the island and were confined there until they gave up trading there in 1854. Engelbert Kaempfer, a physician in the service of the Dutch East India Company who visited Deshima in 1692, has left a description of it. 'It rises,' says Kaempfer, 'about half a fathom [three feet] above high water mark. In shape, it nearly resembles a fan without a handle.... it is join'd to the town by a small stone-bridge, a few paces long, at the end whereof is a strong guard-house, where there are soldiers constantly upon duty.... a broad street runs across the whole island.... That street only, which runs across the island lengthways, hath houses built on both sides.... All the houses are built of wood, chiefly firr, and are withal very sorry and poor, looking more like cottages. They are two stories high, the lowermost of which serves instead of warehouses. The uppermost we live in, and these we must fit up at our own expense, with colour'd paper instead of hangings, as the custom is in the country....'

Vng. Batteau de Iapan dit Champan

A Japanese sampan

A Japanese sampan

Picture of a ship, Sampan, coming from Japan. It is flat at the bow like a scow. At the sides are wooden anchors with sturdy cables of plaited straw. Its sails are of reed and bark, very cunningly plaited. Somewhat in the manner of rolling up a mat, they hoist up these sails with a windlass. Inside, the sampan has many comforts, such as a fireplace and a cistern. It has a very broad rudder on the starboard quarter. There is another rudder at the stern with two lines running from it by which the ship is steered. The Yacht took the sampan and brought it to the Admiral, laden with flour, fish, and numerous hams. (Wording adapted from the original inscription.)

From the account of the voyage of Olivier van Noort. Amsterdam, 1602.

'This is the present state of the Island, the small compass whereof the Dutch have been confin'd by the Japanese; and as things now stand we must be so far satisfied with it, there being no hopes that we should ever be better accommodated, or allow'd more liberty by so jealous and circumspect a nation.' As Kaempfer indicates, the life of the Dutch at Deshima was a far more drab and confined existence than their free and easy life at Hirado during the Company's first years in Japan. In those years, at times at least, the Netherlanders enjoyed themselves hugely. An English captain who put in at Hirado while the Dutch were there wrote with a touch of envy: 'They go staggering drunk up and down the streets slashing and cutting at each other with knives like madmen.' There was no roistering on Japanese streets after the move to Deshima, for there, says Kaempfer, a great number of 'guards, corporations, societies, with their numerous attendants, all upon oath, and themselves jealous and mistrustful one of another, are set to guard, and narrowly to watch us, as if we were the greatest malefactors, traitors, spies, in a word, the worst and most dangerous set of people. . . .' An example of what Kaempfer meant is illustrated by the activities surrounding the arrival of a Dutch ship. When a vessel entered the harbor of Nagasaki, it was boarded by soldiers and officials. The soldiers remained guarding the ship night and day until it sailed for its home port. The officials seized all swords, cutlasses, firearms, and gunpowder and returned these articles to the Dutchmen only when the ship was ready to depart. All aboard were strictly questioned and examined lest there be a lurking Catholic priest among them. One observer reported that 'while our vessels are being inspected and their armaments and cargoes discharged, without any reason whatsoever, our ships' companies—even the chief officers—are beaten with sticks by the inspectors, as if they were dogs.'

The Japanese were especially ubiquitous and paternal in the matter of the mechanics of trade. The Hollanders were provided with 150 interpreters of various grades, each with his salary and fringe benefits fixed by the Emperor but paid by the Dutch. The Netherlanders were also generously provided with five clerks, fifteen inspectors of coolies, and thirty-six officers of the treasury, all receiving ample salaries fixed by the Japanese and paid by the Company. Dutch sailors were forbidden to handle cargo, and twice as many coolies were provided for that task as were necessary. To add a modern touch, the coolies were paid for a full day if they worked any part of it. When a Dutch ship discharged its cargo (if the cargo were other than silk), the potential buyers examined the goods and submitted bids in writing to the chief Dutch

merchant who selected the highest bid. This procedure was customary until 1672, when the system under which silk had previously been sold was extended to all Dutch importations. According to that procedure a board of Japanese merchants examined the newly arrived cargo and placed an evaluation on it. The Governor of Nagasaki then submitted a bid to the Dutch for the goods concerned which the Company might accept or reject, but not discuss. When the bid was accepted, and practically speaking there was no alternative, the Governor of Nagasaki sold the cargo in job lots to Japanese merchants. The chief result of this system, known as the evaluation system, as far as the Dutch were concerned, was to reduce their yearly profits to about five hundred thousand guilders from the more than nine hundred thousand guilder profit they had formerly realized. In 1685 the evaluation system was in turn replaced by the maximum trade system, which provided that foreigners in general might import goods only to the maximum value of 900,000 taels, or 3,150,000 guilders, and might export Japanese commodities to the same amount. Of this maximum amount, the Chinese were to have two-thirds, and the Dutch one-third, so that the Dutch could not import or export goods in excess of roughly one million guilders annually. With the exception of silk, trade was again placed on the basis of sale to the highest bid, submitted in writing. Silk was still to be sold at a price fixed by the Japanese, and of the total value of the goods imported, one-third was to be silk. From time to time also, restrictions were placed on the articles which might be exported or imported. Generally speaking, over the century restrictions on trade were increased and profits were reduced.

In its flourishing period Japan had been a most profitable market. One may gain an impression of how profitable it had been by noting that when the East India Company was formed, its total capital was six and a half million guilders, whereas in the single year 1636 the Japanese trade alone was said to yield a profit of over one and a half million guilders. In 1638, profits were even greater, imports alone yielding nearly two and a half million guilders. These early years coming soon after the Japanese had withdrawn from trade, and when the Portuguese were in disfavor, were record years; but even later, in the period 1651–1671, the profits averaged, as has been indicated, over nine hundred thousand guilders per year. Deshima was at one time the richest of the Company branches and all the more valuable because almost anything found a market there. Raw and worked silk from China; cotton cloth from India; and woolen cloths from Europe; buffalo hides, deer and rayfish skins

from Siam; deerskins from Formosa; and tanned leathers from Persia and India were all prized by the Japanese. They also desired such European articles as spyglasses, magnifying glasses, spectacles, medical instruments, tools, clocks, and medicines. Western armaments, helmets, armor and fire arms, sold well as did the prized products of the East, pepper, cloves, nutmegs, brazil wood, and sandalwood. The Japanese also wanted gin and arak, coral and amber, quicksilver, arsenic, gall stones and unicorn horns. The Dutch incidentally brought to Japan something which intrigued the natives enormously, namely, a wholly new variety of European culture. One of their writers, in 1708, described these strangers for his countrymen. 'Holland,' he reports with accuracy, 'is a very cold country throughout all four seasons.... Hollanders have white skins, red and short hair, high noses and the pupils of their eyes are white. Their clothes are usually made of woollen cloth, whilst both high and low alike wear beaver hats.... The Hollanders are very clever artisans and very skillful in designing various contrivances. They are the best seamen on the ocean seas in the whole world, well versed in astronomy, geography and divination. They are also first-class medical scientists.' Although the Dutch clocks wore out, the spectacles were broken, and the European firearms became obsolete, the knowledge of the strange crafts and exotic customs of the Netherlanders was kept alive in Japan through the nineteenth century. In return for their earthly goods the Dutch got from the Japanese, as has been said, chiefly copper, gold, and silver, but they carried away also considerable quantities of lacquer work, some pottery or porcelain, and kimonos.

It is now necessary to return to the point of beginning, that is to the port of Patani, in the first years of the seventeenth century, and to trace the spread of Company factories and trade to Siam, or modern Thailand, Cambodia, Laos, Quinam or Annam (or Cochin China) and Tonkin. Company activities on the east side of the Bay of Bengal will be described in the chapter on India. Of the countries which have been mentioned, Siam was easily the most important. The Netherlanders first reached the country from Patani, which was a dependency of Siam, in 1604. In that year Wybrant Warwijck sent Cornelis Specx to Ayutia, the capital of Siam, in the hope that from there he could enter into relations with China. Though unsuccessful in opening trade with China, Specx laid the ground work for a Dutch factory in the Siamese capital, and on his return to Patani, he was accompanied by the first Siamese ambassador to the Netherlands. The Siamese capital (spelled by the Dutch Ajudhja, which was quickly corrupted to Judea) and the ports of Ligor and

Tenasserim (both tributary to Siam) were important trading cities before the Dutch arrived. In this area the Dutch found themselves at the center of a trading network stretching to China, Japan, Indonesia, India, and Persia. European travellers were impressed by the commercial traffic at Tenasserim. One of the first of them, Duarte Barbosa, the famous Portuguese navigator, observed that ' . . . . many ships of Moors and from other parts congregate at this port of Tanasary [Tenasserim], and bring there copper, quicksilver, ver- milion, scarlet cloth, silks, coloured velvets from Mekkah, saffron, coral wroght in strings, rose-water from Mekkah in little bottles of tinned copper... opium, Cambay stuffs [cotton cloths from India], and all these goods fetch a high price at this place.' Somewhat later, in the first years of the seventeenth century, John Saris, a captain in the employ of the British East India Company, noted that Tenasserim was a port of call for junks from India. Still later, Van Dam, historian of the Dutch East India Company, remarks that the Siamese had a trade and traffic with Japan, China, Surat, Malacca, and Indonesia, that there were many Chinese merchants in Siam, and that formerly, before they were prohibited from going abroad, the whole hide trade had been in the hands of the Japanese, but that it had since fallen into the hands of the Dutch. Siam remained an important crossroads of trade after the arrival of the Hollan- ders, as it had been before their coming. Tenasserim (the dependent port) was a useful port of call for Dutch ships bound for Formosa and Japan; and the inland factory at Ayutia, the nation's capital, became an important center for Dutch trading activities. The international character of Siamese trade is revealed by the goods for sale in that country. Southward from Canton and Macao came raw and finished silk, porcelain, quicksilver, iron, and copper- ware. Northward from the East Indies came pepper, sandalwood, camphor, and spices. The native junks and Dutch ships brought eastward from India the great variety of cotton and linen cloths made on the Coromandel coast, and the Dutch brought copper from Japan, and mirrors and ornaments from Europe.

Regarding exports from Siam, deerskins, cowhides, buffalo hides and the skins of ray fishes were especially valuable, since they were in great demand in Japan. The skin of the ray was used to rub down woodwork, and the more prettily marked skins had magical powers. There was in fact an important three-cornered trade involving Indian cloths which were sold in Siam for hides, which in turn were transported to Japan and sold for silver, which was used to purchase more Indian cloth for the Siamese market. Tin also was an

important re-export from Siamese and an export from Malayan ports in the seventeenth century, as it has been since. Siam also produced an abundance of foodstuffs, especially rice, and in times of shortage in the East Indies, the Company transported rice from that country. Timber was readily available, and there were quantities of benzoin, shellac, sappan wood, elephants' tusks, gold, and rubies to be had.

Cambodia to the east of Siam was not nearly so important as the latter country for trade. 'For every merchant found in Cambodia,' said Van Dam, the Company historian, 'one can find a hundred in Siam.' Actually, Cambodia both attracted and repelled the East India Company. On the one hand certain articles could be procured cheaply there and there was some market for Company goods; but on the other hand, the unsettled state of the country made trade precarious. The first Dutchman to touch at Cambodia was Admiral Van Neck, who was there in 1601–1602. In 1620, the Netherlanders built a lodge or factory at Lauweeck near the capital city of Pnom-Penh, but this post was eliminated in a period of Company retrenchment in 1622–23. When the Japanese abandoned foreign trade in 1636 and left a number of lucrative markets to the first comer, the Company decided to drive trade wherever the Japanese had abandoned it. Consequently, ships and men were dispatched to Cambodia and a new factory established. Unfortunately, in 1643 the Cambodians destroyed the post, murdered thirty-six Company servants, and made prisoners of fifty more. Only a short time previously, a number of Dutchmen had been murdered by Portuguese refugees from the conquered fortress of Malacca.

Although the Company had been outrageously treated by the Cambodians, hope for trade and profit sprang eternal in the corporate breast, and a reconciliation was effected in 1656. The Dutch purchased a lodge which had been built by English merchants and were again in business in Cambodia, but only briefly. The King of Cochin China was then warring on Cambodia, and in the course of operations his forces destroyed the Dutch factory and killed some of the personnel. Nothing remarkable occurred after the misfortune until 1667, when a raiding party of Koxinga's forces from Formosa destroyed the re-established factory, killed a number of employees, and put an end to the Company branch in Cambodia.

The trade for which these sacrifices were incurred was chiefly in gumlac or shellac, and benzoin, 'as good and cheaper than that gotten in Siam,' says Van Dam. Other items exported by the Company from Cambodia were gold,

black lacquer, sappan wood, sweet-smelling aloe wood, deerskins, cowhides, cardamon, elephants' tusks, ray skins, wax, musk, resin from the tree *garcina cambogia* and from the aloe tree (both gums very efficacious as medicines), and various foodstuffs, principally rice. The principal item sold by the Dutch was cloth of various kinds. The people in the hinterland of Laos also came to trade in Cambodia, and upon occasion the Dutch went into that country. The products obtained in Laos were much the same as those gotten in Cambodia. The Company also opened trade with Annam (Quinam or Cochin China) in 1633. A report compiled by the Company on the possibilities of trade in that kingdom declared that gold, iron, and raw silk could be purchased profitably, and that there was a good market for pearls, porcelain, pepper, and lead. In the first years of the trade, 1633–36, the competition of Chinese and Japanese merchants was murderous, and the Annamese officials were corrupt and quarrelsome. The volume of trade, consequently, was small and the profits unsatisfactory. A factory was actually established in Annam in 1637, but abolished the following year. The Annam post had been rendered unnecessary by the branch which was established at Tonkin in 1638. According to Van Riebeeck who reported to the Company directors on affairs at Tonkin, the chief article to be procured there was silk, which was purchased with silver. To a large extent the silk procured at the port was shipped to Japan. Musk, cardamon, anise, cinnabar de montagne, and gold were also procurable at Tonkin. The gold was particularly desired by the Company since it was needed for their purchases on the Coromandel coast. The Dutch sold at Tonkin those necessities for any ambitious principality, saltpetre, sulphur, and lead. There was also a market for sandalwood, cloths, and various other items. Three factors made the Dutch stay at Tonkin something less than happy: first, there was considerable competition from the Chinese, the Portuguese, and in the later years of the century, the English; second, corrupt officials and unsettled conditions made commerce difficult; and third, the Company allied itself with the Tonkinese in their war with Annam. Still, the Netherlanders for decades continued to hope for better days, and did not finally close the Tonkin branch until 1700. Siam, Cambodia, Annam, and the other small kingdoms in the area were all addicted to war and turbulence. If Malaya and Indo-China in the seventeenth century were to be described in a word, that word would be 'unsettled.' In speaking of Siam in 1618, George Ball, the president of the English East India Company at Bantam, observed that the goods of that country yielded a great profit, and if the country were at peace,

it might have yielded a far greater trade. One must be ready to admit that the wars of the Siamese, Cambodians, Annamese, and other peoples in this area were doubtless fought for reasons which at least seemed as important and substantial to them as we know such questions as the Spanish succession, the Austrian succession, the stamp tax, and the Polish corridor actually were. Still, speaking trade-wise and profit-wise, their wars are to be regretted, for as Ball says, without them, these countries might have yielded a far greater trade than they did.

The Company traded in other places in Indo-China and Malaya than in those which have been mentioned. The capture of Malacca in 1640 from the Portuguese gave the Dutch control of the Straits of Malacca and increased their prestige with the native princes. As a direct result of their new position of power, the Company was able to negotiate a contract (1642) with the Kingdom of Kedah for the purchase of tin. In 1650 they also contracted with the Kingdom of Perak for the purchase of this metal. There was a factory at Batoesawer in the land of Johore, which was strategically placed for trade. There was another post on the east coast to the north of Patani at Sangora, and one at Ligor, south of Tenasserim. On the island of Udjung Salang, lying about a hundred miles north of Malacca, there was a company post that dealt mostly in tin, and this list by no means exhausts the places in the Peninsula where the industrious Company servants negotiated to the profit of the Company, and also to themselves.

CHAPTER IX

India, Ceylon, and Burma

The expansion of the East India Company northward from the East Indies into Malaya and Japan was matched by a similar westward development in India, Ceylon, and Burma. The westward movement was for the Company a necessary complement to the trade in spices in the East Indies, for the only article which could be bartered for spices on any considerable scale in Indonesia was cloth from India. Throughout the East, India was the great source for clothing; muslin, percale, calico, and gunnee (as in gunny-sack) are all words originating in the Indian textile trade. Year after year, the Indonesians were accustomed to buy from the Indian merchants who came to their shores, the same textiles, the same textures and patterns with which they had been long familiar. In their purchases, they were against change, and more specifically, they were against the warm woolen cloths the Dutch brought from northern Europe. To get spices, then, the Netherlanders needed Indian cloths. These, of course, could be purchased from the Gujerat (north-west Indian) merchants, who continued to frequent Indonesia, but they sold the cloth at a fifty per cent advance over its cost in India. This fifty percent profit, someone else's profit, caused the Company considerable pain and made it imperative that the Company have its own factories in India. The Company branches which were subsequently established there may be thought of as being located in six principal areas. The first three of these regions surround the Bay of Bengal. They are the Coromandel coast (the stretch of coast between Cape Calimere and the mouth of the Kistna River), the region of Bengal to the north of the Coromandel coast, and finally the lands on the east side of the Bay which constitute present-day Burma. The three remaining regions are the island of Ceylon, the Malabar coast (the stretch of the south-west India coast), and Northwest India centering at Surat.

The first Dutch establishments were on the Coromandel coast, since the cloths most in demand in Indonesia were manufactured there. There were initially four principal establishments. Two of these four, the factories at Masulipatam and Petapoelie, were at the mouth of the Kistna River, the northern limit of the Coromandel coast. The post at Masulipatam was established in 1605, and that at Petapoelie (or Nizampatam) in the following year. Negotiations for the establishment at Tegenapatam, the southernmost of the four, were begun in 1608, and the factory was established not long after. Permission to establish a factory at Pulicat about midway on the coast was obtained in 1610.

Masulipatam, the site of the first Dutch factory, was the chief seaport for the Kingdom of Golconda. It was described by a contemporary English traveller, William Methwold, as 'a small towne, but populous, unwalled, ill built and worse situated; within, all the springs are brackish, and without, over-flowed with every high sea for almost halfe a mile about.' The neighboring post at Petapoelie was also in Golconda and was also situated on the low delta land at the mouth of the Kistna. The factory at Pulicat, in the dominion of the King of Vellore, was established by permission of the Naik of the Carnatic, the local grandee, under whose jurisdiction the port lay. In granting permission to the Netherlanders to trade, the Naik at the same time excluded all other Europeans, a blow aimed at the Portuguese, who were established nearby at their fort of São Thomé. The Portuguese had long gotten here the painted cloths necessary for the Indonesian trade, and did not give up without a fight. In fact, in 1612, two years after its establishment, the Portuguese raided the Dutch factory and destroyed it. Several employees were killed; others were made prisoners and carried off, together with the Company's merchandise, to São Thomé. The Portuguese action so aroused the Dutch that they constructed a fortress, called Fort Geldria, at Pulicat which gave them a distinct advantage in the fight for the trade on the coast. The same Englishman, William Methwold, observed that Pulicat was 'a badde neighbour to the Portugall since the Dutch possessed their castle in that place; for with the shipping great and smal, which they [the Dutch] constantly kept upon that coast, they so scowre it that a Portugull frigat stirre not but in the confidence of her better sayling, nor dares anchor before the towne....' Under the Netherlanders, Pulicat became something of a Dutch city, one Hollander remarking that there were streets wholly inhabited by Dutchmen, with houses precisely like those found in Holland, 'with three rows of trees in front where it is pleasant to stroll.' The post at Tegenapatam, also under the King of Vellore, had its beginning

in 1610 when the Company ship *De Cleyne Sonne* (*The Little Sun*) with Arendt Martenszoon in charge anchored before that place, and Martenszoon was able to conclude an agreement with the Naik at Gingee which not only excluded the Portuguese from the domains of the Naik but gave the Dutch a dilapidated Portuguese fort at Tegenapatam as a trading center. Later the Dutch moved their principal operation in the locality to nearby Tierepopelier but maintained the post.

The chief *raison d'être* of the establishments on the Coromandel coast, as has been said, was to secure the Indian cloths. The textiles available varied from place to place, each port having its specialties. The Golconda seaports, Masulipatam and Petapoelie, were prime sources for bleached and dyed cloths. Chintzes, percales, muslins, taffetas, worked silks, and turban cloths were made in the neighboring villages. That sure guide to the East, Linschoten, said that in the neighborhood of Masulipatam 'there is excellent faire linnen of Cotton.... of all colours, and woven with divers sorts of flowers and figures, very fine and cunningly wrought.... They likewise make clothes thereof for women to put about them from their navelles downewarde, bound about their bodies....' Goods other than cloth were also available in these ports. Iron and steel were manufactured in Golconda and brought to the ports on the backs of oxen. The country was also noted for its crystal, and was a great source for gems of various kinds, diamonds, garnets, amethysts, topazes, and agates. Salt manufactured in the interior was also brought down the river to the ports. Pulicat, farther south, was the great center for the painted cloths, or *pintados*, for which the coast was noted. 'The paintings [i.e. painted cloths] of this coast of Choromandel,' remarked William Methwold, 'are famous throughout India, and are indeed the most exquisite that are seene, the best wrought all with the pensill, and with such durable colours that, notwithstanding they bee often washed, the colours fade not....' At Tegenapatam in the south, certain grades of both painted and dyed cloths were said to be obtainable cheaper than elsewhere, and saltpetre and indigo were also for sale as they were at other places on the coast. Regarding imports, they did not vary a great deal from factory to factory. They were such condiments as pepper, mace, nutmegs, and cloves, and such metals as lead, solder, tin, and quicksilver. Silk was an important import, as were sandalwood and eaglewood, a fragrant wood used as incense. In addition, a great number of miscellaneous products were wanted on the coast, such as musk, camphor, sulphur, alum, vermillion, and porcelain.

Especially noteworthy was the trade in slaves which were to be had cheaply in time of war or famine. Methwold, who was at Masulipatam from 1618 to 1622, observed that native traders carried rice and grain to southern ports, 'taking children in exchange, which cost not them above three or foure shillings a childe, and they sell againe in Masulipatnam and other places for forty shillings.' The Dutch and English as well as natives were deep in the trade. Thomas Mills, the English factor at Pulicat, wrote to his superiors in July, 1622, to say that he was unable to comply with the request for fourteen or fifteen slaves because of the short notice given him, and because the Dutch were ordered 'to buy as manye as possible can be procured, to the nomber of four or five thousand,' and had already bought all on the market. In the following September when Mills again wanted to buy slaves, the Dutch persuaded him not to, pointing out that competition would merely inflate the prices. They promised that if he stayed out of the market they would furnish him all the slaves he required. In November, Mills noted that a Dutch ship, the *New Zealand*, had sailed from Pulicat with 460 slaves and was ordered to call at Tegenapatam for 650 more. To their trading activities, the Netherlanders added some manufacturing. At Ponnepilly near Pulicat they eventually had a nail factory, where twenty-two native journeymen with their fifty-eight apprentices made nails as good as Holland nails, and in the Kistna River, they built boats and repaired ships as the Indians had done before them. As the century wore away, the number of places where the Dutch traded on the coast was increased, Negapatam becoming important, but the nature of the trade remained essentially the same.

Following the convenient device of envisaging Dutch trade about the Bay of Bengal as being conducted in three principal regions, the Coromandel coast, Bengal, and Burma, the next region to be noted is Bengal. The natives of the Coromandel coast had long traded backward and forward between their home ports and that region, and the Dutch followed their example. The entrance of the Netherlanders into Bengal was made easier by the desire of the Nabob to get rid of the Portuguese. The Dutch were granted in 1634 the right to trade in all of Bengal and to build a factory at Hooghly on the Ganges. In addition to Hooghly, the Hollanders later traded at Cossimbazar, Dacca, Patna, and in other cities, but Hooghly originally was their trading center, and it had been a notable commercial city before the coming of the Dutch East India Company. 'One finds there,' observed a Dutchman, 'paved streets and pleasing walks with here and there stately Bengalese buildings, rich warehouses,

dwellings and shops run by rich Moors, who have a flourishing trade in all sorts of merchandise, but especially beautiful cottons, silks, and other oriental cloths.' The Lowlanders erected a factory in Hooghly which was worthy of the city and of which they were most proud. It was surrounded by a wall and a moat, cannon were mounted for its defense, and there were fine quarters for the Company servants. Later a factory was established at Pippli on the coast.

Regarding the exports of Bengal, cotton and silks were most important. The cotton cloths had a fine reputation, the muslins and gauzes being especially good. Saltpetre was produced in great abundance, and foodstuffs, especially wheat, rice, and sugar, were also plentiful. Bengal was also known as a great opium producer, and some civit was available. Of the last commodity Linschoten reports that 'by the subtiltie and villany of the Bengalians, it is falsifyed and mixed with filth.' Certain towns sometimes specialized in commodities. Cossimbazar, for example, was the chief center for silks, and the Company had its own silk manufactory there. Patna specialized in saltpetre and opium, and the Company did a thriving trade there in these items.

The third region to be noted, much less important than the preceding two, we have designated roughly as Burma. Almost at the head of the Bay of Bengal, and bordering on Bengal, was the independent kingdom of Arakan, and south of Arakan was the kingdom of Pegu, which stretched along the lower Irawady. The Dutch were invited into Arakan by the ruler of the country, Salim Shah, who hoped to secure their aid against the Portuguese. Accordingly at the end of 1607 Pieter Willemszoon sailed for Arakan from Mazulipatam with a cargo of trade goods. Salim Shah not only gave the Dutch permission to trade in his own kingdom, but permission to conduct commerce in Bengal and Pegu, over which he had no jurisdiction. He also kindly presented the Lowlanders with the Portuguese fortress of San Iago (in Pegu) provided they could get it away from the Portuguese. The Hollanders instead, and somewhat later, established a factory at Dianga, the chief port of Arakan.

Although Willemszoon in 1608 had also suggested that trade should be opened with Pegu, the Company did not actually establish a branch in that kingdom until 1635. This first branch in Pegu was at Siriam on the estuary of the Irawady, and was followed by a second trading establishment at Ava, a town up river near Mandalay. Dutch ships also visited the port of Martaban across the gulf of Martaban from their post at Siriam. The exports from the two kingdoms were numerous. Arakan's chief commodity was

slaves which were got by raiding Bengal. There were also available quantities of wax, indigo, rice, and cassoumba, an orange-red dye stuff, which was used also as medicine. The goods for sale in Pegu were in greater variety, and included a number of precious stones, rubies, spinels, sapphires, Iacinthes (a precious blue stone), emeralds, and garnets. Various metals were also obtained in Pegu: gold, silver, bronze, solder, tin, lead, and quicksilver. Other articles got in this kingdom were lacquers of various kinds, benzoin, elephants' tusks, wax, honey, Chinese coins, rice wine, and petroleum, the latter very efficacious for stiffness in the legs. In spite of this apparent richness, trade was not too successful, and was given up at both Ava and at Siriam in 1679.

Moving away from the Gulf of Bengal, the three remaining regions to be considered are the Malabar coast, the island of Ceylon, and northwest India. The first of these, the Malabar coast, is the western littoral beginning near the southern tip of the continent and extending northward as far as the mountains called the Western Ghats, south of Bombay. Two Netherlanders, Wolff and Lafer, explored the trade possibilities on the coast in 1603, but they were captured by the Portuguese. Following them, Steven Van der Hagen concluded agreements with the Zamorin of Calicut, the local ruler, but no factory or trade resulted. Nearly twenty years later in 1626, Herman van Speult also concluded an agreement with the Zamorin. This prince hoped to use the Dutch against his enemies the Portuguese, and agreed that all the pepper of his kingdom should be sold to the Lowlanders at a fixed price and that it be duty free, but again there was no tangible result. The first Company post on the coast was not actually established until 1637, when a branch was opened at Wingurla, with merchant Pieter Paets in charge. Actually there was not a full-blown factory on Malabar until ten years later, when one was established at Kayankulam, between Quilon and Cochin. With this foothold as a beginning, the Dutch gradually pushed their way into the cities which had been the preserves of their Portuguese rivals. Calicut and Kranganur were conquered, and in 1663 the important trade center of Cochin was delivered up to the Netherlanders. The Dutch had also assailed Goa, but it withstood their attack, as it has withstood the attacks of others since.

The chief product of the coast was pepper, somewhat inferior to that of Sumatra. The second product in importance was cinnamon, which was a great embarrassment to the Dutch. It grew over extensive areas in a thickly populated region and defied all of the best techniques for creating scarcity. The outlets for the spices were too numerous, the trees too scattered, and the

population too extensive to discipline. Cinnamon here was a problem in monopoly impossible of solution. Another spice, cardamon, was also produced, very good for meats and to sweeten the breath. A specialty of Malabar was ginger, which indeed grew elsewhere also. There was a good market for ginger in Arabia and Persia, as well as in India itself. 'Being greene, it is much eaten in India, for sallets,' says Linschoten, 'as also sodden in Vineger, which they call Achar.... There is likewise much Ginger conserved in Suger'. As one would expect, ginger was a powerful medicine, but Linschoten was puzzled to know if it should be regarded as a cure for diarrhea or as a laxative. There was also a traffic in palm oil, palm wine, and arrack which was distilled from the wine. Foodstuffs, especially rice and poultry, were also abundant.

The opportunity to enter the fifth region, Ceylon, came as a by-product of the Dutch effort on Malabar. For years the Lowlanders had blockaded Goa in season, and Raja Singa of Ceylon got in touch with the blockading squadron for help against his Portuguese enemies as the squadron was homeward bound. The Portuguese had first visited Ceylon in 1505 and established themselves there thirteen years later. When the Dutch ventured into the East, Ceylon had been one of the first places they explored. In 1598, John Davis, who had previously discovered Davis Strait, sailed for the Orient as chief pilot on a Dutch ship. In the Bay of Bengal the Dutch merchantman was captured by an Indian vessel. 'By these people,' says Davis, referring to his captors, 'wee learned that in Zeilon there is a citie named Metacalou [Batticaloa], a place of great trade, and that there wee might load our ships with sinamon, peper and cloves. They also said that in Zeilon were great store of precious stones and pearles, that the contrey doth abound with all kinds of victuals, and that the King is an exceeding enemie to the Portugals; they also told us of a citie named Trinquanamale [Trincomali], where there was the like trade.' Though Davis and others reported the wonders of Ceylon, the first Dutch voyagers to actually touch at the island were Joris van Spilbergen and Sebald de Weert, both of whom, though independently, reached there in 1602. Ceylon made a tremendous impression on van Spilbergen. He declared that the island was not only rich in cinnamon and pepper, but that there were mountains yielding gold and silver, and many kinds of gems were to be found there such as bacans, rubies, and garnets. In addition, there were fine salt deposits and sound timber for ships and houses. As for the fertility of the soil, it was van Spilbergen's opinion that anything which would grow in any other land would grow in Ceylon. Despite these glowing reports,

The Maharajah of Ceylon and Joris van Spilbergen

The King of Kandy, called in the Sinhalese language Fimala, Darma, Suri, Ada. He has been baptized in Colombo as Don John of Austria of Colombo. This picture has been made in India from the life. His quality and his trade with Joris van Spilbergen are narrated in this history. A contemporary print.

Den Coninck van Candy ghenaemt in Singalesse sprake: Fimala, Darma, Suri, Ada, is tot Coulombo gshedoopt / Don Ian Dauftria van Coulombo, deſe afbeel-
ding is in Indien gshemaeckt / naer tleven van zijn qualiteyt ende handel met Joris van Spilberghen / wort in deſe Hiſtory vertelt.

The Maharajah of Ceylon and Joris van Spilbergen

events moved at the customary pace. An agreement for trade was made with a native ruler in 1610 and another in 1612, but it was not until 1636, the year in which, as has been indicated, the Ceylonese potentate Raja Singa asked the Dutch for help against the Portuguese that the Company gave the island their earnest attention. The Company officials, having in mind the pearls, rubies, sapphires, elephants, and cinnamon, agreed to help the Raja. One by one the Portuguese ports were conquered and the Dutch finally expelled their competitors in 1658. There followed a relatively quiet and generally profitable exploitation of the island by the Company. In this work the Netherlanders were sometimes aided, but usually hampered, by the native governments, if the assembled whims, cruelties, and arbitrary decrees of the native rulers may be identified by that term.

The chief item of trade was, of course, cinnamon, which as usual had been described by Linschoten. He reported that not only was it an aid to digestion, but that it strengthened one's intestines, heart, and liver, and was a sure cure for catarrh, dropsy, and diseases of the kidneys. It was an antidote for poison, and helped women who had difficulty menstruating. Of cinnamon trees, Linschoten explained that 'the tree hath two barkes, the second bark is the Cinamon, it is cut off in square peeces, and so laid to dry.... The tree from whence the barke is taken they let it stand, & within 3 yeres after it hath an other barke....' In addition to the cinnamon industry, the Dutch took over the slave system which the Portuguese had instituted to carry on the business. Another sovereign remedy available in Ceylon for which there was a market was snake-wood. 'Very good and well proved,' Linschoten assures us, 'against the burning fevers.' It was also good for all forms of poison and sickness, especially colic, worms, coldness in the body, and the shakes. The Netherlanders also dealt in gems, pepper, and elephants. They cut the timber and gathered the salt that van Spilbergen had noted in the lagoons, and they stayed in the island until they were expelled by the British during the Napoleonic wars.

The sixth and last region in which the Dutch trafficked, north-west India, actually was the area in which they made their first efforts to gain a foothold on the sub-continent. The territory had at one time constituted the independent kingdom of Gujerat, but at the time it became of concern to the Dutch, it was part of the domains of the Great Mogul. It was the merchants from this area who came to trade the cloths of their own country and of Coromandel for spices in Indonesia. With some chagrin the Dutch compared these traders

in sharpness and shrewdness with Chinese and Jewish business men. The first Dutch post in Gujerat was established at Surat in 1606, but the Portuguese and some of the native authorities so persecuted and threatened the Dutch factor stationed there, David Van Deynsen, that he committed suicide. It was not until 1616, in spite of the best efforts of the English to prevent them, that the Dutch succeeded in establishing a permanent factory at Surat. The number of Company posts or factories in Gujerat is an index of the prosperity of Netherlands trade there. In addition to the factory at Surat about which Company activities centered, there were eventually trading establishments at the coastal cities of Broach and Cambay, at Ahmadabad and Burhanpur, some distance inland, and at the strategic city of Agra, the Mogul's capital.

The region offered an exceptionally wide variety of goods for export. The chief attraction was the fine cotton cloths, blankets, and Gujerat carpets, but a wide variety of small articles was manufactured in the region. Bedsteads, stools, ivory chessboards, fancy backgammon sets, signet rings, ivory ornaments, rock crystal-ware, buttons, and beads were all produced in Gujerat. As elsewhere in India, there was a lively traffic in precious and semi-precious stones, spinels, rubies, garnets, amethysts, agates and jasper. Foodstuffs such as grains, butter, oil, sugar, peas and beans were usually easily obtainable. Indigo was one of the most valuable exports, and there were also available quantities of opium, bangue, and myrobolans. Bangue is a narcotic, and Linschoten declared that those who ate it reeled and acted as if they were intoxicated. Myrobolans were very valuable fruit indeed. Dried or preserved in sugar, they were not only a tasty food, but were good against agues and fevers. They sharpened the wits and cleared the sight and could also be used for tanning and dyeing. The Dutch brought from elsewhere in the East and sold in Gujerat, sugar, spices, benzoin, camphor, silks, satins, porcelain, lacquerwork, ivory and sandalwood. They also supplied the market with such metals as zinc, tin, lead, iron, copper, and Japanese silver. A somewhat peculiar import was cowhides from Russia, which were said to be very cool for sitting on in hot weather. For the ruler, the Great Mogul, the Dutch imported from Holland paintings of respectable Dutch citizens and of Dutch landscapes, which afforded that all-powerful sovereign no end of diversion.

The competitors in this rich trade of India were first of all the same old rivals, the Portuguese and the English, but as was usually the case, the Portuguese were on their way out, and the English had not yet arrived. It was obvious in the first decades of the seventeenth century that the English in India

were no match for the Netherlanders. Thomas Mills, the English agent at Pulicat, wrote in September 1622 that 'The Dutch in their glorie laugh in their sleves att our present miseries,' and noted that the Dutch spoke of the small means of the English East India Company, 'which is very true,' he admitted, 'and not in a tenth degree comparable to theirs.... God send us better means to employe ourselves or a shorte warning to call us home....' Mills' colleague at Petapoeli, Matthew Duke, was even more bitter about Dutchmen. 'Theis buterboxes,' he had observed in December 1618, 'are groanne soe insolent that yf they be suffred but a whit longer, they will make claime to the whole Indies, so that no man shall trade but themselves or by thear leave....' William Methwold at Masulipatam was of the opinion that 'The Dutches insolency, or our impotency, have allmost, and will I feare altogether, deprive us of the best part of this trade.' In Gujerat, the English were well established before the Dutch, but they had no confidence they would be able to maintain their advantage. Thomas Roe, the English Company's ambassador there, a diplomat 'of a pregnant understanding, well spoken, learned, industrious, and of a comelie personage,' warned his Company that the Dutch would 'out-present, out-bribe, and out-buy us in all things.' On another occasion, he observed of the Lowlanders that 'they grow to insuffrable insolencies.... You must speedelye looke to this Maggat... wee talke of the Portugall, but these will eate a woorme in your sides....' The other Europeans, the French and Danes, caused the Dutch no trouble. Actually, the Indian traders themselves probably provided the severest competition. It has been mentioned that the Dutch found the men from Gujerat to be smart traders. The natives of other regions were no less so. Linschoten observed that 'The heathenish Indians that dwell in Goa are verie rich Marchants, and traffique much.' He further noted that these natives 'not onely sell all kindes of Silkes, Sattins, Damaskes, and curious works of Porselyne from China and other places, but all manner of wares of velvet, Silke, Sattin, and such like, out of Portingall.' A special but minor problem in Cochin were the Jews, some of whom were from Portugal, and others of whom had arrived there about a thousand years before the Dutch. These people were divided into two groups, the black Jews and the white Jews. The white Jews were wealthy and, as seems almost inevitable, looked down on their co-religionaires. This white community controlled the trade within this center of Dutch trade until the Napoleonic wars.

In India, as in other regions where the East India Company traded, one

group which diminished the Company's profits as consistently as any rival was the Company's own employees. Pilfering the Company's resources and trading for private profit were the almost universal pleasant pastimes of Company servants. So widespread was this strictly private enterprise that within the Company there was an informal organization known to the initiate as 'the little company,' designed to help employees in their private ventures. 'The little company' transported goods on Company ships, or if the deal were big enough, chartered native craft to carry merchandise. The opium trade of Bengal was particularly well suited to private trading, and it has been estimated that at times half of what might have been the Company opium trade was carried on by Company officials for their private gain. In 1686, it was said that in the period 1678–1686 the Company lost by the private dealings of its employees and unfaithful administration more than three million eight hundred thousand guilders. At Hooghly, one of the measures initiated to stop such malfeasance was to issue an order that widows and unattached Dutchmen must return to Batavia, and that Company officers must live on the Company post. One might be puzzled to know how such an order would lessen dishonesty. The Company historian, Van Dam, has explained that there was so much transportation of goods by the dark of the moon in Hooghly between Company warehouses and private residences that one would think oneself in a city of enterprising free merchants, rather than at a Company post. It could simply have been, of course, that the Company servants were so imbued with the spirit of private enterprise that they found it difficult to restrain their zeal. Each new region opened up to trade meant increased profits for the Company and new opportunities for the private operations of its zealous servants. The two factors operating together increased the rate of expansion of Company activity.

CHAPTER X

Arabia and Persia

Before the arrival of the Dutch in Gujerat, there was already a lively traffic between that country and Arabia. The Great Mogul of India, Jahangir, 1605–1627, was a Moslem, as was his dynasty. He ruled Gujerat through a lieutenant at Ahmadabad, and the Gujerat Ports of Cambay and Surat became the great departure points for Moslem pilgrims bound for Mecca. There was also concomitantly heavy commercial traffic carried on by means of the native craft plying between Gujerat and the Arabian ports. When the Netherlanders finally opened trade with Arabia, they followed this trade route. The new commerce was largely a project of their factory at Surat and the Arabian branches were dependencies of the one at Surat. The Company was aware that it could dispose of in Arabia such items as pepper and cloves, cloth from Gujerat, diamonds, indigo, gumlac, musk, benzoin, radix (a root from China used as a drug) and various other medicines. Some useful articles could also be obtained there—myrrh, pearls, and raisins, for example, but inducements to trade these items were insignificant compared with the great fact that goods could be sold in Arabia for cash. Indeed, it was at one time Jan Pieterszoon Coen's scheme to so develop Arabian trade that he would obtain there the cash to purchase the Gujerat cloth he needed in Indonesia. It was also thought by some Company officials that the presence of Company ships in the Gujerat-Arabia trade would result in the Company's being treated more respectfully than it had been by the native merchants who were busily plying the trade routes of the Arabian Sea.

The first efforts to gain a foothold in Arabia were made by Pieter Van den Broecke. He was a principal or senior merchant, and was aboard the same ship as Governor General Gerard Reijnst when the latter was on his way out to the Indies from Holland. Not far from Madagascar on this voyage, the Governor's Council decided to detach Van den Broecke and the yacht *Nassau*

to investigate the possibilities of trade in Arabia. Accordingly, the *Nassau* sailed for that country and anchored first at Aden. This port was within the domains of the Sultan of Turkey and more directly under the authority of the Sultan's officer, the Pasha of Yemen. That official was not inclined to let Van den Broecke remain, and so the *Nassau* sailed for the neighboring port of Sheher. This latter place was controlled by its own king, one Abdullah, who although he paid tribute to the Pasha of Yemen, was in many ways independent. Here Van den Broecke had better luck, and, with permission of Abdullah, left three men at Sheher with a supply of cash and inferior ironmongery and tinware to open trade. On a second voyage to Arabia in 1616, after leaving more trade goods at Sheher, Van den Broecke continued on to Mocha, an important trade center, and in Company eyes, the most important Arabian port in which to have an establishment. Here the Netherlanders again encountered the difficulty that the port was under the Pasha of Yemen, who was not empowered to grant them the privilege of establishing a factory. Despite this fact, the Pasha and his officers were friendly and Van den Broecke departed in July 1616, after doing considerable profitable trade.

Permission to trade in Arabia was actually obtained through the Dutch representative at the Court of the Sultan at Constantinople, Cornelis Haga. Because of the representations of Haga, the Sultan in July 1618 instructed the Pasha of Yemen to permit the Dutch to have their consuls at Mocha, Aden, and other places and to treat them with honor and friendship. Unfortunately at the time permission to trade in Arabia was obtained, the Company lacked shipping to take advantage of the opportunity, and it was not until August 1620 that Van den Broecke returned to Arabia on a third voyage prepared to establish a Company factory. It being late in the season and being under the necessity of catching the monsoon to sail for Surat, Van den Broecke landed his cargo and several Company servants at Aden, instructing them to tranship the goods by native craft to Mocha and there establish the permanent Company factory. These Dutchmen with the cargo finally arrived in Mocha in January 1621. Unfortunately, not long after their arrival, the period of friendly relations between the Company and the authorities in Yemen came to an end. It had happened that two Dutch ships, the *Samson* and the *Weesp*, bound for Surat and Mocha captured at sea two native craft belonging to the port of Dabhol on the west coast of India. These Indian ships were found to be carrying cargo belonging to the Portuguese at Goa, which the Dutch promptly confiscated, an act which the Hollanders considered judicious and

Portrait of Pieter van den Broecke by Frans Hals
Collection Lord Iveagh, Kenwood House, London.

justifiable, but which had very little chance of being considered by eastern peoples as anything other than robbery and piracy.

Aboard the Dutch ships was the unfortunate Willem de Milde who, when the *Samson* and *Weesp* reached Mocha, was left there in July 1621 to take charge of the newly established factory. He assumed his duties with heavy forebodings. The merchants of Dabhol were highly respected in Mocha, and de Milde suspected that news of the actions of the *Samson* and the *Weesp* would soon reach the port. His fears and forebodings were not unfounded. Reports of the plundering of the Dabhol ships arrived, and de Milde and his assistants were made prisoners. Eventually also the Company goods were confiscated. There now ensued a long period, to 1624, in which agreement after agreement between the Pasha and his officers on the one hand, and the Company officials on the other, for the release of the goods and prisoners and the re-establishment of trade were made and broken. It seems apparent in this affair that the Pasha used the incident of the Dabhol ships as a pretext to plunder the Company factory, and that he used de Milde and other Dutchmen as hostages or pawns in his attempt to obtain as much loot as possible. From time to time small amounts of cash were recovered by the Company and a Company servant occasionally was released or escaped, but the idea of a factory at Mocha was finally given up in 1624. The last heard of de Milde was in 1632, when he was still in an Arabian prison. Although some trading was done, a Dutch factory was not again established in Arabia until 1697.

The experience of the Dutch in Persia was much happier than their Arabian adventure, and of the two countries, Persia was commercially by far the more important. It was a country with a long history of trade and commerce. Babylonians, Assyrians, Greeks, Romans, Parthians, Arabs, Genoese, Florentines, Venetians, Portuguese, and English had all traded there before the arrival of the Dutch. One of the most fortuitous circumstances for the commercial future of Persia had been that in the early centuries of the Christian era, Chinese merchants and other traders brought silks overland as far as Turkestan, and by sea as far as Ceylon. Whichever way the silks came, on their further journey to the markets in the west, they passed through Persian hands. Inevitably the art of making silk became known to the Persians and in place of a Persian silk trade, there arose in the seventh century a Persian silk industry which was to bring great prosperity to the country. By the seventeenth century, it is doubtful if a European venturing into Persia would have found it a country inferior to his own in appearance. In European cities there were

no public parks or museums. Many of the houses were of wood; the streets were narrow and at night unlighted and dangerous. In the same period, Ispahan had broad streets and many beautiful buildings. Don Juan of Persia said of Ispahan that it was so densely populated 'that they call it the city of *Nisf-i-Jahán*, which in the Persian tongue signifies Half-the-World.' This writer goes on to say, probably with some exaggeration, that the city's population might number eighty thousand households, more rather than less, or three hundred sixty thousand souls. He reports that the number of hostels that stood at the entrance gates of the city numbered upward of six hundred, and that there were three hundred bath houses in the city, and ten thousand shops selling all manner of cloths, victuals, and other goods. In addition, many interesting crafts were practiced such as carpet weaving, silk and brocade weaving, and ceramics. Painting was popular, and illuminated manuscripts were produced in great quantities. At the court of the Shah, mathematics and science flourished, as well as medicine, history, geography, and other scholarly pursuits.

Ispahan was only one of a number of teeming cities in the domains of the great Shah. There was Shiraz, a thriving commercial town on the caravan route from Tartary to India, and there was also the city of Herat, which Don Juan claimed had a population of about 450,000 and which enjoyed a thriving trade with India, Muscovy, and Tartary. Not far from the Caspian Sea was the city of Kazvin, where, says Don Juan, 'until very lately, the kings of Persia have been wont to hold their court.' He says that here in Kazvin he had many times counted the mosques, of which there were more than five hundred. It was on the shores of the Caspian Sea also, in Persia's most fruitful province, that the silk industry had developed. In addition to silk, there were other products to be gotten in the country, such as foa, a red dye stuff, rose-water, and horses, but such items were trifling in comparison with the possibilities of the silk trade.

It so happened that about the time that both the Dutch and the English East India Companies were considering the possibilities of trade in Persia, the remarkable ruler of that country, Shah Abbas, was casting about for a suitable avenue for selling his silks in Europe. The overland route to Mediterranean ports by way of Mesopotamia was blocked by his enemies, the Turks, and throughout the sixteenth century the sea route westward via the Red Sea was rendered difficult by the presence of the Portuguese at Ormuz, Muscat, and the Bahrein Islands. Shah Abbas desired chiefly an arrangement with a mariti-

me power that could load the silks in Persian ports. His chief emissaries in Europe were the English brothers, Sir Anthony and Sir Robert Shirley, two of the most talented and unreliable adventurers in Christendom. The Shirleys had organized both infantry and artillery for the Shah and placed the Persian army on such a footing that it could compete successfully with the Turks, and for a time, at least, the brothers stood high in the monarch's favor. First Sir Anthony and later Sir Robert toured the courts of Europe in an effort to form an alliance for the Persians. In 1611, Sir Robert visited Holland. The historian, Emanuel Van Meteren, noted that 'in Holland this summer [1611] arrived an ambassador from Persia, an Englishman, and a knight's son named Robert Sherley.... who sought to have the States General to open and to make a bid for a trade in Persia; then since he came from Spain where he had long lain and there suchlike might have had such a dealings, he was suspected that he might have been sent out by the Spanish in order to hinder or to concern himself with the Netherlands East Indian Trade....'

Although the Shirleys approached both the English and Dutch authorities concerning trade in Persia, and although there were efforts by others in Europe to open trade with that country, as an actual fact in the case of both nations, the trade was brought about by Englishmen and Dutchmen at Surat who saw possibilities of trade before their eyes, as they had seen the opportunities of trade with Arabia. The great obstacle at first was the presence of the Portuguese in the Persian Gulf. The chief stronghold of these rivals was the port of Ormuz, or Hormuz, situated on a small island off the coast. Ormuz was already a famous port when Marco Polo visited it in 1275. 'Were all the world a ring,' went an old Persian proverb, 'then Hormuz would be the jewel therein.' The city had been conquered for the Portuguese by Affonso de Albuquerque in 1514, and this port which had been so praised in the Persian proverb became known to its conquerors as the most 'beautiful pearl in the crown of Portugal.' Of Ormuz, Linschoten said that 'in it is the staple for all India, Persia, Arabia, and Turkie, and of all the places and Countries about the same.' As has been mentioned, the Portuguese were also established at Muscat on the south side of the Gulf and on the Bahrein Islands within the Gulf. Their sway was undisputed throughout the sixteenth century, but at the beginning of the seventeenth century, Shah Abbas brought steady pressure to bear on them. In 1602, he drove them from the Bahrein Islands and in 1615 from Gamron, a town on the mainland opposite Ormuz. In 1622, the troops of his provincial governor, Imam Kuli Kahn, cooperating with a flotilla of English ships,

captured Ormuz itself. With the fall of Ormuz, the power of Portugal in the Persian Gulf was really broken, despite a later attempt by them to recapture the city, and despite the fact that Muscat was still a Portuguese stronghold. With their rival removed, both English and Dutch were enabled to enter the Persian trade. Of the two, the English were the first on the ground, and indeed they unloaded goods and traded at Jask, a port to the south of Ormuz as early as 1616. After the fall of the latter port in 1622, the English moved their post from Jask to Gamron, which was renamed Bender Abbas, or the port of Shah Abbas. It was through this port of Gamron or Bender Abbas also that the Netherlanders first entered the Persian trade. The first Dutchman on the ground was Huybert Visnich, who arrived there in the Company yacht *Heusden* in June 1623, and obtained permission to unload cargo. Almost immediately after, he set out for Ispahan for an audience with Shah Abbas, the great king, and his negotiations with the Shah were profitable and successful. Shah Abbas granted the Dutch trading rights which were practically the same as those accorded to the English, and the agreement remained for a long time the basis for Netherlands trade in Persia. Among other things, the Lowlanders were to have the right to trade where they pleased in the Shah's domains. They were not to be charged more than was charged to Persians for camel hire. The Shah's officers were to see to it that the Netherlanders had housing, food, horses, and whatever else was necessary, including convoy guards when their goods were en route. The Shah's police, or justices, were not to enter the Lowlanders' houses without permission, and when Christian slaves were offered for sale, the Dutch were to have the opportunity of purchasing them.

The first years of the Company in Persia constitute one of the most interesting chapters in the history of the Dutch East India Company. The fact that silk was a royal monopoly meant that here the Dutch were frequently dealing with the high officials of the kingdom. A concomitant of this profitable trade also seemed to be a variety of irregularities in carrying it on, and last, but not least, the pioneer who established the trade, Huybert Visnich, was not only a successful but a colorful merchant. Visnich found that assistants frequently fell below his expectations. Almost at the beginning of the Persian experience, he wrote to one of his underlings to say that he was shocked at the reports on business, that the methods used would lose the Dutch all of their reputation, and that the expenses were not to be endured. These remarks he would have been justified in repeating many times later. He was to find that Company servants connived with Persians to import goods privately, and the market

was flooded with Dutch goods the Company had never imported. Employees also sold Company goods privately and reported the merchandise as lost. They purchased silk from Persian officials with the understanding that a certain percentage of the purchase price would be returned to them by the Persians. They sold goods above the official price and pocketed the difference. They took bribes from the camel drivers and freighters who contracted to carry Company goods, and they carried their private merchandise free in Company ships. The slackness of Visnich's assistants seemed at times to be matched by the indifference of his superiors, as on the occasion when he complained to the officers in Batavia that the camphor they had sent him was of poor quality and that the copper was so poorly refined that it all had to be smelted down and re-refined. His situation was difficult. The officials of the Shah's court, dishonest colleagues, and suspicious superiors at far-away Surat, Batavia, and Amsterdam were able to stir up a wide variety of misunderstandings, fears, and hatreds. The position finally became unendurable, and poor distraught Visnich, although not more dishonest or more guilty of wrongdoing than many another, simply fled from his post in despair. He was succeeded at the end of 1630 by one Antonio del Court, of whom great things were expected, but at the end of two years, it was apparent that he was not equal to his task and he was replaced in February 1633 by Nicolaes Jacobszoon Overschie. Overschie, like Visnich, found himself surrounded by distrust, dishonesty, and envy, but his term of office was generally successful and profitable. At the beginning of 1638 he was summoned to Batavia to answer various charges which had been made against him. The accusations were not proved, and Overschie remained in Company service until he was able to retire to the Netherlands with a great fortune. After Overschie, events were less exciting, but Persian trade continued to be highly profitable, and was almost exclusively in silk. After Overschie's time and until 1647, the Shah was graciously pleased to permit the Dutch to buy silk from merchants but only after purchasing considerable quantities of bad and expensive silk from himself.

During the administration of Visnich, the total profits of the trade amounted to more than a million guilders. The Persian profit was greater at that time than in any other Company factory except that at Batavia. These pleasing dividends caused Jan Pieterszoon Coen to exclaim in November 1627, 'God grant the Company a long and peaceful trade in Persia....' and He was, in fact, graciously pleased to grant a continued high return. For more than a century the Persian establishments were the most important Company posts

on the mainland of Asia. Over the period 1623–1636, the profits on silk (although in some years as low as twenty-five per cent) possibly averaged between thirty and forty per cent. Much later, in the year 1682 a profit of 211 per cent was reported, and in the following year, 153 per cent. In the period 1683–1740 the profits of the Company as a whole amounted to about ninety and a half million guilders, of which approximately twenty million, or twenty-two per cent of the whole, was profit from Persia. It has been mentioned that foa, a dye stuff, and rose-water were also exported, but in comparison with silk, these were negligible items. Although the number of exports was scanty, there seemed to be a market in Persia for all the goods the Company could bring in. The spices and condiments which have been mentioned so many times in these pages, pepper, cloves, cardamon, and tamarind, were imported. Many foodstuffs were brought in also: Chinese and Bengal sugar, candied and plain ginger, coffee, and tea. As might be expected, dyeing materials such as madder and indigo were in demand, as were such drugs as benzoin and sarsaparilla. All of the metals available could be sold in Persia, tin, copper, pewter, steel and such steel products as cuirasses, coats of mail, and gun barrels. Those two woods so favored by Orientals, sandalwood and sappan wood, sold well, as did a host of miscellaneous products: Dutch and Indian cloth, tobacco, porcelain, camphor and Japanese lacquer work. The most important import of all was silver, for the silk trade was a monopoly of the Shah and he demanded that half of its cost be paid in cash. Eventually, in addition to Gamron or Bender Abbas and Ispahan, the Company had branches at Shiraz and Lar, which were on the caravan route between the capital and the port. The maintenance of these factories, the coming and going of ships with their multitudinous commodities, the cares of Visnich and the worries of his superiors were all to the end that certain luxuries might be sold in Europe, in order that Maaike, or Priscilla, or Antoinette might go in silk and smell of roses. Actually European ladies might have been more comfortable in good Dutch or English wool, but such thoughts and their implications are dangerous for any commercial people, including ourselves.

The extension of trade to Persia marked the Company's farthest expansion westward. The Dutch had now explored the trade possibilities to both the west and the north of their headquarters in Indonesia. To the east stretched a vast and largely empty ocean, but what might lie to the south, no one knew for certain. That there might be there a whole new land of untold riches was an exciting possibility to contemplate, and a tempting one to explore.

CHAPTER XI

Australia

The possibility that there might be trade opportunities in unknown lands to the south and east of Indonesia haunted both the Company officials in Batavia and the directors in Amsterdam. Actually, there had been speculation for centuries both in Europe and in the Orient about a vast country somewhere south of Java and east of the Cape of Good Hope. Many a person had observed seals, sea mews, and penguins on the shores of Africa and South America which migrated southward in the springtime, and pondered the fact that such birds and animals bred in the spring and needed breeding grounds on dry land. It is believed by some that the Portuguese knew of Australia long before other Europeans suspected its existence. It has been pointed out by some that there are sixteenth century copies of a Portuguese chart showing Australia in recognizable form, and in roughly the correct geographic location. Others have said that with so much speculation and so many cartographers sketching imaginary southern continents, it would have been strange if some map maker had not scored a near miss on Australia. It has been said often, and mistakenly, that the southern continent was sighted by the Portuguese, Manuel Godhino de Erédia in 1601. If the Portuguese had been cognizant of those distant edges of the world, they were remarkably successful in keeping their knowledge to themselves. Actually, these people had ranged the seas so widely and traded so prosperously that their European neighbors often suspected them of secret designs and hidden knowledge they did not actually possess. Pierre Crignon, a French poet, who himself travelled to the Indies, observed of the Portuguese that 'they seem to have drunk of the dust of the heart of King Alexander, for they think God made the seas and the land only for them, and if they could have locked up the sea from Finisterre to Ireland, it would have been done long ago.' It is also said that the Chinese knew about Australia even before the Portuguese. Arguments have also been produced to show that French,

English, and South Netherlanders were in the antipodes before the Dutch, but all of this talk at best is but of shadowy deserts and infrequented woods.

To the officials of the East India Company, rumors and speculation about new lands was serious business. They considered carefully the evidence for a southern continent and the possibilities of trade in those unknown parts, and finally, in 1605, the president of the factory at Bantam, Jan Willemszoon Verschoor, and his council dispatched the yacht *Duyfken* commanded by Willem Jansz to explore to the south and east. John Saris, an English sea captain who has been mentioned before in these pages, was then at Bantam and was an interested observer of the sailing of the *Duyfken*. 'The eighteenth [November 1605],' he wrote, 'heere departed a small Pinasse of the *Flemmings*, for the discovery of the Land called Nova Guinea which, as it is said, affordeth great store of Gold....' Departing from Bantam, the *Duyfken* sailed along the south coast of New Guinea. Those aboard noted that there might be a passage to the east, where in fact Torres Strait actually is, but the yacht passed into the Gulf of Carpentaria and discovered the east coast of that gulf without actually being aware that Torres Strait existed. The *Duyfken* returned to Java without having discovered anything of commercial value. John Saris was still in the Indies when the yacht returned, and he received news of the *Duyfken* from the skipper of a Java junk recently arrived from Banda. 'He told me,' reported Saris, 'that the *Flemmings* Pinasse which went upon discovery for *Nova Ginny*, was returned to Banda, having found the Iland: but in sending their men on shoare to intreate of Trade, they were nine of them killed by the Heathens, which are man-eaters; So they were constrained to returne, finding no good to be done there....' Later Company officials summed up the practical results of the *Duyfken* voyage by saying that, 'no information was obtained touching the exact situation of the country and regarding the commodities obtainable and in demand there....' Following this voyage, a number of Dutch ships touched Australia, some of them literally and violently, a circumstance which was brought about by a change in the route taken by vessels bound for the Indies. The original route from Europe to Indonesia, learned from the Portuguese, led around the Cape of Good Hope, thence to Mauritius, and from Mauritius in a direct line to Sunda Strait. Between the Cape and Indonesia there were long stretches of calms where the ship rolled on the gentle swells, while the sails hung limply on the yards, and the pitch in the deck seams bubbled and ran liquid in the heat. In these stretches, as the sea and air became hot, still, and silent, the ship's stores stirred into activity.

Weevils crawled through the ship's biscuit, maggots swarmed in the salted fish, and various marine fauna disported themselves in the drinking water. In the heat and discomfort, good tempered voyagers became quarrelesome; the bad tempered became vicious; and the weary sickened and died. Thus the Company vessels in these latitudes were filled with the suffering, the fighting, and the dying, and so burdened, they crawled wearily to the Indies. The almost incomprehensible fact is that such hardships were endured for a number of years, when it was known that there existed a far better and faster route. Specifically, it was realized that if after reaching the Cape of Good Hope, instead of heading for Mauritius, a ship turned slightly south and then steered due east, it would encounter only fresh spanking breezes which would carry it quickly to the longitude of Java. Having reached that longitude it was only necessary to steer northward to reach Batavia quickly and without hardship. Hendrik Brouwer, at the direction of the Company, had taken this route in 1611, and made the voyage from the Texel in Holland to Java, which usually took more than a year, in less than six months. Despite Brouwer's experience, ships continued to swelter in the southern seas while the Directors in Amsterdam considered the advisability of making a change. The resolution to employ a new southern route did not come for five years after Brouwer's voyage. One of the first skippers to steer the southern course was Dirk Hartogszoon of the ship *Eendracht*, or 'Concord.' The *Eendracht* headed due south from the Cape of Good Hope, and those aboard were surprised one day to see land dead ahead. What they saw was, of course, the weast coast of Australia, or more accurately, a small inshore island which is still known as Dirk Hartog's Island. Having reached the coast at 25 degrees south latitude, Hartogszoon explored northward until he reached twenty-two degrees. Once Dutch ships had adopted the new route, they sighted the Australian coast with a fair degree of regularity. About a year and a half after the *Eendracht* voyage, the commander of the ship *Zeewolf* was surprised to come upon a lowlying coast where his chart showed open ocean. 'We do not know,' he reported, 'whether it forms an unbroken coast line, or is made up of separate islands. In the former case, it might well be a mainland coast, for it extends to a very great length, but only the Lord knows the real state of affairs.' Following the *Zeewolf*, other Company ships, first the *Mauritius*, than the *Dordrecht* and *Amsterdam*, and then the *Leeuwin* sighted the coast on their way from the Netherlands. These events kept interest alive in the southern continent, and speculation on the possibilities of trade there continued.

After further considering the matter for several additional years, the Directors in Holland wrote the Governor-General and Council at Batavia, observing that something might be done in these new lands to the honor and profit of the Company, and asking that a yacht be fitted out to explore from 'Eendrachts-land' (roughly, the coast from twenty-two to thirty-two degrees south latitude) to the lands lying to the northward. The letter of the Directors, written in 1620, arrived in the Indies in 1621. The Governor and Council thereupon went briskly to work and in the fall of 1622 the yachts *Haringh* and *Hasewint* were gotten ready for the exploration the Directors had requested. 'You will moreover go ashore in various places,' ran the instructions to the yachts' commanders, 'and diligently examine the coast in order to ascertain whether or no it is inhabited, the nature of the land and the people, their towns and inhabited villages, the divisions of their kingdoms, their religion and policy, their wars, their rivers, the shape of their vessels, their fisheries, commodities and manufactures, but especially to inform yourselves what minerals, such as gold, silver, tin, iron, lead, and copper, what precious stones, pearls, vegetables, animals and fruits, these lands yield and produce. To all which particulars and whatever else may be worth noting, you will pay diligent attention, keeping a careful record or daily journal of the same, that we may get full information of all your doings and experiences, and the Company obtain due and perfect knowledge of the situation... in return for the heavy expenses to which she is put by this expedition.... According to the written statements of Jan Huygen [Van Linschoten] and the opinion of sundry other persons, certain parts of this South-land are likely to yield gold, a point into which you will enquire as carefully as possible.

'For the purpose of making a trial we have given orders for various articles to be put on board your ships, such as ironmongery, cloths, coast stuffs [Indian cloth] and linens; which you will show and try to dispose of to such natives as you may meet with, always diligently noting what articles are found to be most in demand, what quantities might be disposed of, and what might be obtained in exchange for them; we furthermore hand you samples of gold, silver, copper, iron, lead and pearls, that you may inquire whether these articles are known to the natives, and might be obtained there in any considerable quantity....

'When you get near the northern extremity and the east coast of the South-land, you will diligently inquire whether it yields anywhere sandal-wood, nutmegs, cloves or other spices....

In places where you meet with natives, you will either by adroit management or by other means endeavor to get hold of a number of full-grown persons, or better still, of boys and girls, to the end that the latter may be brought up here and be turned to useful purpose. . . .'

So instructed, the yachts sailed south to explore the new lands, but they had barely gotten outside Sunda Strait between Sumatra and Java, in other words, they had barely begun the voyage, when they sighted two Company ships bound for Java from Holland. The two vessels were in such dire distress that they could no longer make headway and had come to anchor. The *Haringh* and *Hasewint* assisted the stricken vessels and brought them safely into Batavia, but when this had been accomplished the season was too far gone to undertake exploration. The same instructions which had been prepared for the *Haringh* and the *Hasewint* were later given to Jan Carstenszoon, who sailed in January 1623 in command of the yachts *Pera* and *Arnhem* to carry out the proposed exploration. Reaching the coast of New Guinea, Carstenszoon ordered his subordinates to treat the natives kindly and 'if possible to lay hands on some of them, that through them, as soon as they have become somewhat conversant with the Malay tongue, our Lords and Masters may obtain reliable knowledge touching the productions of their land.' So poorly were these kind intentions reciprocated that when the skipper of the *Arnhem* and a landing party went ashore, the skipper and nine of his men were slain by the savages. Carstenszoon found the New Guinea natives not only bloodthirsty but entirely lacking in the urge to play a part in world trade and commerce. 'We threw out to them,' he says, 'some small pieces of iron and strings of beads, at which they showed great satisfaction; they paid little or no attention to the gold, silver, copper, nutmegs and cloves which we showed them, though they were quite ready to accept these articles as presents.'

At the end of March the yachts passed from the New Guinea coast to the Australian coast as the *Duyfken* had done. The explorers, like their predecessors, were unaware that they had passed from one land mass to the other. The two ships entered the great gulf which Carstenszoon named Carpentaria, after the then Governor General in the Indies, Pieter de Carpentier. Landings were made in a number of places on the east coast of the Gulf. Mindful of the instructions to procure a few useful natives, Carstenszoon's men 'seized one of the blacks by a string which he wore around his neck' and carried him off. 'As regards their customs and policy and the nature of the country,' Carstenszoon remarks, 'Your Worships will in time be able to get information from

the black man we have got hold of....' The commander also offered ten pieces of eight to his boatmen for every additional native they were able to capture. Despite diligent investigation, no possibilities for profitable trade could be found. 'We have not seen one fruit-bearing tree, nor anything that man could make use of,' the commander reported; 'there are no mountains or even hills, so that it may be safely concluded that the land contains no metals, nor yields any precious woods, such as sandal-wood, aloes or columba.'

In the same year, 1623, in which the *Arnhem* and *Pera* made this voyage, the ship *Leijden*, or *Leyden*, bound from the Netherlands for Java, came upon the western coast of Australia. The *Leijden* sailed and drifted northward along the shore for ten days to the great anxiety of the skipper. The following year the *Tortelduiff (Turtledove)* sailed along the coast. In 1627, the *Gulden Zeepaard (Golden Seahorse)* discovered the south-west coast, and in the same year the *Galias* suddenly came upon the breakers along the beach when the reckoning showed the ship to be still three hundred miles at sea. The *Wapen van Hoorn (Arms of Hoorn)* was the third ship to sight the shoreline in 1627. In the following year, the *Vianen* was the unwilling discoverer of the north-west coast. Sailing from Java late in the season she struck a reef off the Australian shore, and was 'forced to throw overboard 8 or 10 lasts of pepper and a quantity of copper, upon which through God's mercy she got off again without further damage....' In 1628, there was the sad case of the *Batavia*, skipper François Pelsaert, which on a fine clear night with all sails set, ran upon the dangerous off-shore Houtman Rocks on the south west coast. Other vessels also, in addition to those mentioned, sighted the Australian shore.

The many reminders that there was a great unknown land to the south which might contain undreamed-of wealth at last stirred the Company into renewed activity. Another expedition was readied. In 1636, the ships *Klein-Amsterdam* and *Wesel* were fitted out and placed under the command of Gerrit Thomaszoon Pool. Pool's instructions reminded him that for a long time past the Company Directors had been insistently recommending the exploration of the Southland, that they 'still continue to do so, and we have frequently discussed the matter....' The commander was instructed to treat the natives with great kindness, using 'wary caution, and skilful judgment... slight misdemeanours on the part of such natives, such as petty thefts and the like, which they should commit against you, you will suffer to pass unnoticed, that by so doing you may draw them unto you, and not inspire them with aversion to our nation. Whoever endeavours to discover unknown lands and tribes,

has need to be patient and longsuffering, noways quick to fly out, but always bent on ingratiating himself.

'We have put on board your ship various kinds of merchandise and minerals, which you will show to the people whom you should come to parley with, partly that by so doing you may come to know whether any of these goods are produced by their country, partly in order to see what desire and inclination they evince to our mercantile commodities, and what goods they might be ready to offer in exchange for the same.' Actually, the minerals and trading goods proved useless. The expedition was even less successful than that of Carstenszoon. The commander was killed by New Guinea natives soon after the departure, and although the ships continued under the command of the supercargo, they brought back from Australia none of the hoped-for gold, copper, sandalwood, or any other commodity, nor any report on anything of value.

After this voyage, being occupied with more pressing problems, the Company neglected Australia until 1642, when the ship *Heemskerck* and the flute *Zeehaen (Gurnard)* were fitted out and placed under the command of the illustrious Abel Janszoon Tasman for the discovery of 'the apparently rich lands to the south and east.' The Governor and Council at Batavia declared that they were anxious for the opening up of important countries to trade or 'leastwise of convenient routes to well-known opulent markets.' As on previous occasions, the vessels' cargoes included all manner of articles useful and useless to delight the eye of a noble or ignoble savage, as well as samples of gold and silver to exhibit to the natives in the hope that the metals would be recognized by them. Among the trade goods aboard the *Heemskerck* were cloth, knives, blankets, Chinese coral, small Chinese mirrors, nineteen pounds of elephant tusk, two packets of tinsel, two hundred pounds of ironmongery, and twenty-five assorted iron pots. If he encountered savages, Tasman was instructed to treat them with kindness and win them over so that he might learn if there was anything profitable to be gotten in their country. If he encountered civilized men, he was to explain that he had come for the sake of commerce, and to enquire after gold and silver, 'making them believe that you are by no means eager for precious metals, so as to leave them ignorant of the value of the same; and if they should offer you gold or silver in exchange for your articles, you will pretend to hold the same in slight regard, showing them copper, pewter or lead and giving them an impression as if the minerals last mentioned were by us set greater value on.'

So instructed, Tasman set out on what is certainly one of the great voyages of history. Leaving Batavia, he sailed southwestward to Mauritius, then south and eastward around the south coast of Tasmania, thence along the western coasts of New Zealand. From New Zealand, he steered northeast to the Friendly Islands, from there westward around the northern shores of New Guinea, and so back to Batavia. He thus discovered Tasmania and New Zealand and dispelled the notion of another great southern continent immediately below Australia. Yet from the point of view of the Company, this voyage was also a failure. In reporting on it to the Directors, the Governor, Antonio Van Diemen, and his Council observed that 'the said commander has been somewhat remiss in investigating the situation, conformation, and nature of the lands discovered, and of the natives inhabiting the same. . . .'

Despite the disappointing results, Governor Van Diemen resolved to send Tasman and Franchoys J. Visscher, who had accompanied Tasman, on a second expedition to the southland. Tasman was not only to look for profitable trade for the Company, but to determine if a strait existed between New Guinea and Australia. Such a passage, it was thought, could be of great importance to the Company. Far away on the west coast of South America, the people of Chile lacked for European goods of all kinds. Despite the laws of Spain, the Chileans were eager to buy from whoever happened along, and the Dutch East India Company saw a fine opportunity to open up a profitable South American trade if a route east to South America could be found where, in fact, Torres Strait actually is. Accordingly, Tasman was instructed to coast along the south shore of New Guinea, and if it proved to be an island, he was then to turn south along the east coast of Australia. If there were a passage between the newly discovered Van Diemen's Land (Tasmania) and Australia, he was to steer through this passage westward and thus eventually return to Batavia. If at the outset, he found New Guinea to be joined to Australia, he was given alternative orders to pursue. Actually, both sets of instructions proved useless, since Tasman made the time-honored mistake of leaving the coast of New Guinea, passing into the Gulf of Carpentaria and concluding that Torres Strait did not exist. Emerging from the Gulf, he followed down the west coast of Australia to 23 degrees, 30 minutes south latitude, and then turned homeward. Needless to say, Governor Van Diemen was again most grievously disappointed. There had been no bartering and no profit, and instead of rich kingdoms, Tasman reported only naked, destitute savages. It was unreasonable to suppose, thought Van Diemen, that in this vast island which had now

What was seen on the island of Mauritius
From Begin ende Voortgangh.

practically been circumnavigated, nothing profitable to the Company could be found, and he concluded his report to the Directors by praying that despite these disappointments, God would grant 'that in the one or the other part of the world some prolific silver or gold mine be hit upon, to the solace of the general shareholders and the signal honour of the first discoverer. . . .'

Following the expeditions of Tasman, the possibilities of Australian profits seemed small and interest waned. From time to time a section of the coast was charted, or a shipwreck resulted in new knowledge of the land, but no exploration comparable to Tasman's was undertaken until 1696, when, largely through the efforts of a remarkable man, Nicolaas Corneliszoon Witsen, an expedition under Willem de Vlamingh was sent out from Amsterdam. This expedition also, to the disappointment of Witsen, and despite the fact that significant exploring was done, including marches overland, found nothing but arid, barren, and wild country. There was another expedition in 1705, somewhat interesting anthropologically but not commercially, and after that it was about fifty years before the Company, nagged by the hope that something of value might be found, again sent an expedition southward. This last expedition of the Company was sent out in 1756, probably with the same high hopes but certainly with the same barren results. It seemed incredible that such a large mass of land should contain so little. It was a cruel fortune that after so much effort, expense, hardship, and nearly a century and a half of intermittent exploration, the Company should be rewarded with not a single log of sandalwood nor a pound of spices. Seventeenth century merchants were sometimes called adventurers, and in this instance the Dutch had been more adventurers than merchants.

A review of trade in the Orient ought not to be concluded without some word about the establishment at the Cape of Good Hope, and about the islands of Mauritius and Madagascar. Regarding the Cape, the development of Dutch activity there is largely a story of the eighteenth rather than the seventeenth century. During the latter century, Table Bay was primarily a place for rest and refreshment on the long passage to the Indies. It was also an informal postal station, letters being left in certain designated places to be picked up by ships going in the opposite direction. About mid-century the region became more useful as a refreshment point. In 1647, the East Indiaman, *Haarlem*, was wrecked in Table Bay. The crew were marooned for a year before being picked up by a passing ship. During that interval, they caught fish and game,

raised a few crops, and became somewhat acquainted with the natives whom they found friendly. On regaining Holland, certain members of the crew recommended that the Company plant gardens, and gather provisions at the Cape for the convenience of passing ships. Accordingly in 1652, Jan van Riebeeck was dispatched with three ships, and landed at Table Bay. He planted vegetable gardens and traded with the natives for sheep and cattle, giving them copper bars, beads, brandy, arrack, and tobacco in exchange. Although originally the establishment was entirely a Company undertaking, after a number of years some of the employees were granted land under certain restrictions where they might raise vegetables and cattle on their own. They might sell the produce of their farms, again under certain restrictions, to Company ships. The object in having settlers at the Cape was not to form a colony in the usual sense of the word, but to provide necessary ship provisions at minimum cost. As has been said, the transformation of the supply station into a colony and the trekking of Dutchmen into the interior are largely matters of the eighteenth century.

The island of Mauritius was visited by Warwijk and Van Heemskerck in 1598, and was used occasionally from that time forward as a refreshment point. In 1606, the ships of Cornelis Matelief coming out from Holland let loose some pigs and goats which enhanced the value of the island as a place where long voyages could be broken. In 1634, a ship was sent to Mauritius especially to gather ebony and returned to Holland with a cargo of the wood in 1636. The voyage influenced the directors to take possession of Mauritius in 1638. Amber was found on the coast, and tin in the interior, but the greatest attraction was the ebony. The wood was cut along the coast, but difficulties in getting out the timber were experienced when cutting proceeded into the interior. A commandant was appointed to the island, and a fort, called Fort Frederik Hendrik, was erected, which was manned by a small complement of men.

Madagascar, like Mauritius, was visited by Dutch voyagers before the end of the sixteenth century, and this island also was used from time to time as a place where a ship might put in for fresh food, wood, and water. In 1641, the commander on Mauritius sailed to Madagascar, where he made a treaty with one of the native rulers, the Prince of Antongil. This potentate placed himself under Dutch sovereignty and promised to supply the Dutch with slaves, rice, and meat. As a result a few men were left behind to establish a small trading post. Unfortunately the slaves obtained soon died when they

The cutting and shipping of Brazil-wood

From the Beschryvinghe *by Jan Huygen van Linschoten. Amsterdam, 1596.*

were transported to Mauritius or to India. Consequently the Company decided to give up slave trading in Madagascar and withdrew its servants from the island in 1647. Dutch ships continued to stop at the island from time to time after this date for rest and refreshment.

What has been said about the East India Company in the Orient will give an impression of the remarkable speed with which the Corporation developed trade throughout the East and the surprising variety of the goods in which it traded.

The West India Company, trading in the New World, had an equally far-flung operation, and if its activities were not as profitable, the adventures experienced by the Company servants, being nearer home, are perhaps more exciting and interesting for us.

CHAPTER XII

The West Indies and Guiana

In the chapter on trade with the Iberian peninsula, it was pointed out that several European wars and specifically the Spanish-Dutch war broke the traditional pattern of Netherlands-Iberian trade, both because South Netherlanders with trade connections abroad migrated to the United Provinces and because the Iberian trade was difficult. It was there said that the Netherlanders, casting about for profitable means to employ ships and seamen, had made voyages to the Arctic, Iceland, Africa, the Mediterranean, the Orient, and the Americas. Of these regions, something has already been said about commerce in Africa, the Mediterranean and the Orient. This chapter and the two following are devoted to a brief description of trade in the Americas. For convenience, Dutch activity in the new world has been thought of as being carried on in three principal areas: first the West Indies and Guiana; second Brazil; and third New York, or New Netherland. The present chapter will be concerned with the first of these sections, the West Indies and Guiana.

It had been the Spanish intention not only that the greater part of South America, Mexico, and the West Indies should be Spanish, but that the Caribbean should be a Spanish lake, a highway for Spanish ships carrying Spanish goods to the profit of Spanish merchants, and by the laws of Spain, foreign merchants were excluded from trade with Spain's colonies. The desire of Spain was understandable, but not reasonable, since as has been indicated, Spain had little to trade and few ships to carry it in. The weakness in the Spanish design appeared almost immediately after it was conceived. There were many Portuguese in Spanish service and in this way Spain's neighbor became acquainted with the needs of the colonists and with the colonists themselves. Armed with such knowledge, the Portuguese were soon making clandestine voyages to Spanish America on their own account, carrying slaves and merchandise they

knew they could sell to the colonists. As the power of Portugal waned, the Iberian smugglers were succeeded by Dutch smugglers, and one glimpses their activities from time to time in official reports and private papers. The beginnings of Dutch trade in the New World have been traced by Professor Engel Sluiter. By 1572, the Netherlanders had appeared off Panama, and by 1587, they were trading clandestinely in Brazil. Some years later it was reported to the Spanish crown that in 1596 two Dutch vessels had traded both at Cumana on the present Venezuelan coast, and at the island of La Margarita, just off the coast, and that they had filled these two provinces with English and Dutch cloth to the value of eighty thousand ducats, smuggling it in at night. It was also reported that Dutch smugglers stationed themselves near the pearl fishers and obtained such a quantity of pearls by their illicit trading that such jewels disappeared from circulation, and this same report maintained that the Spanish authorities along the coast were bribed by these illegal traders. When Samuel de Champlain voyaged to the Indies in 1599, the Spanish fleet in which he sailed sighted off the north coast of Española, according to Champlain, 'thirteen great ships, French, English, and Flemish [i.e., Dutch], half armed for war, half with merchandise.' The town of Nueva Ecija de los Cumanagotos near the city of Cumana was described by the Spanish governor in 1603 as a notorious smuggling center where the Dutch traded openly and every Spaniard was in business. So industrious were the Dutch merchants that by 1609 they had outstripped all rivals and could fairly claim to be the foremost smugglers of merchandise and slaves in the Indies. The Netherlanders also carried the never ending quest for salt to the New World, and were fortunate in finding (in addition to other deposits) a vast, seemingly inexhaustible salt pan on what is now the Venezuelan coast, a very short distance inland from Punta de Araya. The salt deposit was approximately five miles long and from one to two miles wide. In a six and a half year period, 1599–1605, more than seven hundred and fifty Dutch ships arrived off this sector of the coast. Except the few vessels intent solely on smuggling, all were loading salt. Later, salt was also gotten from the islands of Tortuga and Saint Martin, and elsewhere.

As in the case of oriental trade, such individual voyages were the forerunners of a great monopolistic company. The West India Company which was subsequently formed was, in fact, modeled on the East India Company. The idea of such a corporation was conceived by Willem Usselinx, a testy, shrewd old bachelor, something of an idealist, and a fiery Calvinist. The objective of the company, as conceived by Usselinx, was to be somewhat different from

that of the East India Company in that the chief business would be the raiding of Spanish colonies and commerce. By such onslaughts, Usselinx pointed out, the Spanish enemy would be weakened, Holland would be enriched by plunder, and the theater of war would be far removed from the Netherlands. In addition to this prime objective, there were subsidiary aims. The West India Company would establish colonies where none but the true reformed Calvinist religion would be tolerated, and where the good Dutch colonists would educate the natives and instruct them in Christianity. These establishments in the New World would produce raw materials and serve as bases for the raids on the Spanish. It would be forbidden to develop any industry in the colonies which might compete with home industry. Although Usselinx was himself opposed to slavery, a subsidiary objective of many who supported his scheme was to obtain a large share, if not all, of the slave trade.

Since the principal objective was to raid the enemy, an essential part of Usselinx' scheme was that war should continue. Unfortunately for the plan, there were by 1608 persistent rumors of peace. In the interests of his idea, Usselinx wrote a book to point out the advantages of the war and the calamities which might ensue if peace were declared. He recalled to his readers the fact that the Dutch factors, agents and merchants scattered over the world were almost all South Netherlanders. This was natural since Antwerp in the South or Hapsburg Netherlands had been the great commercial city before the Spanish-Dutch war, and these Dutch overseas connections had been largely Antwerp connections. As a war measure, the Dutch had closed the Scheldt and had thus cut off outside access to this famous port of Antwerp. If, said Usselinx, peace were declared, the Scheldt would be opened, Antwerp would once again become the great commercial city of the Netherlands, and the highly important South Netherlandish agents and merchants throughout the world would swing their allegiance back to Antwerp firms, thus causing the collapse of Dutch commerce. The picture of things to come painted by Usselinx was, from the Dutch point of view, an appalling one, but his words had little effect. The political party in power at the moment in Holland was the peace party, led by the great statesman Johan van Oldenbarnevelt. In spite of the efforts of Usselinx, the United Provinces declared a truce with Spain in 1609. A West India Company, as Usselinx had conceived it, that is a company to plunder the enemy, was then impractical. It was not until 1619, when the peace party was overthrown and Oldenbarnevelt put to death, that the way was again open for war and profits through Usselinx' Company. The West

India Company was actually chartered in 1621. Like the East India Company, it was divided into a number of chambers situated in different areas. Of the nineteen directors composing the governing board, eight were to be from Amsterdam, four from Zeeland, two from the Maas, two from Friesland and Groningen, and the nineteenth was to be appointed by the States General.

As far as the Company's activities in the West Indies and Guiana are concerned, they may be thought of roughly as raids for plunder, and the establishment of trading posts in the Indies, and attempts to found colonies in Guiana. From 1625 until 1640, the Company sent fleet after fleet of commerce raiders to the Caribbean. The most spectacular and successful of the raids was that of Piet Heyn, the great man with the little name, and as the ideal raid his exploit is of some interest. Heyn sailed from the Texel in May 1628 with a fleet of thirty-one ships and three thousand men. Reaching the Caribbean, he cruised off Havana where the two Spanish treasure fleets, that from New Spain and that from the Spanish Main, rendezvoused before beginning the long voyage home. Because of rumors of Heyn's presence, the squadron from the Spanish Main remained safely at Cartagena, but the fleet from New Spain of twenty-one or twenty-two ships loaded with passengers, merchandise, gold and silver, set out in August for Havana, oblivious of the Dutchmen beating up and down before that harbor. Near Havana these Spanish ships were scattered by a storm. In the darkness and confusion some of them reached port safely, but in the morning the greater number of them found that they had sailed unknowingly into the midst of Piet Heyn's squadron. The Dutch commander immediately captured nine of them. In desperation, the Spanish Admiral, Juan de Benavides y Bazan, together with the larger ships containing the valuable cargoes headed for the bay of Matanzas, which was not far off, with the Dutch in hot pursuit. In this attempt to escape, Benavides suffered his crowning misfortune, for his flagship drove bows on into a sand bank, and was followed in this melancholy manoeuvre by four other great Spanish ships. The Dutch poured shot into the unfortunate vessels which were unable to return it effectively, and so to Heyn fell the rich prize, nearly 200,000 pounds of silver, 135 pounds of gold, and pearls, spices, indigo, cochineal, sugar, logwood, and hides to the total value of fifteen million guilders, a sufficient sum to pay the West Indian stockholders a dividend of fifty per cent. Heyn's was, as has been said, the ideal case of plunder on the high seas, and there was never again a cruise as profitable. Much more typical of the fortunes of the commerce raiders was, except perhaps for its conclusion, the voyage of Captain Cornelis

Corneliszoon Jol. This skipper sailed from the Texel in December 1634, and reaching the Indies boldly entered the port of Santiago de Cuba flying a Burgundian flag. Here he cannonaded the fort and boarded seven empty frigates. The total loot gathered in the daring exploit was a few bundles of tobacco and a few crocks of syrup. Two weeks later, Jol destroyed a small Spanish vessel hunting turtles, and about a week later captured another turtle hunter. At the end of May he took a bark with a cargo of maize and one chest of sugar, and in June a ship with a hundred and fifty passengers, but no cargo of value. He burned this vessel after putting the passengers ashore. He later captured two barks laden with corn. In the first days of August he took a frigate with a cargo of cacao, seven or eight pounds of silver, and a few hides. A few days later he got his first worthwhile prize, a small ship carrying 1800 hides, 4300 pounds of sarsaparilla, and 4800 pounds of tobacco. In September he plundered a frigate with some sugar and salt aboard and a ship laden with 140 canisters of tobacco, 73 bars of copper, nine cases of indigo, and six or seven thousand pieces of eight. Jol had now been at sea nine months and had boarded at least seventeen enemy ships. His plunder, while not spectacular or especially valuable, had filled his holds, and so he steered homeward. Unfortunately, in sight of Holland, his ship was captured by pirates out of Dunkirk. The voyages of Heyn and of Jol may serve as examples of other Company voyages seeking to make a hard guilder at the expense of the Spanish. Johannes De Laet, the chronicler of the West India Company, estimated in 1637 that the Company had sent out in the years 1623–1636, 806 ships manned by more than 67,000 men at a cost of not less than forty-five million guilders. De Laet does not distinguish between commerce raiders and Company vessels bent on legitimate business, and probably it would be impossible to make such a distinction. One cannot be sure then of the cost of the plundering expeditions, but De Laet is specific about the results of the activity. He says that the Company captured enemy ships and cargo worth approximately thirty-six million guilders and in addition destroyed Spanish ships, cargoes, and shore establishments, and deprived Spain of possible revenue to a total of an additional thirty-seven million guilders. He asserted that the cost of fitting out the Company ships had been defrayed by plunder gathered by the commerce destroyers. He was therefore able to say that the cost of all voyages and shipping (45 million guilders) plus the value of the booty (36 million guilders) plus the damage to Spanish property (37 million guilders) represented a total damage to Spain for the period considered, 1623–1636, of

118 million guilders. Such a report, certainly, would make the heart of any patriotic Dutchman swell with pride in the activities of the West India Company, but actually the plundering ventures, however laudable from the patriotic standpoint, were not well paying business; and by the time De Laet wrote his report the charges of the Company had exceeded returns by 18 million guilders.

It was noted previously that a subsidiary aim of the Company was to obtain all or part of the slave trade. The importation of slaves had begun soon after the advent of Spain into America, the first Negro slaves being brought from the home country to the Antilles in 1502. Throughout most of the sixteenth and seventeenth centuries, the importation of Negroes into the colonies was a monopoly, and was called the Asiento. The Asiento was sometimes sold to an individual or group of individuals by the crown, and sometimes was given to a royal favorite. Regardless of who held the Asiento, actually the slaves had to be purchased from the Portuguese who controlled the West African coast which was the source of supply. As has been previously noted, the Dutch in the early part of the seventeenth century made inroads on the Portuguese West African preserve, and in the years 1637–1642 gained possession of practically every African slave-trading post of importance. By 1638, English, French, and Spanish were buying slaves not from the Portuguese, but from the Dutch, and at prices fixed by the Netherlanders. In 1640, a situation arose which gave the Lowlanders a golden opportunity to exploit the foothold they had already gained in the slave trade. In that year the Portuguese rebelled and threw off the yoke of Spain. The Spanish were averse to giving the Asiento to any of their newly rebellious subjects, the Portuguese, or to any of their old rebellious subjects, the Dutch, and certainly were averse to giving it to the perfidious Englishmen. To give it to any of their own countrymen would mean in effect, certainly, that one or the other of these nations had the profits of the Asiento, since the slaves would have to be bought from them. In this perplexing situation, the Asiento was given up and for about twenty years (1641–1662), although occasional slaving licenses were granted, there were no asientistas. The lack of any official and legal slave supply created the great opportunity for the Netherlanders. In 1634, they had seized the island of Curaçao, and they turned it into a great entrepôt for slaves, supplying illegally the market for which no regular provision had been made. The slave pens of Curaçao sometimes contained thousands of Negroes. With their own sources of supply on the African coast, and their ample shipping, the Dutch could

furnish unheard-of numbers of Africans, and slaving grew by leaps and bounds. As an example, there were only a few hundred Negroes in Barbados in 1640 at the time the Asiento lapsed, but within five years there were about six thousand, and by 1651 there were twenty thousand. The Dutch did not completely control the trade, for the Portuguese, as was noted in Chapter IV, regained São Thomé, their island slaving station on the African coast, soon after they had lost it, and in 1654 the British also gained a foothold on the slave coast, but for the remainder of the seventeenth century the Dutch remained dominant in the commerce. This was so even though the Asiento was revived and given in 1662 to two Genoese, Domingo Grillo and Ambrosio Lomelin. These new asientistas were empowered to purchase their slaves from any power at peace with Spain, which practically speaking could only mean the Dutch. Actually, the only difference the revival of the Asiento made was that whereas before the Lowlanders from their pens at Curaçao had sold slaves to all comers, they now sold nearly all of them to Grillo and Lomelin. Throughout the period of the Asiento, although some Negroes were supplied by the English, the great bulk was supplied by the Lowlanders. An idea of the volume of the trade can be gathered from the fact that at the time the Asiento was granted, Grillo and Lomelin undertook to import 24,000 'pieces of the Indies' within seven years. A 'piece of the Indies' was defined in this case as a prime male slave between twenty-four and thirty-five years of age or his equivalent in value in women and children.

The two Genoese were succeeded in the Asiento by one Antonio Garcia, whose bankers were the Dutchmen, Balthasar and Joseph Coymans, and probably from this time on the Asiento was financed with Dutch capital. The two Coymans also represented Garcia in his negotiations with the Dutch West India Company for a supply of slaves. In 1675, the Company agreed to supply Garcia with 4,000 Negroes per year as long as a state of war continued, and 3,500 per year if there should be peace in West Africa. All were to be healthy 'pieces of the Indies' which were here defined as Negroes between the ages of fifteen and thirty-six inclusive. Children from fourteen to seven were to be counted as two-thirds of a 'piece of the Indies,' while six-year olds on down to sucklings were to be counted one-half. The Company sold a 'piece of the Indies' in Curaçao for about 265 guilders. Since the actual cost to the Company of laying down a slave at that island was about eighty guilders, there was a satisfactory margin of profit.

The Netherlanders not only sold slaves to the holders of the Asiento, but

also to the French and English planters in the West Indies who early in the seventeenth century had established themselves there. At first these planters had engaged in tobacco culture, but in the 1630's when the price of tobacco fell, they were faced with ruin. Dutch traders suggested to the planters that they turn to sugar culture, and supplied them with the long term credit and expensive equipment needed for boiling sugar. The Hollanders thereby not only increased their trade in the islands, but created in the new sugar plantations a fresh market for slaves. Although Curaçao was primarily a vast slave pen, almost inevitably other commercial activities developed there also. Cocoa and tobacco brought from Venezuela were stored on the island, just as the island of Saint Eustatius, where the Dutch had also established themselves, became the warehouse for indigo, cochineal, and logwood from Honduras and Campeche. These islands also served as supply bases for trade goods used by Dutch agents at Rio de la Hacha, Maracaibo, La Guayra, and Puerto Cabello, and as convenient centers for the good old game of smuggling. At times the Dutch were also established on Tobago, and held (and do still hold) Aruba and Bonaire in the Leeward group. In the Windward group, they seized Saba, Saint Eustatius, and part of Saint Martin. Thus firmly established, they soon added to their commercial activities by dominating the inter-island carrying trade.

At the beginning of this chapter, it was said that the plan of the West India Company was to plunder the Spanish, to appropriate the slave trade, and to plant colonies. The last objective was achieved in a limited way in Brazil, and was successfully carried out in New Netherland, but there were also many attempts at colonization in Guiana, despite the fact that the climate of these regions has been described as a cross between a Finnish steam bath and an orchid hot house. In general it might be said that the Dutch first settled in what is now British Guiana, although there were colonizing efforts elsewhere, rather than in present Surinam or Dutch Guiana. This region between the Amazon and the Orinoco, which we know as British, Dutch, and French Guiana was, in the seventeenth century, often called 'the wild coast.' As early as 1599, the Spanish authorities were complaining of the numbers of Dutch ships visiting this wild region, and the nearby islands of Trinidad and Margarita. These Netherlandish visitors, as well as other Europeans, traded with the natives for tobacco, and it was not long before they had established themselves, however precariously, on this nominally Spanish but entirely neglected strip of coastline. From this time onward, one can trace the efforts of individuals

and small companies independent of the great West India Company to exploit the area. Shortly before 1600, there was a Dutch establishment at the mouth of the Orinoco, two other small forts on the Amazon, and a fourth settlement on the Essequibo. Shortly after that year, Dutch establishments became larger and more numerous. From trading with the Indians, the interlopers progressed to growing tobacco for themselves, and by 1613, there was a Dutch fort on the Corentyne, and in 1616, two Lowlands expeditions were fitted out to plant colonies on the Oyapock and on the Amazon. In the latter year also, two powerful Dutch merchants, Jan de Moor and Peter Courteen, resolved on a trading venture to Guiana. They were lucky enough to enlist as the man to carry out their plan one Aert Adriaansz Groenewegen, a native of Delft, who had been a factor at the Spanish fort of Santo Thomé on the Orinoco. He left the Spanish service to command the expedition sent out by de Moor and Courteen, and established for them a post on the estuary of the Essequibo, where he conducted trade with great success. An Englishman, Major John Scott, visited Groenewegen's establishment and remarked of the Dutchman that he had the affection of the natives 'whose humours the gentleman understood perfectly.' Scott also noted that Groenewegen was actually trading clandestinely with the Spanish, or as he put it 'he managed a great Trade with the Spaniards by the Indians with great Secrecy.' In point of fact such clandestine trade using Indians as intermediaries had grown to large proportions. In the year following Groenewegen's arrival, Sir Walter Raleigh noted in his 'Apologie for his voyage to Guiana' that 'In a letter of the Governours to the King of Spaine of the eighth of July he not only complaineth that the Guianians are in arms against him, but that even those Indians which live under their noses, doe in despight of all the Kings edicts trade with Los Flemnicos & Engleses enemigos.' The clandestine trade continued to expand for many years, for in 1637, twenty years after Sir Walter Raleigh wrote, the Spanish governor declared that the Dutch trade with the Indians continued to increase, that they still had their settlement on the Essequibo and had new settlements among the Carib and Arawak nations.

Although Guiana was, of course, within the area granted as a monopoly to the West India Company, these Dutchmen of whom the Spanish were complaining were independent merchants. In addition to those already mentioned, there were other efforts at trade and colonization by such sturdy individualists. An attempt to found one settlement on the Oyapock has already been noted, and there were two later efforts on the same river, in 1623 and 1627. There was

an attempt to found a settlement on the Cayenne in 1627 and two merchants of Flushing, Abraham van Pere and Pieter van Rhee, had a small trading colony on the Berbice in 1624. With so much individual effort being expended and profits made within the territory, the West India Company also bestirred itself to exploit this corner of its vast empire. A Company colony was established under Jan Adriaanszoon van der Goes in 1624 on the Essequibo and competed with that of de Moor and Courteen. Twenty years later, in 1645, the Company sadly noted that 'the River Essequibo has now for some time been navigated with small profit to the company, for the reason that private colonists are permitted to trade there as well as the company, so that goods coming from there cannot fetch their proper price on account of competition.'

Dutch efforts in the region had begun in a thoroughly haphazard way, and they continued throughout the seventeenth century to lack the organization and order which characterized commercial ventures of the Netherlanders elsewhere. The Lowlanders' position in Guiana was greatly strengthened in 1645–46, when on the departure of Johan Maurits from Brazil a large body of Jews left Pernambuco and settled on the Pomeroon. Twenty years later, at a time when the English were attacking the Lowlanders, an Englishman said that there was a total of seven colonies on the coast of Guiana, one English, two French, and four Dutch. The largest Dutch settlement was this colony on the Pomeroon. The second was the old post of de Moor and Courteen which Groenewegen had established on the Essequibo. In addition there were small colonies on the Oyapock and on the Berbice.

In 1665–67 the Dutch position was strengthened by the victories of a Zeeland expedition over the English, and the English settlements were ceded to the Dutch in exchange for New York by the Treaty of Breda. The efforts of the West India Company in Guiana had been the special concern of the Company directors of the Zeeland Chamber. On the basis of this fact, the Province of Zeeland, in the latter half of the century, laid claim to Guiana, not as a possession of the United Provinces of the Netherlands in general, but as the particular possession of Zeeland Province. The claim was vigorously opposed by the States General of the United Provinces. The dispute was settled in 1672 in an ambiguous, but thoroughly satisfactory manner. It was agreed that while the States General held the supreme authority, Zeeland had the possession and the right to govern the colony. Actually, Zeeland soon found that it could not bear the financial burden of Guiana, and sold it in 1682 to the West India Company. The Company in turn also found the burden too great and in the

following year made over a third interest to the City of Amsterdam and a third interest to a nobleman, Cornelis van Aerssen van Sommelsdijk. Van Aerssen went to Guiana as governor, and so well did he govern, that within a few years the number of sugar plantations increased from fifty to two hundred. He was killed in 1688, but near the end of the century another governor reported that in addition to plantations there were a hundred and fifty sugar mills in the country.

It cannot be pretended that Dutch exploitation of Guiana in the seventeenth century was anything more than a very minor branch of Netherlands commercial activities. Actually, there was little to exploit. A certain amount of tobacco could be gathered in; a limited number of settlers could plant and refine sugar; a certain amount of trade with Indians and smuggling with Spanish could be carried on. But the sugar was overshadowed by that of Brazil and the West Indies; the tobacco was insignificant compared with that of the West Indies; and as a place for settlers, Guiana when compared to New Netherland was not attractive. De Laet had boasted of the profits made from raiding Spanish commerce and Spanish possessions in the West Indies, and Zeelanders had been fascinated by the commercial possibilities of Guiana. Robbery and tropical jungles have, of course, always been good news items, yet actually those two other regions assigned to the Company, Brazil and New Netherland, had far more interesting possibilities.

CHAPTER XIII

Brazil

The second region in which the West India Company was extremely busy was Brazil, or 'New Holland,' as the Dutch called it when they were finally able to gain control of it. In the first half of the seventeenth century, Brazil was the great sugar producing country of the world, and the Dutch were attracted to that area as bees to honey. Actually, ships from the Netherlands had visited Brazil before the century began. Three Dutch ships touched at that country in 1587, and in the years following there were many more visits of Dutch vessels, some on ostensibly legal voyages, and others outright smugglers. Dutch bribes were ample, Portuguese official flesh was weak, and Lowlands vessels obtained sugar cargoes so easily that in the early part of the seventeenth century, a pound of sugar cost less in Amsterdam than it did in Lisbon. In 1622, there were twenty-five sugar refineries in Amsterdam, and the Hollanders exported sugar all over Western Europe. When the West India Company was formed, the incorporators had well in mind the profits which would accrue to them if they could conquer the sugar-rich Portuguese colony. Since at the time the enemy Spain controlled Portugal, there would even be virtue in such armed robbery. A contemporary writer declared that 'The West India Company could find nothing more profitable for itself, nothing of greater service to the republic, and nothing more calamitous for the kingdom of Spain than the conquest of Brazil.' The writer pointed out that many people of small means might go to Brazil; and, by raising sugar or tobacco or by keeping shops, could gather a fortune and return to the fatherland, as was constantly being done by Portuguese and Spanish migrants to the colonies. Also, if the Dutch possessed the source of sugar, English, Scots, French, and Easterlings who began to be troublesome could be squeezed out of the sugar trade. Without sugar, refineries in other countries would be forced to

shut down, and deserving Dutch merchants would then begin to receive their just and more ample deserts. In such words, the author doubtless expressed the sentiments of many sensible Dutchmen. The importance which the West India Company attached to possessing Brazil is indicated by the fact that at the end of 1623, roughly two years after the formation of the Company, an expedition was equipped for the conquest of the country. From what has gone before, the reader will realize that this was remarkably speedy action. This expedition, consisting of twenty-six vessels, 1600 sailors, and 1700 soldiers, appeared off the town of Bahia (or Salvador) in May, 1624, and caught the defenders by surprise. Although the Portuguese fought courageously, they were overpowered by the superior Dutch forces, who were led by that same hero, Piet Heyn, who later captured the silver fleet. With the conquest of the port completed, the Dutch placed a garrison in the city and the remaining forces sailed away. Lulled by the pleasant atmosphere of Brazil's oldest city, the garrison became as somnolent and unmilitary as the former Portuguese soldiery had been. Consequently, when in the following year Portuguese forces appeared before Bahia, they in turn had no difficulty in recapturing the town from the Dutch. In 1627, a second Dutch expedition under Piet Heyn was dispatched in an attempt to regain what had been lost, but the Portuguese in Bahia were not to be surprised a second time. Heyn and the Dutch fleet found the shore batteries and the garrison alert, and the enemy ships anchored in the shelter of the batteries. The enemy position appeared impregnable, but Heyn boldly attacked the shipping and gained a great victory, not to mention four shiploads of booty. The main objective of the expedition, the recapture of the port, remained unachieved, and a later attempt on Bahia by Heyn a few months later also failed. In 1629 the Netherlanders prepared yet another attack on Brazil with the most powerful fleet ever assembled by the Company. There were fifty ships and yachts, thirteen sloops and two smaller vessels. The fleet mounted a total of 1,170 guns, was manned by 3,780 seamen, and transported 3,500 soldiers. The expedition was commanded by Hendrik Corneliszoon Loncq, who had been Piet Heyn's second in command when he had captured the silver fleet off Havana. At various times during the latter half of 1629 the vessels left the Dutch ports where they had been outfitting, and on the 22nd of December rendezvoused off the island of Saint Vincent in the Cape Verde group to begin the long voyage across the Atlantic. A few days after the fleet sailed, there were eight hundred sick, and as the vessels lumbered along, more fell ill. At the end of January, 246 had died and there

The Capture of Bahia

1. The Sand-Bay, where the soldiers were put ashore.
2. The narrow road through which they had to pass and where they could be stopped with little trouble.
3. A Corps de Guarde or big guardhouse deserted by the enemy from fear.
4. A large level square where the soldiers drew up in order of battle, marching then on to the suburb, where they encountered some resistance, but which, repeating their efforts, they captured.
5. A little Chapel outside the town.
6. The suburb, where the soldiers the first night played havoc.
7. A Gate at the South-end of the Town, where our soldiers entered first.
8. A stone fort lying so far from the shore that one may (at high tide) sail with a barque behind it; on this lay 11 large pieces of artillery and incredibly many soldiers.
9. Another Battery ashore which fired fiercely.
10. A large Warehouse wherein much sugar was found.
11. These ships all having come near the shore, have been set on fire by us.
12. Two other Castles of which the nearest to the above-mentioned Battery was called S. Philippo.
13. Two big Windlasses. Heavy things were pulled up along two big steep runners (made of wood) by these windlasses to the Upper-Town, which lay about a hundred fathoms above the water.
14. A Gate situated at the North-End of the Town.
15. The Convent of S. Francisco, where the Jesuits have their College.
16. The Prison.
17. The Artillery-House.
18. A newly begun Church.
19. The great Market Place.
20. A Watchhouse.
21. The House of the Governor.
22. Two fountains, where the townspeople get their fresh water.

The Ship *Samson* and the Ship *Star* moved in to be near the wateringplace, marked A and B. The Ships were fired upon by the Castles on the seashore, and they returned the fire on the Castles, continuing the fire on the morning that the Town was captured.

From the Iaerlick Verhael of Johannes de Laet. Leyden, 1644. (Wording adapted from the original Dutch inscription.)

S SALVADOR

S.Antonio

BAYA DE TODOS OS SANCTOS

The Capture of Bahia

were 1,200 ill, but the fleet pushed steadily toward Brazil, still a mighty force for its day.

Meanwhile the Portuguese had not been idle. Through spies in Holland they had known of the Dutch preparations from the beginning. They soon learned also that the expedition was aimed not at Bahia, which had proved so difficult a problem for the Lowlanders, but at Olinda, the second city of Brazil. Mathias de Albuquerque, who had distinguished himself in the defense of Bahia, was ordered to Olinda to put the city and the surrounding province of Pernambuco in a state of defense. The wise and vigorous appointment was somewhat nullified by the fact that Albuquerque was given no funds to prepare the defenses, but fortunately he was a man of resolution. Arriving at Olinda in October 1629, he immediately began repairing the ruined fortifications and increased the army from two hundred to two thousand. Consequently when the Dutch invaders arrived, they were met by an enemy which, while much weaker than themselves, was not entirely unprepared. The harbor at Olinda was formed by the confluence of the estuaries of the Capiberibe and the Beberibe rivers. The estuary of the Beberibe was parallel to the coast, being separated from the sea by a narrow tongue of land. On the tongue of land was Recife, and at the head of the Beberibe estuary was Olinda. At the confluence of the estuaries was the island of Antonio Vaz on which Mauritsstad was subsequently built. Arriving off the port, the Dutch fleet found that it could not force a passage into the anchorage, but where the fleet was unsuccessful, the Dutch soldiery were. Landing on the coast, the invaders set out for Olinda. At several points they met resistance, but the hearts of Albuquerque's raw soldiers were not in their work, and the Dutch captured Olinda with the loss of less than sixty men. While the Netherlanders were conquering this city, Albuquerque's forces were active in Recife. Before the Dutch could take that city, the Portuguese burned the twenty or thirty merchantmen in the harbor and set afire the warehouses in the town, destroying in a most awe-inspiring conflagration seventeen thousand chests of sugar, vast quantities of Brazil wood, and other merchandise. One account said that the total destruction amounted to two million ducats. To the Company raiders bent on profits rather than glory, nothing Alburquerque could have done would have caused greater sorrow. Having lost the city, Albuquerque harassed the Dutch by hit-and-run raids launched from outside Olinda, but the superior forces of the Netherlanders made themselves felt, and they gradually pushed back the Portuguese. At the end of 1634, with the loss of thirty dead, they captured

the city of Paraíba, and by the following year four of the principal captaincies or provinces of Brazil, Pernambuco, Itamaracá, Paraíba, and Rio Grande, recognized the supremacy of the Dutch.

Despite these Dutch successes, the Portuguese still held out in Bahia, and indeed during the Dutch occupation the country as a whole was not completely pacified. Raids of irregulars from bases in the hinterland and sporadic uprisings of Portuguese in the settled areas continued throughout the period. The spirit of resistance never completely died, and eventually proved the undoing of the Dutch. Yet in the first flush of victory, in the first gathering of plunder, the tough, successful endurance the Brazilians were to exhibit was not, of course, apparent. The first loot gathered was of such proportions that if it had only been clear profit, it would have satisfied the most avaricious of stockholders. Yet while the booty was substantial, the overhead expense of getting it was frightful. Fleets had to be fitted out, armies trained, numberless functionaries paid, war material and provisions shipped overseas, and the other endless costs of an occupying power in a hostile land provided for. The melancholy result was that as was previously said, in those same fourteen years, the debits of the West India Company outran the credits by about eighteen million guilders. From the stockholders' standpoint the situation in Brazil was beyond endurance, and thoroughgoing reform was called for. It was decided to appoint a governor of the newly conquered dominion, a general manager actually on the ground, who would bring order and economy to the country and profits to the Company. The person selected for the post was Johan Maurits of Nassau, a relative of the Prince of Orange. The new governor landed at Recife in January 1637 and set to work with vigor. The principal reason for the West India Company's presence in Brazil was of course sugar, and one of the first cares of Johan Maurits was to rehabilitate this industry. During the battles of the conquest, sugar mills, boiling houses, and the cane fields themselves went up in flames, what was not destroyed by the retreating Portuguese being laid waste by the advancing Dutch soldiery. To aid the recovery of the planters Johan Maurits discontinued sales for bankruptcy, and confiscated properties were returned to their owners. Portuguese refugees who found themselves homeless were provided with homes, and the time for payment of old debts was extended. Free loans were available for repairing sugar mills, and as an inducement to getting acreage back in production, the high export duties on sugar were reduced. A grave weakness in the revived industry, at least from the Dutch point of view, was that the planters to a very

View of Olinda

A. The big Church, Saint Salvador
B. Cloister of the Jesuits
C. Cloister St. Francisco
D. The Hospital and the Church
E. The cloister St. Bento
F. The Fort of the Company
G. The Fort of Iuan d'Albuquerque
H. The Foundry
I. The Pottery
K. The Townhall
L. Church of St. Peter
M. Reefs under water on both sides of the channel
N. The Jetty
O. The Courthouse
P. The Beacon
Q. The Road to Recife
R. The Convent of the Carmelites

From Johannes de Laet, Iaerlyck Verhael. Leyden, 1644.

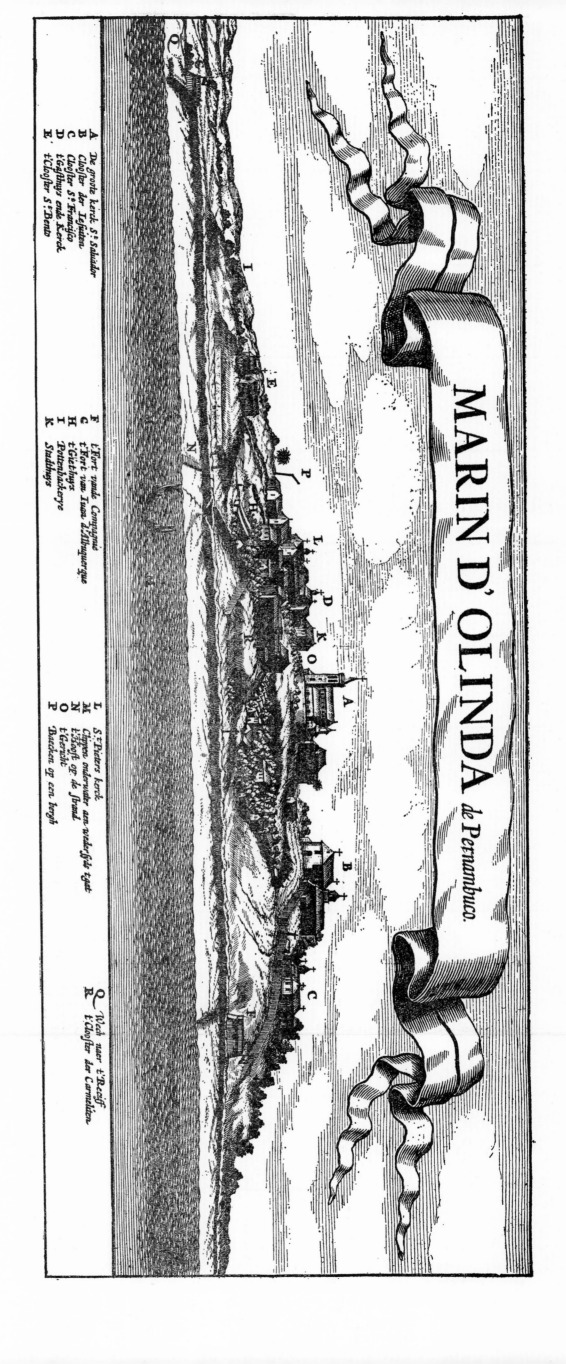

MARIN D'OLINDA de Pernambuco.

A   De groote kerck S:t Salvador
B   Cloofter der Iefuiten
C   Cloofter S:t Francifco
D   't Gafthuys ende Kerck
E   't Clooster S:t Bento

F   t'Fort vande Compagnie
G   t'Fort van Iuan d'Albuquerque
H   t'Giethuys
I   Pottenbackerye
K   Stadthuys

L   S:t Pieters kerck
M   Clippen onderwater aen-wederfijds t'gat
N   t'Schip op de Strand
O   t'Gericht
P   Baecken op een bergh

Q   Wech naer t'Recijf
R   t'Clooster der Carmeliten

View of Olinda

large degree remained Portuguese. Although Netherlanders have usually proven adaptable and successful in commercial ventures, in Brazil, even when they took over plantations, comparatively few of them learned the intricacies of raising, grinding, and boiling sugar. Thus the business remained basically a Portuguese occupation.

Having rejuvenated the sugar industry, the Governor turned his attention to that great concomitant commerce of sugar, the slave trade. 'The fruits of the land,' ran a report on Brazil to the Company directors in 1640, 'can never be secured or garnered save through their [i.e., the slaves'] work; and consequently there is not the smallest doubt that the more slaves are imported, the better will the land be cultivated, and the greater will be the Company's profits.' Despite discouragements and setbacks, this trade was made to prosper also. As was mentioned in the previous chapter, for the proper carrying on of the slave trade, factories or bases on the African slave coast were needed. The Jesuit father, Antonio Vieira, who spent a great part of his life in Brazil, described the situation succinctly by saying that, 'without negroes there is no Pernambuco, and without Angola there are no negroes.' The Company had conquered slaving stations on the African coast, and drew Negroes not only from Angola, but from the Congo and Upper Guinea also. The Negroes from Angola were most highly esteemed as tractable and willing workers. Those from Upper Guinea exhibited a sinful spirit of independence and were viewed with less favor, although their women were said to make excellent mistresses. Exactly who the slaves were, to what tribes and racial stocks they belonged were facts which remained largely unknown to Company officials. Their concern, after all, was with profits rather than ethnography. There was of course, as in any business, a technique to slaving, and although the Dutch could forcibly displace the Portuguese, they could not by so doing immediately become expert slavers. An agent of the Zeeland chamber of the Company reported in 1643 that the Portuguese 'bring over 500 slaves in a small caravel with ease, while we get only 300 in a large ship,' and, he continued, 'Through cleanliness, good food, and care, it comes about that they seldom have a death. Moreover, they get negroes used to slavery before bringing them over. When we follow their example we shall have a better commodity, fewer deaths, and get higher prices in Brazil.' The technique of transportation the Dutch gradually learned, and eventually they probably shipped slaves more efficiently than the Portuguese had. The slave business can be thought of as involving three phases: the acquiring of the poor lost souls, their transportation, and

finally their marketing. It was in the final phase of the business that the Com-any experienced in Brazil the most difficulty. Economists in their barbarous way observe that monopolists tend to maximize profits while minimizing production. Since the Company had a monopoly of the slave trade, there was exhibited at times, in line with this sage observation, a tendency to import fewer slaves and to ask higher prices, which made difficulties for the planters and inevitably for the Company. There were other problems also. At first the Company sold Negroes to planters with the understanding that they would be paid for at harvest time in sugar, but frequently the harvests were insufficient to cover the cost of the slaves purchased. The Company then ruled that slaves could only be bought for cash. Since the planters had no cash, the slaves were actually purchased by Jewish middlemen who were willing to extend credit to the sugar growers for a consideration. The influx of slave dealers also decreased Company profits, since, when whole cargoes of slaves were pur-chased by a few individuals, these buyers as a group could largely dictate the price of the slaves. Despite such damaging developments, slaving remained profitable for the Company. Statistics were given in the last chapter on the cost and selling prices of slaves, and additional figures are available for the trade in Brazil. In the first years of the Dutch in that country, it was said that a Negro could be gotten in Angola for forty or fifty guilders worth of trade goods, and could be sold in Brazil for anywhere from two hundred to eight hundred guilders, with the average price being between two hundred and three hundred guilders. In the period 1636–1645 inclusive, 23,163 slaves were brought into Brazil by the Company. The numbers sold at auction increased from about a thousand in 1636 to about 2,500 in 1645, an increase in sales which must have gladdened the hearts of the stockholders.

In addition to slavery and sugar, other segments of the economy were rejuvenated in Johan Maurits' time. The Governor reformed the Brazil or dye-wood industry, which was in a chaotic state, so that within a short time a larger share of money was rolling into the coffers of the Company, and a smaller share into the pockets of the Brazil-wood cutters. He also brought about reforms in the infant tobacco industry, and relieved the chronic food shortage by directing that all plantation owners who were not raising sugar should plant manioc, from which the great staple food, manioc meal, was made. Not only did Johan Maurits bend his best efforts to reviving the eco-nomy, but he also attempted to give Brazil a good civil administration gener-ally. He returned to Holland a number of officials who had conducted them-

selves badly. He shook up the judicial system so that it became more vigorous and more just. He founded institutions to nourish and treat the sick, the poor, and the orphaned. Catholics were allowed to practice their religion almost unhindered, and Jews were permitted to keep their Sabbath. Those Portuguese who had fled from the Dutch, Johan Maurits invited to return, promising them restoration of their property and liberty of conscience. He made an effort to convert the Indians, and opened to them the schools conducted by Dutch ministers. He put an end to the host of abuses in the distribution of foodstuffs, and saw to it that each received his fair share. From the standpoint of Brazilians, natives, Dutch, and even Portuguese, the Company could have made no better choice of governor. Yet despite all these great and good works, there were fundamental and insoluble problems in the Governor's task which were of three varieties. First, there were the minor difficulties which were due to the personal characteristics of Johan Maurits himself; second, there were the problems which arose from the fact that while the West India Company was avowedly bent only on profits and plunder, it now found itself involved in the responsibilities and expenses of governing a nation; and third, there were the grave troubles which resulted from the fact that the Dutch had conquered Brazil and maintained themselves there by force. Regarding Johan Maurits, it may be noted that his training was not that of a merchant, nor was he a man who could regard profits as one of the more worthwhile aims in life. He was a nobleman, trained to play the part of the good, the just, and the gracious prince. Regardless of who employed him, he could only act in accordance with this training. Professor C. R. Boxer gives a most interesting account of Johan Maurits in his *The Dutch in Brazil*. Maurits kept about him a whole host of scholars, artists, and scientists, and patronized the arts in a lavish way in the tradition of a European prince. He had not one, but two residences, and he gathered at his magnificent country seat all manner of Brazilian plants. 'He also,' says Manuel Calado do Salvador, a valuable contemporary Portuguese historian, 'brought thither every kind of bird and animal that he could find; and since the local *moradores* knew his taste and inclination, each one brought him whatever rare bird or beast he could find in the back-lands. There he brought parrots, macaws, *jacijs*, *canindes*, wading-birds, pheasants, guinea-fowl, ducks, swans, peacocks, turkeys, a great quantity of barnyard-fowls, and so many doves that they could not be counted. There he kept tigers, ounces, *cissuarana*, ant-bears, apes, *quati*, squirrel-monkeys, Indian boars, goats from Cape Verde, sheep from Angola, *cutia*, *pagua*, tapirs,

wild boars, a great multitude of rabbits—and in short, there was not a curious thing in Brazil which he did not have, for the *moradores* sent him these with a good will, since they saw that he was kindly and well-disposed towards them.' In addition to maintaining his two residences in Brazil, Johan Maurits also sent home to Holland great quantities of Brazilian woods for the construction of a sumptuous residence at The Hague, which is now the Mauritshuis Museum. As reports of the magnificence of Prince Maurits came in, many a stockholder must have wondered sorrowfully how he could ever afford such an expensive employee.

In addition to supporting a veritable monarch, the Company had, as has been said, all the other cares of government, and one of the most serious of these cares was that of the currency. At the coming of the Netherlanders, many Portuguese made haste to bury their beloved Spanish reales, so that coinage became extremely scarce. At one period, the West India Company was forced to pay its soldiers by giving four or five of them collectively a single gold piece. In desperation, the Company authorized the circulation of paper money and soon the country was flooded with it. Vouchers for manioc meal and meat also came into circulation. The value of such paper fell swiftly. Speculators bought it in large quantities at low prices and paid their debts and taxes with it. More troublesome than currency for the Governor and his administrators were the types of Netherlanders who flocked to Brazil. Actually they were not greatly different from those who flocked to California in the days of the gold rush, or those who flocked to Australia in the days of that country's gold fever, or those found in any region which suddenly promises adventure and easy fortune. Recife was described as crowded with discharged soldiers, laborers, former school masters, ex-university students, hussies, and 'other lost souls.' In this new society obligations were taken lightly, manners and morals were at a discount, and marriage especially was something less than highly regarded. It was rather common for a man to have one wife in Holland and another in Recife. Many a soldier's faithless wife stood in the pillory in that city, and many a *fille de joie* was whipped in public and banished from the town. The sudden influx of Netherlanders also caused an acute housing shortage. A large part of the newcomers were young men, sometimes as many as eight of them occupying a single room, and warehouses were cut up into bedrooms for single men. Duelling was widespread and impossible to stop even when the death penalty was imposed. While the Portuguese remained abstemious, the Dutch consumed incredible quantities of alcohol,

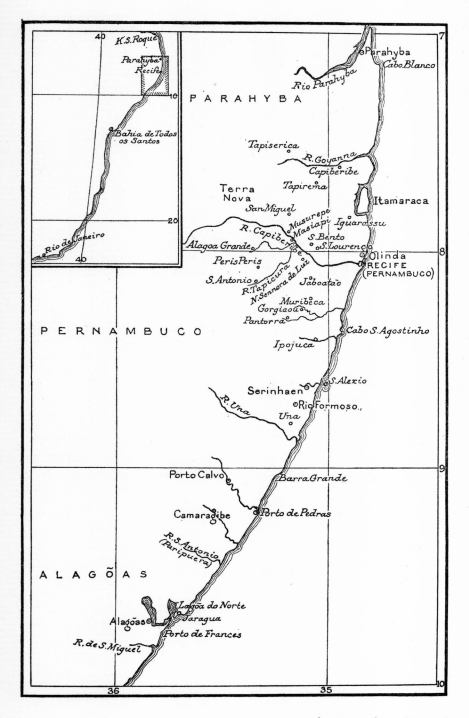

The Coast of Dutch Brazil

From Johannes de Laet, Iaerlyck Verhael, *in 'Werken van de Linschoten Vereeniging'*
vol. XL.

one Dutchman observing that the Company officials 'knew nothing but how to drink themselves drunk.' To the problem of discontented Portuguese and tumultous Dutch was added that of displaced free Negroes and runaway slaves, and the troubles of the Jewish community. Those Negroes who drifted to Recife became merely part of the general problem of a large floating population, but others formed themselves into troublesome brotherhoods of bush Negroes, or went over to the bands of Portuguese rebels. The Jews were a difficulty of another kind. As has been so often the case, their numbers were exaggerated, and the evils they were held responsible for were legion. As an example, a document presented to Johan Maurits in 1641 by the Christian merchants charged that the Jews had gotten trade into their own hands by lying, cheating, and using false weights and measures. All of the sugar, it was charged, passed through Jewish hands. The document enquired why Jews in Brazil were not required to wear red hats or yellow insignia as they were in other countries. It has also been said that the Israelites had a strangle hold on the slave trade, selling Negroes only at enormous profits. Recife showed the strain imposed by its suddenly acquired heterogeneous population by having its streets transformed into quagmires. Incidentally, an analogous situation developed in San Francisco in the days of the gold rush, when the masses of new citizens churned the streets there into mudholes. In Recife, Johan Maurits, acting with his usual vigor, gave the roads a coating of ashes, at the cost of, but over the protests of, the citizenry.

The problems of population and civil administration drained away Company resources by the expense which they involved, but the Company by its involvement with government was perhaps damaged in a more serious way. The first objects of the Company ought to have been to provide the Portuguese sugar planters with necessary supplies, and to import into Brazil, as the Dutch had done elsewhere, cargoes of trade goods which could be sold to Portuguese, Indians, free Negroes and others. Instead, a large share of the available cargo space was devoted to goods which were needed, or thought to be needed, by the hosts of Company merchants, clerks, soldiers, laborers, and civil administrators. Brazil could provide a bountiful supply of delectable foods: manioc, yams, bananas, oranges, papaya, and other fruits were easily available, as were the more prosaic items, beef, pork, fish, and wild game. Despite this situation, the ostensible trading vessels labored across the Atlantic well filled with the salt herring, bacon, bread, dried codfish, butter, cheese, wine, and beer so cherished by the legions of Dutchmen in Brazil. Also, Americans realize that

131

frontiersmen are able to work out their own way of life, and that a soldier in a buckskin shirt is nonetheless a soldier, but in Brazil in order to keep the Company troops and servants respectable, great quantities were imported of table linen, bed clothes, pillows, shirts, underwear, shoes, stockings, hats, gloves, shirt ruffles, buttons, silver and gold lace, scarfs, combs, brushes, mirrors, tableware, and glasses. To these items were added those absolutely indispensable supplies for a civilized conquering power, small arms, shot, gunpowder, flints, slow-matches, sabers, knives, pikes, drums, trumpets, tents, and cannon. In Holland the land is marshy and rock and gravel scarce, so that roads are built expensively of imported rock, eked out by ashes in some cases. The same absence of stone has resulted in the fact that the typical Dutch building material is brick. Brazil on the contrary has ample supplies of rock, yet the Company laboriously loaded and shipped to Brazil such indispensable items as klinkers for street paving, timber, tile, lime, and good Dutch brick for building. The shortage of shipping space rendered acute by the Company's burden of civil administration was aggravated by the fact that Company vessels were also deflected to coast guard and other governmental duties. An inevitable consequence of the Company's failure to bring in sufficient supplies for the population, or to provide enough cargo space for the export of the sugar crop was that the monopoly of the Company began to be invaded. There were protests in Brazil that trade should be free to all rather than a corporate monopoly, and Johan Maurits, ever the good and just prince, rather than the dependable organization man, insisted vigorously that without more freedom of trade, a really prosperous Brazil was not possible. In 1638, the Company gave way before the clamor. In that year the ports of Brazil were opened to all independent Dutch traders who held shares in the West India Company, and all non-Dutch inhabitants of Brazil were accorded trading privileges. The Company retained only the monopoly of dye-wood, war materiel, and slaves.

The relatively minor expense of maintaining a magnificent prince, and the more serious problems of governing a nation were lesser troubles than those arising from the disagreeable fact that in Brazil the Company maintained in subjection a race different in religion, race, and temperament from its own. The Company, and Johan Maurits particularly, had sought to gain the goodwill of the Catholics, but narrow Calvinists on the one hand, and fanatical Roman Catholics on the other made goodwill impossible. Franciscans and Jesuits in the occupied area plotted revolution with the Portuguese still holding

out in Bahia, and righteous, Godly officials of the Dutch Reformed Church inveighed against tolerance and human kindness being extended to Papists. Despite the many Dutchmen in Brazil, the great bulk of the population remained Catholic Portuguese, and the Calvinists became more stern as they felt themselves less secure. As has been mentioned, the Portuguese were never completely subdued; from time to time there were raids by bands of patriots, or terrorists depending on one's point of view, and minor rebellions occurred at various times and places. The fact that in 1640 the Portuguese at home regained their independence also had its effect on the Portuguese in Brazil. In 1642 there was a serious Portuguese uprising in Maranhão. The Dutch commander there, Henderson, who was really an Englishman, wrote that 'Things go badly for us in Maranhão. I see in this God's punishment for the brutal treatment which... our compatriots have meted out to the Portuguese, taking their property and their sugar out of pure greed, under the most flimsy subterfuges, and not paying a stuiver for it.' As Portuguese armed opposition increased, the thrifty Company helped the enemy by decreasing defense budgets. The congeries of races, religions, and conflicting economic interests was really held together by one man, Johan Maurits. All could recognize in him that which he was sincerely trying to be, the just and merciful ruler. When in 1644, he resigned and sailed away to Holland, Dutch control began to disintegrate. Still, if the Company had displayed more wisdom, all need not have been lost. In 1647 the Portuguese ambassador proposed an arrangement whereby (among other advantages) the conquests made by the Portuguese insurgents in Brazil would be peaceably restored to the Company, but this offer was refused. Instead, a powerful fleet under Admiral Witte de With was sent to punish the rebels. In the following year the Portuguese crown offered to buy back Brazil, but this offer was refused also. In 1651, after the insurgents had repeatedly shown their superiority to the unpaid, demoralized Company soldiery, the Portuguese proposed an arrangement whereby they would pay an indemnity to the Dutch of eight million florins and an additional indemnity to Zeeland province of eight hundred thousand florins. The West India Company would relinquish its claims to Brazil, but would have the right to trade in the country, and would also have the entire salt trade from that great source of the commodity, Setubal, in Portugal. The Dutch also refused this offer. They could not bring themselves to accept anything less than all the profits and riches of Brazil. The Dutch merchants were not, of course, the first group whom greed, or love of power, or ease of living had

blinded to the necessity for compromise, but in the case of Brazil the attitude of all or nothing ended in the Dutch having nothing. In 1652, Holland went to war with England. The cost of that conflict put a strain on the United Provinces, and powerful English squadrons roamed the seas. There was neither time nor money to attend to the problem of Brazil. Recife, the chief Dutch stronghold, capitulated to the Brazilian insurgents in January 1654. The fortresses of Itamaracá, Rio Grande, and Paraíba were included in the capitulation, and New Holland was a thing of the past. This part of the plan, then, of Usselinx and the West India Company had gone awry. The English and others were not to be eliminated from the sugar business. There were to be no tidy fortunes gathered in Brazil and spent at leisure in Holland. But there is still left to consider that third region assigned to the Company, New Netherland, on the Hudson, where it was planned to establish many prosperous properties, and to gather in many expensive furs, and as a matter of fact, both of these activities are carried on there, by one person or the other, at the present day.

CHAPTER XIV

New Netherland

The third region in which the West India Company operated, New Netherland, was one whose history is so well known to American readers that it is only necessary to indicate here those phases of the colony's history which affected Dutch trade. The area differed in several aspects from others in which the Dutch had been active, and as a consequence the program envisaged by the Company for New Netherland was unlike that followed by Dutch merchants in other quarters of the globe. In the Orient, the Lowlanders had entered a vast and populous area dotted with towns and cities. The region was covered by a well developed commercial system of which the Dutch became a part. In Spanish and Portuguese America, the Dutch forcibly injected themselves into only a sketchy commercial network which the Iberians had established, but at least in both the Orient and in South America, the Netherlanders had the benefit of some civilization, of accepted avenues or methods of trade, and of established markets. The situation in New Netherland was wholly different. Here was a forest wild, filled with noble and ignoble savages, and here the West India Company intended to accumulate profits by establishing farms and gathering furs. The farms and settlements would serve as bases for trade with the Indians. The settlers would raise foodstuffs for Company colonies or possessions in the West Indies and in Brazil. They would also ship raw materials to the homeland and would buy great quantities of Dutch goods imported for them by the Company. It thus appeared that settlers would probably be profitable, and furs would certainly be so.

In New Netherland as elsewhere there were Dutch on the scene before the West India Company was formed. As early as 1609, as every schoolboy knows, because all the schoolbooks say so, Henry Hudson sailed up the river which

now bears his name. He had not intended to do any such thing. This Englishman in the previous year had tried to find a northeast passage to the East Indies for the English Muscovy Company, and in 1609 proposed that he should make a similar effort for the Dutch East India Company by following a course around the northern end of Novaya Zemlya, but says the historian Emanuel Van Meteren, the seas were full of ice, and 'the cold, which some of his men, who had been in the East Indies could not bear, caused quarrels among the crew, they being partly English, partly Dutch, upon which Captain Hudson laid before them two propositions. The first of these was to go to the coast of America, to the latitude of 40 degrees, moved thereto mostly by letters and maps which a certain Captain Smith had sent him from Virginia, and by which he indicated to him a sea leading into the western ocean, by the north of the southern English colony.' The second proposal, which was to find a northwest passage by way of Davis Strait, the crew rejected. Accordingly, Captain Hudson drove the *Half Moon* and his mutinous seamen across the Atlantic and into lower New York Bay, where it was found that 'The Land is very pleasant and high, and bold to fall withall.' A few days later, it was reported that '...the people of the Countrey came aboord of us, seeming very glad of our comming, and brought greene Tobacco and gave us of it for Knives and Beads. They goe in Deere skins loose, well dressed. They have yellow Copper. They desire Cloathes, and are very civill. They have great store of Maiz, or Indian Wheate, whereof they make good Bread. The Countrey is full of great and tall Oakes.' Hudson proceeded to sail through the passage to the Pacific which seemed to stretch before him. Had it actually proved to be a passage, it would today, a few railroads excepted, be a great convenience to everyone. Hudson found the waterway a mile broad with high land on both sides and full of fish. From time to time Indian visitors came aboard, and on one occasion the Master and his mate 'determined to trie some of the chiefe men of the Countrey, whether they had treacherie in them. So they tooke them downe into the Cabbin, and gave them so much Wine and *Aqua Vitae*, that they were all merrie: and one of them had his wife with him, which sate so modestly, as any of our countrey women would doe in a strange place.' In fact, all ladies since in that province during a wine drinking, have not sate so modestly. Finding that the river grew continually more shallow, and was obviously no passage to the Pacific, the *Half Moon* turned about and dropped down river again to 'Manna-hata,' and so gained the open sea, and eventually Dartmouth in Devonshire.

In the years following Hudson's voyage there was occasional trading to New

Netherland, and in March 1614, the States General decreed that whoever discovered unknown places, might have the monopoly of trade there during the space of four voyages. In that same year a group of Amsterdam and Hoorn merchants applied for and were granted for four voyages to be accomplished in three years, the exclusive right 'to frequent or cause to be visited, the above newly discovered lands, situate in America between New France and Virginia, whereof the Sea coasts lie between the fortieth and forty fifth degrees of Latitude, now named New Netherland.' Subsequently this Amsterdam company attempted to extend the period of its monopoly under the pretext that it had made additional discoveries in the New Netherland area, but these claims were not allowed and the company lost its monopoly in January 1618. The merchants comprising the company then, as individuals, carried out voyages to the region, and at the same time preserved, to some extent at least, their corporate association. As late as 1620 they were negotiating with the Puritans to establish a colony in New Netherland. It was said by the officials of this company, who petitioned the States General for the right to establish a colony, that there resided '...at Leyden a certain English Preacher, versed in the Dutch Language, who is well inclined to proceed thither [i.e., to New Netherland] to live, assuring the petitioners that he has the means of inducing over four hundred families to accompany him thither....' The petition was refused by the States General, and indeed permission to individual traders to make voyages to New Netherland came to an end with the establishment of the West India Company in 1621.

The plan of the West India Company for the region, as has been said, was to establish settlements and to carry on a trade in furs. Actually, there were two flaws in the plan. First, settlements and the fur trade were incompatible, as a number of fur companies were later to learn to their sorrow; and second, in establishing settlements, the Company was entering into the activities of government, which while frequently laudable, seldom produce dividends. In the task of settling the country, the Company sought to build forts, which would serve as the nuclei of towns, and also to dot the countryside with farms and plantations. The first colonists were largely Walloons, and were sent out in 1623. Fort Nassau was established but was later replaced by Fort Orange (now Albany). The House of Hope, or Fort Good Hope, was founded in 1633 within the present limits of Hartford. A new Fort Nassau was built on the Delaware, and Fort Wilhelmus on the Hudson, half way between Fort Orange and the sea. On an island at the river's mouth grew up the town of New

Amsterdam. The Company's plan for the settlement of the countryside was to encourage both small farms and large plantations. The patroon system, a device somewhat analogous to the *capitanias* of the Portuguese, was to provide the large plantations; and was employed in the West Indies and Guiana as well as in New Netherland. Each patroon was to receive title to a parcel of land which was to have, in some cases, a frontage on a navigable river of sixteen miles and was to extend inland as far as 'the situation of the occupiers will permit.' Each patroon also was to bring over fifty colonists of his own choosing, all of whom were to be at least fifteen years of age. A patroon might also administer justice on his lands, enjoy the exclusive fishing, hawking, hunting, and milling rights, be privileged to engage in the fur trade where there were no Company agents, and might also engage in coastwise trade from Newfoundland to Florida. There was thus provided, at least on paper, a pleasant country covered by lordly holdings. These manors would shelter multitudes of industrious workers who would produce goods which could be profitably sold in Holland and who would need a variety of articles of Dutch manufacture. The forts or towns would house other multitudes, also requiring coats, shirts, ruffles, buckles, buttons, hats, and shoes, and these townsmen would produce manufactured articles which, while not competing with anything made in the Netherlands, would nevertheless be useful and salable there. Unfortunately, although towns developed to some extent, they left something to be desired, and the patroon system did not populate the countryside as had been hoped. Some of the more enterprising and perhaps avaricious Company directors immediately became patroons. Samuel Godijn, Samuel Blommaert, and five other directors laid claim to the land surrounding Delaware Bay and named their colony Swaanendael. Another director, Kiliaen van Rensselaer, claimed for his estate of Rensselaerswijck all of the land about Fort Orange. His colleague, Michiel Pauw, established the manor of Pavonia on the Hudson. Of these, the only one which had any durability and success was Rensselaerswijck. There was, of course, much grumbling on the part of those who possessed no manorial estates.

David De Vries, a merchant sea captain who had a part in the founding of Swaanendael, wrote that Godijn, Blommaert, and Van Rensselaer had established their colonies with the means of the Company. Later the size of the land grants was much reduced and the requirements lowered for those desiring them. Turning to the towns or settlements, Fort Orange, as has been said, became eventually Albany, and although other trading posts were not so

t' Fort nieuw Amsterdam op de Manhatans

The Fort New Amsterdam on the Manhattans, showing the original pentagonal
Fort Amsterdam

An Engraving of 1651.

successful, they nevertheless formed the nuclei of settlements. The most lively town was, of course, New Amsterdam on Manhattan Island. It was described soon after its establishment in Nicolaes van Wassenaer's *Historisch verhael* for 1626. 'The colony is now established on the Manhates,' runs Wassenaer's account, 'where a fort has been staked out by Master Kryn Frederycks, an engineer.... The counting house there is kept in a stone building, thatched with reed; the other houses are of the bark of trees. Each has his own house. The Director and Koopman [merchant or factor] live together; there are thirty ordinary houses on the east side of the river, which runs nearly north and south.... François Molemaecker is busy building a horse-mill, over which shall be constructed a spacious room sufficient to accommodate a large congregation, and then a tower is to be erected where the bells brought from Porto Rico will be hung.' By 1664, New Amsterdam was a thriving town of shippers, and ship agents, of sailors, jobbers, and traders, of speculators, and adventurers. 'The town is compact and oval,' runs a description of that time, 'with very fair streets and several good houses... built most of brick and stone, and covered with red and black tile... after the manner of Holland, to the number of about four hundred... and the land being high, it [*i.e.*, the city] gives at the distance a pleasing aspect to the spectators.... The city has an earthen fort... within [which]... stand a wind mill and a very high staff upon which a flag is hoisted whenever any vessel is seen in the lower bay. The church rises with a lofty doubled roof, between which a square tower looms up. On the one side is the prison, and on the other side of the church is the governor's house.... At the waterside stand the gallows and the whip [*i.e.*, the whipping post] and a handsome city tavern adorns the furthest point.'

It perhaps bears repeating that it was through the residents of town and countryside that the Company hoped to realize profits both by buying what the settlers were able to raise or manufacture, and by selling them what they needed. All did not go according to plan. Actually, on the one hand, aside from furs, the goods shipped to Holland from New Netherland were negligible. On the other hand, here, as in Brazil, the Company simply did not bring in enough goods to supply the colonists, and the settlers charged that they were gouged by the Company for what goods were available. A complaint of 1649 alleges that 'The duty is high; of inspection and seizures there is no lack and thus lawful trade is turned aside.... Meanwhile the Christians are treated almost like Indians in the purchase of necessaries which they cannot do without; this causes great complaint, distress and poverty. Thus, for example:–the

merchants sell their dry goods, which are subject to little loss, at a hundred per cent advance, and that freely, according as there is a demand for, or scarcity of this or that article; petty traders who bring small lots and others who speculate, buy up these goods from the merchants, and sell them again to the common people who cannot do without them, often at another advance of cent per cent [*i.e.*, of 100%]....'

Long before the date of this complaint there were here, as in Brazil, out-cries that trade should be free to all. As a result of the clamor, in 1638, all inhabitants of the United Provinces and of friendly countries were granted permission to trade in New Netherland provided only that cargoes for either Holland or New Netherland be carried in Company ships; and in 1645 all Dutchmen were allowed to use their own ships. In 1647 a committee of the West India Company itself gave it as their opinion that the settlers in New Netherland should be allowed to trade in Brazil. The committee pointed out that the products of New Netherland were precisely like those of other colonies in North America. As a consequence there was no nearby market for what could be raised in the Dutch settlements, but if the New Netherlanders could sell their agricultural produce in Brazil, they could then buy slaves from the Brazilians. With the labor of these slaves the New Netherland colonists would be able to increase the quantity of their produce, which of course would enable them to buy yet more slaves. There would thus be developed a profitable slave market in Brazil, and a flourishing agriculture in New Netherland. The report is vague on the question of how in any appreciable degree the West India Company was to benefit from this interchange of goods by free merchants, except to re-echo the generalization heard also when there was agitation for freedom of trade in Brazil, that the Company could not be prosperous unless the colony was prosperous. In New Netherland, although some settlers certainly did well, it cannot be said that the colonizing effort was profitable for the Company.

That other hope, that the fur trade would yield good dividends, also proved to be unfounded. The Company officials stated in 1633 that the trade did not bring in more than fifty thousand guilders per year. Part of the reason for the small volume of business was certainly due to the fact that the patroons and others deflected the furs from the Company. The patroons were given the privilege of trading in furs wherever there was no Company agent, and the additional privilege of exporting beaver skins to Holland in Company ships at a very low rate, one guilder per skin. Several patroons were zealous

fur traders, and they thus presented the interesting spectacle of endeavouring by their private enterprise to decrease their dividends as Company stockholders. The fur trading was not confined to the patroons, but was spread generally throughout the population. It was said of the settlement of Rensselaerswijck that there were as many traders as people. It was impossible to control the fur trading of individuals, and in 1639 the pretense that the Company had the fur trade was abandoned and the trade thrown open to all. In 1644 in a report of the Company's board of accounts it was said that the colonists to advance their own interests separated themselves from one another and settled far in the interior of the country, the better to trade with the Indians. The settlers then vied with one another in luring Indians to their houses, it was said, and became so excessively familiar with the natives as to earn their contempt. It was the opinion of contemporaries that the disastrous Indian wars which struck the Dutch settlements with intensity in the years 1643–1645 were in part at least due to the friction which developed in fur trading. The Dutch traders freely supplied the Mohawks with firearms and amunition, some New Netherlanders even continuing to do so while the Indians were warring on their countrymen.

The possibility of the Company's being prosperous in New Netherland was lessened by those two ever present problems, the expenses of government and the avariciousness of servants. Here in North America the two problems were remarkably intertwined. The administration of the colony has been severely criticized on a great number of occasions for its inefficiency, but it is well to bear in mind that the colony survived and grew; that if the Company did not make money, at least a great number of the colonists appeared to be fairly prosperous and happy; and that a spirit of freedom and enterprise developed which has been a valuable asset to America. During the period of its existence the colony had seven governors: Cornelis Jacobsen May, 1624–1625; Willem Verhulst, 1625–1626; Peter Minuit, 1626–1632; Sebastiaen Janszoon Krol, 1632–1633; Wouter van Twiller, 1633–1638; Willem Kieft, 1638–1647; and Peter Stuyvesant, 1647–1664. Of these, Minuit, Van Twiller, Kieft, and Stuyvesant, because they were colorful men, have caused a great deal of discussion. Van Twiller was fortunate in that the influential patroon and Company director, Kiliaen van Rennselaer, was his uncle. Actually Van Twiller had need of distinguished connections, for his administration was often characterized as incompetent. A few instances may adumbrate the character of his reign. On one occasion the governor denied permission to an English

ship to sail up the Hudson. When the vessel proceeded without permission, 'Commander Wouter van Twiller assembled all of his forces before his door, had a cask of wine brought out, filled a bumper, and cried out for those who loved the Prince of Orange and him, to do the same as he did, and protect him from the outrage of the Englishman, who was already out of sight sailing up the river. The people all began to laugh at him; for they understood well how to drink dry the cask of wine, as it was just the thing that suited them, even if there had been six casks. They did not wish to trouble the Englishman, since they regarded the English as friends.' It should be added in fairness to Van Twiller that he subsequently did force the English ship to depart. David de Vries, who has been mentioned earlier, was especially critical of the administration. 'I said to the secretary,' he reported on one occasion, 'that we were surprised that the West India Company would send such fools into this country, who knew nothing, except to drink; that they could not come to be assistants in the East Indies, and that the Company, by such management, must come to naught.' On one occasion de Vries sailed into the harbor and found New Amsterdam sound asleep. At dawn, he maliciously fired a three-gun salute, whereupon the town's defenders awoke and ran to their stations pulling on their clothes as they did so, Van Twiller bringing up the rear, flourishing a pistol and also endeavoring to dress himself. One of this governor's notable administrative acts was to inaugurate private land grants, incidentally granting a tract to himself.

Willem Kieft, Van Twiller's successor, was also responsible for an administrative act worth noting. He fixed the number of the governor's council at two, himself and a friend, Dr. Johannes La Montagne, a Huguenot physician, assigning La Montagne one vote and himself two votes. In addition to inventing this interesting administrative device, Kieft was also to a large extent responsible for the Indian wars which beset the colony. He attempted to fix a tax or tribute payable by the Indians in corn which was resisted by war. Though certainly memorable, Kieft was surpassed in picturesque qualities by Petrus Stuyvesant. A remonstrance addressed by the people of New Netherland in 1649 to the States General emphasized his unusual characteristics. It was complained that Stuyvesant when acting in his capacity as a judge was accustomed to 'browbeat, dispute with and harass one of the two parties; not as beseemeth a judge, but like a zealous advocate.' It was said that he was busy almost every day issuing proclamations, most of which were never observed. 'Mr. Stuyvesant's promptness at confiscating,' it was added, 'causes also great

discontent among the inhabitants. Scarce a ship comes in or near this place, that he does not look on as a prize, unless it be the property of a friend.' Stuyvesant was in, and carried on, the Remonstrance stated, 'all sorts of business all over the country, for he hath various stores of his own; he is a brewer, hath bouweries, is part owner of ships, a merchant and a trader both in lawful and contraband articles.' The vice-director Lubbert van Dincklagen wrote to the directors of the Amsterdam Chamber in September 1651 to say concerning Stuyvesant that, 'It were yet more commendable, were attention paid to those who [meaning Stuyvesant] on the means of the Honorable Company, or of the stockholders support, in foreign parts, great pomp and expensive style; retrieve, moreover, their wretched affairs in a remarkable manner; consume by thousands, and... take everything at the expense of the Company.... It is a plague, a punishment, and the total ruin and confusion of the Honorable laudable West India Company, that such a man [Stuyvesant] who dares to sell and give away not only the Company's goods but their real estate... should still be upheld and protected by some, as I see with my own eyes.' Not only were Stuyvesant and his fellow governors charged with being somewhat less than ideal administrators, but men in lesser capacities were also found wanting. Of Paulus Leendertsen, a naval storekeeper, for example, it was remarked that although his salary was small, he had become wealthy in a remarkably short time.

As though the problems of small profits, the cares of government, and avaricious servants were not enough, the Company was haunted from time to time by the dreadful spectre of peace between the Netherlands and Spain. To combat the impending calamity, the Company pointed out to the States General the great and useful damage the Company had inflicted on the enemy, but as peace would remove the necessity of inflicting damage, the argument was a dubious one. It was also pointed out that the Company employed many people, and purchased numerous articles in Holland. Because of these facts, the Company directors advanced the thesis, which has sometimes been advanced by other company directors in other countries, that 'the security and welfare of our beloved Fatherland is most intimately connected with the preservation and prosperity of our Company.' Fortunately for the Honorable Company's affairs, the war continued officially until 1648.

One more tribulation must be added to the list of those besetting the Company, which has been mentioned only incidentally heretofore, and this was the Indian wars which raged for a number of years in New Netherland. The

Dutch often and for considerable periods got on well with the natives, but the Mohawks, Mohicans, and others remained in European eyes idolatrous and ignorant savages. In fairness it should be said that by Indian standards the Dutch also appeared less than thoroughly admirable. A Dutch clergyman, Johannes Megalpolensis, said of the Indians that when he delivered a sermon, 'sometimes ten or twelve of them more or less, will attend, each having a long tobacco pipe, made by himself, in his mouth, and will stand awhile and look, and afterwards ask me what I am doing and what I want, that I stand there alone and make so many words while none of the rest may speak. I tell them that I am admonishing the Christians, that they must not steal, nor commit lewdness, nor get drunk, nor commit murder. . . . Then they say I do well to teach the Christians; but immediately add, 'Why do so many Christians do these things?" The friction caused by trade, by lack of mutual respect, by injustices, and murder finally resulted in war which was at its fiercest by 1643. It was said that no less than eleven tribes were warring on the Dutch at one time, and that at least a thousand Indians and hundreds of colonists and soldiers were killed. It was Governor Kieft's opinion that the Indians ought to be exterminated, but wiser council prevailed. Company officials pointed out that it would be not only both 'impossible and unchristianlike so to do, but it would not be advantageous to the Company to incur so great an expense as it requires on so uncertain a result, and so small an appearance of profit.'

It is not surprising that with such afflictions as have been described the financial status of New Netherland should be somewhat dismal. Several statistics are available which indicate how dismal. In 1638 the States General propounded certain questions to the West India Company. One of these was, 'Has the Company realized profit or loss since the planting of New Netherland?' The answer was, 'Loss, but it could afford profit, principally from grain.' In 1644, a report of the Company on the condition of the Colony stated that New Netherland instead of being a source of profit had cost the Company from the year 1626 to the year 1644 inclusive, over 550,000 guilders, deducting the returns therefrom. Five years later, in 1649, after the Company had been established in New Netherland well over twenty years, the value of Company property there was between sixty and seventy thousand guilders, and the debts against the property amounted to somewhat more than its value. The solution of the New Netherland financial difficulty was generally thought to be subsidies, either from the States General, or, since the colony was the special concern of the Amsterdam Chamber of the West India Company,

from the City of Amsterdam. The argument for subsidies was naturally that money so expended was in the national interest, that the Colony would eventually be profitable and benefit a great number of Dutchmen, that the Company was a most effective weapon against the national enemy, and that by employing a great number of people and buying a great deal of goods, the Company was an essential part of the national economy. A number of petitions for help addressed to the States General, or complaints that aid had not been received, are on record. In 1634, the Company directors complained that the States General had never actually voted the subsidy for the Company which the Council of State had approved. Eleven years later (1645) the Company again stated that, 'The promised subsidies of the state are most necessary for the support of the West India Company in its backward and feeble condition.' In 1648 it was complained that the promised subsidies were in arrears approximately seven and a half million guilders. Regarding financial help received by the colony from the city of Amsterdam, it was reckoned in November 1659 that over a number of years the city of Amsterdam had borrowed for the Delaware River Colony in New Netherland a total of 132,000 guilders, and the colony secured loans in the same manner after that date. In addition, the city granted outright subsidies, such as the 25,000 guilders granted to the colony in 1663.

The troubles created by avaricious and arbitrary officials, warlike Indians, insufficient trade, insolent settlers, and deficits in the treasury were really terminated by the English. That nation had claimed the lands of New Netherland since the colony's inception. There were English colonies to the south and for years the English had been pressing down from their northern colonies. In 1635 they had established Hartford on the Connecticut, to the great indignation of the Netherlanders. Cromwell had been on the point of conquering the Dutch colony when the Peace of Westminster put an end to the plan. Finally, in 1664, an English fleet sailed into New York harbor, and the colony was actually surrendered without a fight. In 1673, the Dutch recaptured it, but it was returned to England the following year by the Treaty of Westminster, and since that time, contrary to its sad previous history, has enjoyed a rather remarkable prosperity.

CHAPTER XV

Iceland

The development of the trade of the United Provinces first in Europe and then in the Orient and the Americas is, to a degree, an orderly sequence, but the Icelandic trade does not appear to be, except in a very general sense, part of the general pattern. Neither was it an important trade, but it added another area to the far flung Dutch trading empire. Iceland is usually considered to have been settled by Vikings from Norway in the latter half of the ninth century, although a small band of Irish had preceded the Norwegians. In the first years of the Viking settlement there was continual passing and repassing between the island and Norway. Icelanders loaded their narrow high-prowed ships with hides and coarse woolen cloth which they sold in the Faroes, the Shetlands, Scotland, and the homeland. In Norway they loaded timber, flour, and small luxuries for the long voyage home.

A sad and significant fact was that if an Icelander needed a piece of timber he had to import it from Norway, for the only tree growing in his own land worth mentioning was the birch, and it seldom grew over ten feet in height. The result was that eventually timbered halls, wagons, ploughs, and most disastrous of all, ships, largely disappeared from Icelandic life. Whenever an Icelandic ship wore out, was destroyed, or sold to a Norwegian, there was simply one less Icelandic ship. By the thirteenth century, Icelandic vessels were a rarity. Goods were carried back and forth by Norwegians, and the Icelanders became utterly dependent on them. When the Hansa merchants in the first half of the fourteenth century became the dominant commercial group in Norway, the Icelanders depended on these German merchants. In the first half of the fifteenth century there were interlopers in the Icelandic trade, the chief of whom were the English, but there are records that indicate that at this time the Dutch were also doing some trading in the island. By the end of

the century, the commerce of interlopers was flourishing for in 1490 King John of Denmark confessed that he could not control the voyages of the Dutch and others, and as a consequence, he extended to Dutch cities in general and Amsterdam in particular, the right to trade in his kingdoms of Denmark, Norway, the Shetlands, and Iceland on the same terms as he had extended to the Hansa merchants. Germans, English and Dutch continued to trade in Iceland throughout the sixteenth century, but in 1602 Icelandic trade became a Danish monopoly and remained so until 1787. The monopoly though always Danish underwent several transitions. In the period 1602–1619 the monopoly was given to the citizens of Copenhagen, Malmö, and Helsingör. From 1620 until 1662, it was held by the Danish Icelandic Company, which was displaced in the latter year by four individual merchants known as the chief participants. This group gave way in 1684 to an arrangement whereby the trade monopoly was parcelled out by districts and this scheme endured until 1733. The goods which the monopolists could procure in Iceland were not numerous. Whaling was profitable for part of the century at least. Codfish were caught in large numbers; dried, these became the stokfish which were a staple food from Italy to Norway. Cod was also salted in casks like herring. Thornback or ray was a valued catch, and salmon fishing was also carried on. To these sea products may be added those yielded by the land, fox skins, falcons, and talc. There was also what might be termed a cottage industry which produced stockings, mittens, and butter salted in casks. Generally speaking, the Danes could sell in Iceland the necessities and small luxuries of life. The Icelanders of course needed the tackle and equipment for fishing, lines, nets, cordage, hoops, staves, baskets, salt, tar, keels, and other boat timbers. They needed also such household articles as soap, wool, and iron and copper kettles. They imported a variety of cloths and such foodstuffs as bread, flour, meal, and grits. Finally they purchased small luxuries, tobacco, beer, brandy, anise, and wine.

Since the Icelanders were dependent on oversea trade, the Danish king in creating a monopoly entrusted the fate of a people to a single group of merchants, or to one company. Unfortunately the Danish Icelandic Company, particularly, did not have the resources to supply Iceland. The failure of the Company to satisfy the market had the same consequences as have been noted in the case of South America. Here, as in Latin America, smugglers provided what the legitimate merchants could not furnish, and here also the smugglers and quasi-legal traders were usually Dutch. Throughout the century there is evidence that Iceland lacked an adequate supply of goods. In the first years

of the monopoly the Icelanders complained of high prices and shoddy goods. By 1630 they were saying that they could not get salt, flour, or fishing tackle, the bare essentials of their simple lives. In that year the people of one Icelandic port reported that although a Danish ship had visited them in 1607, no vessel had been to their port since. In the second half of the century there is a record of the people of a district sending a representative to a Dutch fishing vessel begging the Netherlanders to come to their part of the coast to trade. On three occasions when the Danes were at war, trade with Iceland was suspended entirely.

The Dutch infiltrated this under-supplied market in a number of ways. Some were outright smugglers, others combined smuggling with a legitimate activity and others were legally involved in Iceland trade. The legitimate activities which could be combined with smuggling were fishing, whaling, and catching falcons. Dutchmen might be legally involved in the Icelandic trade by chartering their ships to Danes, by being shareholders or partners in a Danish-Icelandic enterprise, or by furnishing the capital for such an enterprise. Of course, various combinations of relationships were also possible.

Falcons might be thought to be a strange item of commerce, but in the seventeenth century no sport was more popular among the wealthy classes than hawking or falconry. Iceland was the home of a large and much prized falcon, and in the first half of the century, the Danish crown granted to the falconers of the Prince of Orange, the right to catch falcons in Iceland. The privilege was granted and extended on a number of occasions. Difficulties arose when the falconers did not confine themselves to catching birds. In 1606 the Danes complained that the English had invaded the west and the north of the island and were trading there, and later on numerous occasions it is apparent that the Dutch falcon hunters also traded with the natives. In 1631, the Danish sovereign protested to the States General that the Dutch falcon hunters and whalers were trading with the Icelanders. The falcon hunters were said to be the chief offenders since by virtue of their patents, they ranged far and wide over Iceland. No privileges to catch falcons were granted after 1662, but actually the sport began to wane somewhat in popularity about that time.

Regarding whaling, as early as 1616 the Danish king complained that Dutch whalers landed on the coasts of Norway, Iceland, and the Faroes in violation of the privileges which he had granted to his own subjects. When in 1631 the Danish Icelandic Company took up its privilege to catch whales off Iceland, it had neither the ships or equipment for the enterprise. The greater part of the

necessary gear was purchased in Holland, very often the harpooners and boat-men were hired there, and Dutch ships were often chartered for the voyages. The Netherlanders were not content to take part in the business only as the em-ployees of the Danish Icelandic Company. There was, indeed, a combination of merchants at Delfshaven also calling themselves the Icelandic Company who fitted out ships for whaling off Iceland. In 1635, a protest was lodged with the Danish Company by a Danish merchant stating that a party of Dutch-men had set up tents and rendering kettles in the Icelandic harbor of Stengels-fort. The Danish merchants also reported that the Lowlanders were not only whaling off the Icelandic coast but were openly trading with the inhabitants. As a matter of fact, illicit trading was made easy by the government officials in Iceland who, realizing the dire need of the people, did nothing to prevent it. The year following the complaint noted above, King Christian IV of Denmark forbade whaling voyages to Iceland by foreigners, or Danish voyages employ-ing foreign equipment, and it was also forbidden for foreigners to render blubber in the ports of Iceland, Greenland, or Norway. If in the latter years of the century the complaints about Dutch whalers were fewer, it was because the Icelandic coast became a much poorer hunting ground for the monsters.

The Dutch cod fishermen, like the whalers, were frequently smugglers. Contraband commerce, incidentally, is not an activity which leaves many records of its existence, and usually such activities come to light only when someone gets caught. This misfortune befell the Netherlands ship *Abrahams Offerhande* which was captured by the Danes in an Icelandic harbor and taken to Copenhagen. In the resulting controversy the Dutch, on the one hand, pointed out that the ship was equipped with fishing tackle and the necessary casks in which to pack the codfish it was intended to catch. The Danes, on the other hand, pointed out that the vessel also had aboard a cargo of brandy, tobacco, and iron cooking utensils. They implied that while it was possible, though highly improbable, that these valuable stores were intended to be consumed by the crew, it was at least certain that fishermen would have no earthly use for a large consignment of cooking utensils. While smuggling under the cover of a legitimate activity such as codfishing, whaling, or catching falcons was perhaps the more common variety, there were certainly Dutch voyages to Iceland which were solely for the purpose of illicit trade. The Amsterdam merchant, Hugo Davelaer, for example, who in 1648 chartered the ship *Fesant* for a voyage to Iceland, the Faroes, and all 'free and unfree places,' had evidently no respect for the laws of the king of Denmark. In the

periods when the Danes were at war and suspended the Iceland trade because of the need for ships, Dutch vessels visited the island in great numbers to the joy of the Icelanders and the profit of the Netherlanders. In the years 1644–1645 when the Danes required ships for war, the Althingi, or Icelandic parliament, decided that in such a time of stress it was perfectly permissible to buy at least altar wine and fishing tackle from the Dutch interlopers. A few years later in 1647, the Icelandic Company complained that these interlopers had so thoroughly taken advantage of their opportunity that Danish ships were forced to return from Iceland empty or with half cargoes since the Dutch had bought up all available goods. The next year (1648) the Danish resident at The Hague protested to the States General about the smuggling Netherlanders. The States General referred him to the authorities of Amsterdam who blandly informed him that they had no information about their fellow citizens trading in the island. The smuggling was particularly exasperating to the Danes since Holland was the chief market for their Icelandic goods and the contrabandists were supplying the Dutch demand.

Turning from the illegal or quasi-legal trade to activities in which the Dutch could legitimately engage, the most common and widespread was the chartering of Dutch ships by the Danish monopolists. This activity began as soon as the monopoly was inaugurated. In 1602, the first year of the monopoly, two Dutch ships are mentioned in the Sound toll registers as being bound for Iceland with cargoes belonging to Danish merchants. About seventy years later, actually in 1671, the Dutch resident at Copenhagen, Jacob Le Maire, wrote that 'here with the spring according to old custom, several Netherlands ships have come in ballast hoping to get a charter for Iceland, but the king has now made it clear that only Danish bottoms may be used.' Evidently the Danish king did not remain firm in his resolution, for in 1677 Le Maire wrote that a great number of Dutch cargo vessels were employed in the trade to Iceland and the Faroes, taking out food, and other goods and returning with cargoes either to Copenhagen or direct to Holland.

As has been said, Netherlanders also became involved in the Icelandic trade by entering into partnerships or other combinations with Danes. The activities of Johan Marcuszoon Mom are an example. Mom was a falconer of the Prince of Orange and as such made voyages to Iceland and had numerous dealings in that country in connection with his privilege to catch falcons there. In 1648, the Danish resident at The Hague obtained from his sovereign the privilege of fishing for salmon off certain areas of the Icelandic coast for the

space of twenty years. He took as associates in the enterprise two prominent fellow countrymen and the Dutchman, Mom. Although one of four associates, Mom put in one third of the capital, and when one of the Danes who also was to furnish one third of the capital found that he did not have the funds, Mom loaned him the money. Later, about 1660, Mom became associated with another Dane established at Amsterdam, Jonas Trellund, who had obtained a fishing privilege.

The way in which Dutch capital financed Icelandic trade is perhaps best illustrated by the story of this same Jonas Trellund and his Dutch family connections. Trellund was born in Ribe, Denmark, about 1630, where his father was a member of the council. As a young man he was engaged in the business of importing Jutland oxen into Holland. He settled at Amsterdam, and married into the powerful merchant family of Pelt of that city. In the first years after his marriage, Trellund was chiefly engaged in shipping wine and textiles to his native country, but with the support of his wife's powerful family he rapidly expanded his operations. By 1658, although not yet thirty, he was trading in the Barbary States, Portugal, and Iceland, and was a well known and successful merchant. The Danish-Swedish wars of 1657–1660 when Danish voyages to Iceland were suspended gave Trellund his great opportunity to enter the Iceland trade. From available documents it is clear that Trellund's ventures into this commerce were financed by members of his wife's family, and indeed, some of the Pelts had been previously involved in the trade. Trellund sent a number of ships to the island in 1658, and in 1659 had his great year, chartering seven ships for Iceland voyages and going to the island himself to supervise their loading. His activities in these years can be traced by means of the ship charters. One of the vessels chartered by Trellund was the *Joncker Willem*. The ship was to sail wherever the charterer or his supercargo thought it should sail, except that it was not to go further north than Trondheim, nor east through the Sound, nor further west than Bordeaux, nor was it to go to England, Scotland, or Ireland. There was little else left in the way of a destination other than Iceland and that was in fact where the vessel actually did go. In 1660, Trellund obtained privileges from the Danish crown for both fishing and whaling, and the right to enter certain harbors. The Icelandic Company complained that he was not restricting himself to fishing and whaling, but was also trading with the natives. By 1661, Trellund's trade was seriously injuring the Company. That Corporation complained that he had bought so many fish in the island that their own vessels were

151

forced to return with half cargoes. The Company identified the welfare of Copenhagen with the welfare of the Company and pointed out that the collapse of the organization would mean the loss of a great source of income for the city. Despite the protests it was clear that the Company actually could not handle the trade nor could it oust Trellund, and some compromise was necessary. As has been previously said, the commerce was reorganized in 1662. The old company was replaced by a combination of four powerful merchants, and of these Trellund was one. He continued in the trade until 1670 when he turned over his privileges to another member of the Pelt family, Cort Adeler. From time to time there had been other members of the Pelt family in this particular branch of oversea shipping. Paulus Pelt, for example, the uncle of Trellund, had been one of the chief merchants in the commerce in the years 1660–1662.

As has been said, viewed in relation to Dutch overseas commerce as a whole, the Icelandic trade was not of great financial importance, but it adds one more area to the vast panorama of oversea shipping in the century, and gives one more indication of the power and vigor of Dutch merchants at that time.

CHAPTER XVI

Conclusion

This fleeting view of Netherlanders in various corners of the world has perhaps given an impression of a nation intent only on the pursuit of the almighty guilder. Actually it is remarkable how often those who were involved in trade took the view that profits and corporate interests ought not to be the only guides to conduct. Numerous East India Company servants protested against the cruelty and hardship inflicted on the Indonesians as a result of Company policies. There was also a Company director who insisted that the Corporation ought not to pursue only profits but ought to explore the Pacific region merely to extend the bounds of knowledge. On one occasion the Company officials at Batavia protested vigorously when the ministers sent to Formosa by the Company attempted to coerce the natives into being Christians. The indignation of at least one West India Company official in Brazil over the treatment accorded the Portuguese has already been noted. Although no attempt has been made to collect examples of humane and just views, it does appear that there was usually a number of merchants or employees who would protest against greedy or unjust methods whenever they occurred. It seems probable that in this respect Dutchmen were much more to be commended than any of their contemporaries.

An interesting fact about the seventeenth century Netherlands was that while the merchants were engaged in the amazing commercial expansion which has been described, other Dutchmen were making Holland remarkable in other ways. Almost anyone in any part of the world, for example, recognizes the genius of the great Dutch painters of the age, Rembrandt, Hals, Ruysdael, Vermeer and numerous others. It has been reckoned that some two hundred thousand paintings were produced in the country during the century. In the field of science, Holland numbered among its citizens Christian Huy-

gens, Simon Stevin, and Leeuwenhoek; in philosophy, Spinoza; in religion, Arminius; in law, Grotius. It seems fair to say also that the University of Leyden was in that century as renowned as any university in Europe. In the cities, the social life to a considerable extent revolved around literary clubs and drama societies. In such an atmosphere, the fact was that a merchant did not particularly seek to be known as a go-getter or hard man of business. He aspired to know painting and to buy paintings, to belong to a literary group and to know literature, to be acquainted with philosophy and the new science. In short, he was apt to take the view that he should not only be a good business man, but should also be a gentleman of some taste and erudition. Thus, while Dutchmen were spreading out all over the globe in search of profit, they contrived at the same time to bring the arts and learning to such a high pitch that forever after Netherlanders have looked back upon this epoch as their golden age. May all commercial nations at the zenith of their prosperity do as well.

Bibliographical note

The herring fishery. There are rather numerous sixteenth and seventeenth century accounts of the Dutch herring fishery. Semeyns' work is entitled *Een corte Beschrijvinghe over de Haringvisscherije in Hollandt.* Guicciardini, in his history of the Low Countries, describes the fishing in a passage which has been quoted many times. John Keymor described the fishery in a pamphlet which appeared in 1664. This essay is often wrongly attributed to Sir Walter Raleigh, and has been reprinted a number of times. Actually Keymor depended a good deal on another Englishman who had sailed with the Dutch fishing fleet, Tobias Gentleman. Gentleman's work, entitled *England's way to win wealth*, first appeared in 1614. It was reprinted in Edward Arber, *An English Garner* (Westminster, 1903–04). Needless to say, accounts are to be found in the general economic histories, such as E. Lipson, *The Economic History of England* (London, 1929–31), H. E. Sée, *Modern Capitalism* (London, 1928), E. Baasch, *Holländische Wirtschaftsgeschichte* (Jena, 1927), and H. C. Diferee, *De Geschiedenis van den Nederlandschen handel...* (Amsterdam, 1908). One of the more interesting accounts is to be found in that wonderful book which ought to be translated, R. J. Fruin, *Tien Jaren uit den Tachtigjarigen Oorlog, 1588–1598* ('s-Gravenhage, 1941). In this chapter A. Beaujon, *Overzicht der geschiedenis van de Nederlandsche Zeevis-scherijen* (Leiden, 1885), H. A. H. Kranenburg, *De Zeevisscherij van Holland in den tijd der Republiek* (Amsterdam, 1946) and K. Jagow, *Kulturgeschichte des Herings* (Langensalza, 1920) have been relied upon to a considerable extent. Three periodical articles have been most useful: P. E. van Renesse 'De evolutie van onze Noordzee-Haringvisscherij' in *Haagsch Maandblad*, Ve jg. (1928); C. P. Burger, Jr. 'De Haring in de Geschiedenis en in de Literatuur' in *Het Boek*, 10e jg. (1921); and H. E. Van Gelder 'Gegevens betreffende de Haringvisscherij op het einde der 16de eeuw' in *Utrechtsch Historisch Genootschap*, B. & M. vol. 32 (1911).

For the biological description of the herring, four books have been relied upon, T. W. Fulton, *The Sovereignty of the Sea* (Edinburgh, 1911), J. R. Norman, *A History of Fishes* (London, 1931), H. M. Kyle, *The Biology of Fishes* (London, 1926), and A. Meek, *The Migrations of Fishes* (London, 1916).

The Baltic, Russia, and Sweden. An account of the Lowlands as a center for cloth trading and manufacture is contained in H. van Werveke, *Bruges & Anvers; huit siècles de commerce*

flamand (Bruxelles, 1944). Dutch trade to the Baltic ports was noted or described by Emanuel van Meteren, *Historien der Nederlanden, en haar naburen oorlogen tot het jaar 1612* (Amsterdam, 1663), Theodorus Velius, *Chroniick van Hoorn* (third edition, Hoorn, 1648), P. D. Huet, *Mémoires sur le commerce des Hollandois* (Amsterdam, 1718), and by Pieter de la Court, *The true interest and political maxims of the Republick of Holland* (London, 1702). For modern writers on the subject, basic documents have been the Sound Toll Registers edited by Nina E. Bang under the title *Tabeller over skibsfart og varetransport gennem øresund 1497–1660*, (København, 1906–1933).

Of modern writers on the trade, the most useful for the present chapter have been A. E. Christensen, *Dutch Trade to the Baltic about 1600* (Copenhagen, 1941), J. G. van Dillen, 'Stukken betreffende den Amsterdamschen Graanhandel omstreeks het jaar 1681' in *Economisch-Historisch Jaarboek*, 1917, and a contribution by the same author to the *Economisch-Historisch Jaarboek*, 1918, entitled, 'Stukken betreffende den termijnhandel in graan in de laatste jaren der zeventiende eeuw.'

Material on the first Dutch trade with Russia is to be found in J. H. de Stoppelaar, *Balthasar de Moucheron: een bladzijde uit de Nederlandsche handelsgeschiedenis* ('s-Gravenhage. 1901), in various biographical sketches of Oliver Brunel, and in the accounts of individual voyages to the Arctic, Russia and the North, as published by the Linschoten-Vereeniging and the Hakluyt Society. Volume 8 of the Linschoten series, entitled *Reizen van Jan Huyghen van Linschoten naar het Noorden*, ('s-Gravenhage, 1914) is particularly useful. The voyages of Barents, Heemskerck, and Rijp to the Arctic have also been published by the Linschoten-Vereeniging, being volumes 14 and 15 in the series.

With regard to Sweden, two especially useful books are F. Breedveld-van Veen, *Louis de Geer, 1587–1652* (Amsterdam, 1935), and E. P. Heckscher, *An economic history of Sweden* (Cambridge, 1954).

France. Regarding France, general works on French commerce, commercial methods, and commercial policy have been useful. These include: C. W. Cole, *Colbert and a century of French mercantilism* (New York, 1939); E. Levasseur, *Histoire du commerce de la France* (Paris, 1911–12); and J. Savary, *Le Parfait Négociant* (Paris, 1757). Two useful works are concerned specifically with Dutchmen and other foreigners in France: J. M. H. Mathorez, *Les Étrangers en France sous l'ancien régime* (Paris, 1919–1921) and Henri Sée, 'Le Commerce des Hollandais à Nantes pendant la minorité de Louis XIV,' in *Tijdschrift voor geschiedenis*, 41ste jg. 1926.

Concerning Bordeaux, another port favored by Dutchmen, a useful work is T. Malvezin, *Histoire du commerce de Bordeaux depuis les origines jusqu'à nos jours* (Bordeaux, 1892), Because both Dutch and French were concerned with sugar, J. J. Reesse, *De Suikerhandel van Amsterdam, van het begin den 17de eeuw tot 1813* (Haarlem, 1908), has proved useful in this chapter. J. Accarias de Sérionne, *La Richesse de la Hollande* (Londres, 1778), and Violet Barbour, *Capitalism in Amsterdam in the Seventeenth Century* (Baltimore, 1950), have been used to some extent, as they have been relied upon in preparing other parts of the volume.

Spain, and the Dislocation of the Western Trade. The great book about trade with the Spanish

enemy is J. H. Kernkamp, *De Handel op den vijand, 1572–1609* (Utrecht, 1931). There is also an important article on this subject by P. J. Blok, 'De Handel op Spanje en het begin der groote vaart' in *Bijdragen voor Vaderlandsche Geschiedenis en Oudheidkunde*, 5e reeks, vol. I. H. E. Van Gelder also gives interesting information on the trade with Spain in an article, 'Zestiende-eeuwsche vrachtvaart-bescheiden...', in *Economisch-Historisch Jaarboek* ('s-Gravenhage, 1917).

A number of documents on English trade with Spain are contained in R. H. Tawney and Eileen Power, *Tudor Economic Documents* (London, 1924).

With regard to Africa, interesting accounts of the activities there of the Portuguese and others are to be found in *Europeans in West Africa, 1450–1560* (London, Hakluyt Society, 1942), translated and edited by J. W. Blake. The Linschoten Society has published three illuminating volumes concerning Dutchmen on the West African Coast, Dierick Ruiters, *Toortse der Zee-Vaert*, edited by S. P. L'Honoré Naber, 1913; Pieter De Marees, *Beschryvinghe ende historische verhael van het gout koninckrijck van Gunea*, 1912; and *Reizen naar West-Afrika van Pieter van den Broecke, 1605–1614*, edited by K. Ratelband, 1950. Useful here also is that wonderful series of documents on the activities of the Dutch in the East, *De Opkomst van het Nederlandsch Gezag in Oost-Indië* (18 v. in 17, 's-Gravenhage, 1862–1909). Purchas also contains material on the Dutch settlements in Africa. Certain general books have proven useful, especially J. C. de Haan and others, *Nederlanders over de zeeën* (Utrecht, 1940), P. L. Muller, *Onze Gouden Eeuw* (Leiden, 1896–98), and *Algemene geschiedenis der Nederlanden*, Vol. VI (Utrecht, 1953). Books on the voyages to the north have been mentioned in connection with the trade to Russia.

Mediterranean. A number of books previously mentioned, those of Violet Barbour, Fruin, Romein, Accarias de Sérionne, and Diferee, have been used in preparing this chapter. In addition, F. Dekker, *Voortrekkers van Oud Nederland* (Den Haag, 1938), has been of service. More specialized works consulted are H. I. Bloom, *The economic activities of the Jews of Amsterdam...* (Williamsport, 1937), and H. Brugmans, *Opkomst en bloei van Amsterdam* (Amsterdam, 1911). For the trade with Italy, in addition to the books which will be mentioned, one article was most helpful, J. H. Kernkamp, 'Scheepvaart en Handelsbetrekkingen met Italië tijdens de opkomst der Republiek' in *Mededeelingen van het Nederlandsch Historisch Instituut te Rome*, second series, part VI ('s-Gravenhage, 1936). Books of great utility for the Italian section of the chapter include J. C. De Jonge, *Nederland en Venetie* ('s-Gravenhage, 1852) and H. A. W. Van der Vecht, *Cornelis van der Myle* (Sappemeer, 1907). For information on the Levant trade, the documents in *Bronnen tot de geschiedenis van den Levantschen handel* ('s-Gravenhage, 1910–17), edited by K. Heeringa have been found most interesting and valuable.

East Indies. An invaluable source for the chapter has been the documents published in the work already mentioned, *De Opkomst van het Nederlandsch gezag in Oost-Indië* ('s-Gravenhage, 1862–1909). There are two most interesting histories of the East Indian archipelago written in English by Dutchmen, E. S. De Klerck, *History of the Netherlands East Indies* (Rotterdam, 1938), and B. H. M. Vlekke, *Nusantara* (Cambridge, 1943), the latter written

in a style that one whose native tongue is English might envy. Linschoten's *Itinerario*, first published in 1596, has been frequently consulted here as it has in subsequent chapters. When this work is quoted, the translation by W. Phillip reprinted by the Hakluyt Society (1885) has been used. F. W. Stapel's *Geschiedenis van Nederlandsch Indië* (Amsterdam, 1938–40), has been used for Indonesia, and other regions where the Dutch East India Company traded.

The accounts of an Englishman, a Dutchman, and a German, Edmund Scott, Pieter Floris, and Christoph Frick have been consulted to a limited extent. Scott's work, entitled *An exact discourse of the subtilties... of the East Indians*, is contained in the volume edited by W. Foster, *The Voyage of Sir Henry Middleton to the Moluccas, 1604–1606* (London, The Hakluyt Society, 1943), Series II, volume 88. Floris' book is called *Peter Floris, his voyage to the East Indies in the Globe* (London, Hakluyt Society, 1934), and Frick's work is translated as *Voyages to the East Indies* (London, 1929).

Particularly useful has been the volume for the colonies of the *Geschiedkundige Atlas van Nederland* ('s-Gravenhage, 1924–1938).

Formosa. The chief sources for the chapter have been the collection of translations of Dutch documents concerning Formosa published by W. Campbell with the title *Formosa under the Dutch, described from contemporary records* (London, 1903), and C. C. Imbault-Huart, *L'île Formose, histoire et description* (Paris, 1893).

The trade in porcelain is described in T. Volker, *Porcelain and the Dutch East India Company, as recorded in the Dagh-registers of Batavia Castle, those of Hirado and Deshima, and other contemporary papers, 1602–1682* (Leiden, 1954). F. W. Stapel's *Geschiedenis van Nederlandsch Indië* has also been used, since it is really a history of the East India Company. There are also rather numerous articles on Formosa in periodicals, such as that by A. R. Culquhoun and J. H. Stewart-Lockhart entitled 'A sketch of Formosa,' in *China Review* (November and December, 1884).

Japan and the Malay Peninsula. The three items which have been most used in the preparation of the sections on the Malay Peninsula are first, an article by W. J. M. Buch entitled 'La Compagnie des Indes Néerlandaises et L'Indochine,' in *Bulletin de l'école française d'extrême-orient*, vol. XXXVI, 1936; second, a publication of the Linschoten-Vereeniging, H. P. N. Muller, *De Oost-Indische Compagnie in Cambodja en Laos* ('s-Gravenhage, 1917), and third, P. Van Dam, *Beschryvinge van de Oostindische Compagnie* ('s-Gravenhage, 1927–1943). J. Anderson, *English Intercourse with Siam in the Seventeenth Century* (London, 1890), has also been helpful.

In preparing the section on Japan, general books, such as Stapel's history of the East Indies, and the work of Van Dam already referred to have been used. For the background of Japanese history, J. Murdoch, *A History of Japan* (London, 1925–26), has been relied upon. A number of more specialized works have also been used, such as J. W. IJzerman, *Dirck Gerritsz Pomp* ('s-Gravenhage, 1915), published by the Linschoten-Vereeniging, E. Kaempfer, *The History of Japan* (Glasgow, 1906), and C. R. Boxer, *Jan Compagnie in Japan* (The Hague, 1936).

India. The chapter on India has been prepared to a considerable extent from books already mentioned, such as those of Linschoten, Van Dam, De Klerck, and Stapel. A valuable work for this chapter has been Philippus Baldaeus, *Naauwkeurige beschryvinge van Malabar en Choromandel...* (Amsterdam, 1672). H. Terpstra, *De Nederlanders in Voor-Indië* (Amsterdam, 1947), has also been consulted a good deal. This volume is one of the series, *Patria, Vaderlandsche Cultuurgeschiedenis in Monografieën.* The volumes in the series are generally admirable and have been consulted in connection with other chapters.

For the English in India and what they thought of the Dutch, the series of documents and letters originally edited by Sir William Foster under the title *The English Factories in India* (Oxford, 1906–1927), has been invaluable.

A number of the Hakluyt Society volumes have also been relied upon, such as Sir Thomas Roe, *The Embassy of Sir Thomas Roe to the Court of the Great Mogul, 1615–1619* (London, 1899), W. H. Moreland, *Relations of Golconda in the Early Seventeenth Century* (London, 1931), and Pieter Floris,... *His voyage to the East Indies* (London, 1934).

Arabia and Persia. The two books used to greatest advantage for the section on Arabia and Persia have been first, the documents edited by H. Dunlop under the title *Bronnen tot de Geschiedenis der Oostindische Compagnie in Perzië* ('s-Gravenhage, 1930) and H. Terpstra, *De Opkomst der Westerkwartieren van de Oost-Indische Compagnie* ('s-Gravenhage, 1918). Use has also been made of *Don Juan of Persia, a Shi'ah Catholic, 1560–1604, translated and edited by G. Le Strange* (New York, 1926), and of general histories of Persia and of Dutch trade in the East.

Australia. The three works which have been the principal mine for the chapter on Australia have been: first, the documents and original narratives published by J. E. Heeres under the title *The part borne by the Dutch in the Discovery of Australia, 1606–1765* (London, 1899); second, the same editor's *Abel Janszoon Tasman's Journal of his discovery of Van Diemens land* (Amsterdam, 1898); and third, F. W. Stapel, *De Oostindische Compagnie en Australië* (Amsterdam, 1943).

R. H. Major, *The Discovery of Australia by the Portuguese in 1601* (London, 1861), and the same author's *Early Voyages to Terra Australis, now called Australia* (London, Hakluyt Society, 1859), have also been consulted. One of the recent examinations of the Portuguese claims to prior discovery is O. H. K. Spate's 'Manuel Godinho de Eredia: quest for Australia', in *Meanjin,* Vol. XVI, 1957. Spate has written elsewhere on this subject also.

West Indies and Guiana. Several treatments of the West India Company such as W. R. Menkman, *De West-Indische Compagnie* (Amsterdam, 1947) have been useful here. The contemporary accounts by J. De Laet, *Iaerlyck Verhael van de Verrichtinghen der Geoctroyeerde West-Indische Compagnie* ('s-Gravenhage, Linschoten Vereeniging, 1931–1937), is very valuable. Two items on the Dutch in the Caribbean have been drawn upon a great deal. The first is a long article by E. Sluiter, 'Dutch-Spanish Rivalry in the Caribbean Area 1594–1609' in *Hispanic American Historical Review,* vol. 28, 1948; and the second, I. A. Wright, *Nederlandsche zeevaarders op de eilanden in de Caraibische zee...* (Utrecht, 1934–35).

Bibliographical note

Concerning Usselinx, the biography by C. Ligtenberg, *Willem Usselinx* (Utrecht, 1914) is admirable. Concerning the slave trade, the work usually cited is E. Donnan, *Documents illustrative of the history of the slave trade to America* (Washington, 1930). For the discussion of the Portuguese and Spanish slaving included here, more useful items have been G. Scelle, *La traite négrière aux Indes de Castille* (Paris, 1906), and S. Van Brakel, 'Bescheiden over den slavenhandel der West-Indische Compagnie' in *Economisch-Historisch Jaarboek*, IV, 1918. A. P. Newton, *The European Nations in the West Indies, 1493–1688* (London, 1933), puts the Dutch activities in the area in perspective. In preparing the material on Guiana, the writer unfortunately did not have access to the material published by the Venezuela Boundary Commission. The treatment here has been pieced together mainly from the following items: G. Edmundson, 'The Dutch in Western Guiana' in *English Historical Review*, vol. XVI, 1901; V. T. Harlow, *Colonizing Expeditions to the West Indies and Guiana, 1623–1667* (London, The Hakluyt Society, 1925); the same author's *Ralegh's Last Voyage* (London, 1932); and J. J. Hartsinck, *Beschryving van Guiana* (Amsterdam, 1770).

Brazil. The three books most used in the preparation of this chapter have been H. J. E. Wätjen, *Das Holländische Kolonialreich in Brasilien* (Haag, 1921); P. M. Netscher, *Les Hollandais au Brésil, notice historique sur les Pays-Bas et le Brésil au XVIIe siècle* (La Haye, 1853); and C. R. Boxer, *The Dutch in Brazil, 1624–1654* (Oxford, 1957).

In the Utrechtsch Historisch Genootschap *Chronik*, 27 jg., 1871, a pamphlet is reprinted with the title, 'Advies tot aanbeveling van de verovering van Brazilië door de West-Indische Compagnie,' which is most interesting. Some material on Brazil is to be found in J. H. de Stoppelaar, *Balthasar de Moucheron* ('s-Gravenhage, 1901). General histories of Brazil such as J. P. Calogeras, *A History of Brazil* (Chapel Hill, 1939), have also been consulted.

New Netherland. The two principal sources for this chapter have been the documents published by J. R. Brodhead, *Documents Relative to the Colonial History of the State of New York; procured in Holland, England and France* (Albany, 1856); and the documents published by J. F. Jameson, *Narratives of New Netherland, 1609–1664* (New York, 1909). The journal of Robert Juet of Hudson's voyage of 1609 has been published by the Linschoten-Vereeniging, and is most interesting.

Several histories of New York have been consulted. Those most used are J. R. Brodhead, *History of the State of New York* (New York, 1859); D. M. Ellis and others, *A Short History of New York State* (Ithaca, 1957), and W. R. Shepherd, *The Story of New Amsterdam* (New York, 1926). The trade with the Iroquois is described in a superb book by G. T. Hunt, *The Wars of the Iroquois* (Madison, 1940).

Iceland. Aside from general histories and encyclopedic articles which have been used for background reading, the sole source for this chapter is M. Simon-Thomas, *Onze IJslandvaarders in de 17de en 18de eeuw* (Amsterdam, 1935).